Also by George Sibley

Water Wranglers

Dragons in Paradise (1ˢᵗ edition)

Part of a Winter

Long Horns and Short Tales: A History of the Crawford Country
(co-author)

A Crested Butte Primer

A list of other writings is at www.gard-sibley.org/george.html

DRAGONS IN PARADISE
(PLUS)

❧❦

LIFE ON THE EDGE IN THE MOUNTAIN WEST

GEORGE SIBLEY

Raspberry Creek Books, Ltd.

RASPBERRY
CREEK

BOOKS

DRAGONS IN PARADISE (PLUS)

ISBN: 978-0-9851352-5-6
Library of Congress Control Number: 2014955295

Printed in the United States of America

www.raspberrycreekbooks.com

Raspberry Creek Books, Ltd.
Gunnison, CO   Tulsa, OK

Cover Photograph by George Sibley
Author Photograph by Larry K. Meredith

Cover Design by: The M-O Group

For the mountains
And valleys
And those who love them

CONTENTS

Foreword to
Second Edition

M. John Fayhee, *Mountain Gazette* Editor 2000-2013

It was with both pleasure and pride that Mountain Gazette Publishing launched the first edition of George Sibley's *Dragons in Paradise* a decade ago. Even though that publishing venture has gone west, I am equally happy to see a new press bringing out a second edition. Most of the essays herein – including new ones in this second edition – originally appeared in the *Mountain Gazette* magazine, most of them under my editorship.

Mountain Gazette has gone through three incarnations: its antecedent publication, *Skiers Gazette*, which existed from 1966 to 1972, the original *Mountain Gazette* (1972-79), and the resurrected *Gazette* which I helped revive and edited from November 2000 through the winter of 2013, at which time it again ceased to exist as a print publication. George Sibley has had more bylines and more plowable acreage of ink in all of those incarnations than anyone else – to the degree that, in my mind, he has both set the tone and helped define the *Mountain Gazette*.

He has been a personal hero of mine since the mid-'70s, when I first emigrated from the fetid swamplands of eastern Virginia to the Gila

Country of New Mexico, with less than $100 in my pocket and all my earthly possessions happily ensconced in my bright orange Sears external-frame backpack – which, according to Sibley-osophy, is pretty much the only way you should ever arrive in a new place: destitute, hungry, humble and badly disoriented.

Soon after arriving in New Mexico, I found myself, for the very first time, holding a copy of the *Gazette*. Though I do not recollect how it came into my possession, I do remember vividly that is was MG #39, which contained, among other stunning pieces of writing, a very long story titled, "Part of a Winter, Part 2: Red Mountain Pass," by Sibley. Even though it was many years before I managed to get my hands on parts 1, 3 and 4, that story essentially changed my life in both symptomatic and aggregate ways.

First, it served as a conceptual springboard for my new life in the Mountain Time Zone, even though George was writing primarily about Colorado and I was down in the land of cactus and world-class chiles rellenos. "Part of a Winter" – even part of "Part of a Winter" – served as much as anything as a conceptual social primer for new immigrants to the West. And, man, fish out of water that I was, such a primer was much appreciated. Simultaneously, it served as a primer for those who have long lived in the West and who have to deal, for better and for worse, with the millions of newcomers who suddenly find themselves with zip codes starting with "8."

Second, that one lengthy article served as a primer for what the writer's life should be, or at least my then-neophyte take on what the writer's life could be. My take then, and (though I have strayed into the kingdom of darkness often in my career) my take now is that a true writer cares more about his or her writing than he or she does about making money from that writing. It could even be argued that a true writer cares more about the work than about the publication of that work. Fortunately, Sibley and the original *Mountain Gazette* co-existed – a man who cared first and foremost about his writing, and a publication that cared first and foremost about writers who cared first and foremost about their writing. It is doubtful, and I mean no disrespect to George here (quite the contrary), that "Part of a Winter" could have seen ink anywhere else, so complex and challenging and stylistically ground-breaking an article it was.

When the *Gazette* disappeared in 1979, the name George Sibley fell off my radar screen. Shortly thereafter, I moved from New Mexico to Summit County, Colorado, where, a decade or so later, some friends and I started seriously entertaining the notion of resurrecting the Gazette. Along about that same time, I was reading the editorial pages of the *Denver Post* and – whoa! – there it was again: a guest column, not only by George Sibley, but with an author's bio to boot. Living in Gunnison. Teaching journalism at Western State College. Ergo: Easy to hunt down.

As if that was not good enough, the column itself was as astute a piece as I had read in years, even though, daily papers being daily papers, it was only about 700 words long, which is sometimes an opening paragraph length for Sibley. It was a veritable neutron star of profundity for a Summit County inhabitant, talking as it did about how things had changed on the immigration front in the Rockies: where earlier, people had arrived in small mountain towns broke and humble, looking and listening to see how things were, these days people were tending to arrive with bags of money, full of a sense of themselves and talking way more than they listened about how thing should be.

During its seven-year life span in the '70s, the Mountain Gazette was considered by readers to be as much Scripture as periodical. Hell, I can't even use the word "readers" - we were devotees, apostles. When we decided to forge ahead with our lunatic plan to relaunch the *Gazette*, because of its near-spiritual following – I felt compelled to attempt to contact as many of the old writing alumni as I could, to establish my particulars as much as to alert them to the second coming, as it were. I've been in this business a long time and have a c.v. I'm not ashamed of. So, even though I worshiped at the altar of the *Gazette* throughout my 20s, I was not abashed at the notion of contacting *Gazette* contributors from the '70s like Dick Dorworth, Bob Chamberlain, Gaylord Guenin, Rob Schultheis, Gregory Harris, or even contacting by-then-famous ex-Gazette writers folks like Galen Rowell, John Jerome and David Roberts, to let them know who I was, what I was going to do and why.

With regards to Sibley, however, I was nervous, but contacted him anyway, and he turned out to be human in most respects. And shortly after we announced our plans to relaunch, he submitted an essay, which is included in this book, titled, "Ghosts and Growing Up in the Mountains." So there I was, in possession of a manuscript penned by the only man I have ever thought of as a personal hero. To say that I was hesitant to pull out my red editor's pen is, well, accurate.

But Sibley became a good friend over the 13 years I edited the *Gazette* for a string of owners and angels. Between college and community involvements in the Upper Gunnison country, he sometimes needed reminding that he was also a writer, but he took editorial suggestions well and appreciated getting story ideas. Once I sent him a box of "Simple

3

Life" magazines and books, and asked him if he could make any sense of the simplicity movement. He came back in a few weeks with a long essay ("Simpletopia," included herein) that I would put forward as the best critique ever written, not just of that contemporary movement, but of the movement's proto-advocate Henry Thoreau.

Gazette founder Mike Moore originally called the journal "a magazine generally about the mountains," but Sibley tended to take that a little further, making it "a magazine generally *from* the mountains." He seems to genuinely believe that a society is – or at least should be – best built from the community level up, rather than from the national level down. He long ago decided to raise his flag in Colorado's Gunnison River valleys, and he writes for all of us who have chosen to raise our flags in a given place, or who wonder why we have not raised a flag in our place, or who have yet to find (and wonder why) the place we wish to raise our flag. That goes way, way past the borders of the Gunnison watersheds without ever leaving them.

I am thus delighted to see Raspberry Creek Books committing to keeping *Dragons in Paradise* in print. George Sibley has made me understand on levels I never would have the places I have called home for several decades. He has opened both my eyes and my mind to the foundational truth about life here in the mountains: We could very well make for ourselves something closer to paradise here, if only we think, and care, about what we're doing, and where we're doing it. (And maybe in a decade or two or three, someone will bring back the *Mountain Gazette* again to host the discourse about that....)

Hello ...

My name is George, and I'm a recovering writer.
Sometimes, anyway; sometimes I'm recovering,
Able to talk like a newspaper talks in polite society,
Academizing like a dictionary in front of a class,
Capable of fold, beat and puree on the word processor.

But all that time my addiction is latent, lurking,
And I'm thinking about words, words lining up in front of me,
Words like shots in the dark, shots from the dark,
Shots like lightning before me, lighting me up,
Words pouring into me, out of me,
Words dancing on the table in front of me,
Words, words, me drunk on words, words pouring out in
A flood of feeling, flood of meaning, flood of words
Trying to say the unsayable, speak the unspeakable,
Make it all make a higher sense, high, higher,
High on words trying to say something, say —
Something, please, something, anything....

Usually just drunk on words, soggy, smitten,
Words down the drain, down the head of the thirsting soul –
Remembering that once, maybe once, or maybe once imagined
When the words fired, took fire, burned with the white heat
Of joy, anguish and its cousin ecstasy—
No hate, no fear, nothing but the joy beyond fear,
And the love, the love for –.... Well.
Drunk again, drunk on words
And where they take me, take me away....

Sometimes I'm a recovering writer
But mostly I'm just drunk on words and where they take me.

Author's Introduction
to the Second Edition

This is the second edition of a collection of essays, stories and poems first published ten years ago, and reprinted twice. I'm grateful to Larry Meredith and his Raspberry Creek press for wanting to keep *Dragons in Paradise* available, in an "enhanced" second edition.

Since the book needed to be reformatted anyway it seemed like a good time to clean up and prune some of the shaggy writing, and also to add a few new pieces that seem to fit with what's already in the book. The new essays herein include one on climate change, which is emerging as the challenge of the century; a collection of essays about modern life that doesn't include some meditation on the cultural meaning of that challenge seems to me to be lacking something essential. There are also some musings on mortality (fitting enough for someone now in his seventies), a Dionysian look at bars, reflections about sleeping with a forest fire, a look back at Ed Abbey and his importance to us, and a couple reflections on friendship. Also a few new poems.

Not a new book then, but an old book with a new look and some new content. I can excuse this by noting that Walt Whitman spent most of his writing life reissuing *Leaves of Grass* with new content. Not that I'm trying to put myself in that league – or threatening to reissue this forever.

There's another change over the past decade that I want to note here, in introducing or justifying or apologizing for a new edition, and that is a loss: the "demise" of the original publisher of *Dragons in Paradise,* Mountain Gazette Publishing, not coincidentally also publisher of the *Mountain Gazette* magazine in which most of these essays first appeared. I put "demise" in quotes, because there are entities that from time to time disappear, but never really die – King Arthur comes to mind, or Count Dracula. *Mountain Gazette* has been that kind of a phenomenon.

The *Gazette* first emerged in 1972, as the expansion or maybe the transformation of a '60s publication called *Skiers Gazette* – to the "ski industry" what gadfly "indie" papers like the *Village Voice* were to the mainstream media. The genius behind first the *Skiers Gazette,* then the *Mountain Gazette,* was Mike Moore, a Denverite who seldom skied or hiked, never climbed, and hardly did anything outdoors in the mountains except play golf. What he did do was read a lot in an omnivorous way, and he found what he saw as an ornery freshness in the writing of often desperate people who were hanging out in the mountain towns, or out beyond the towns in the mountains themselves. People like myself. That is roughly why he foresook his job as editor of the *Skiers Gazette* to pursue a vision of a magazine "generally about the mountains." "Why not?" he asked rhetorically in the first issue in 1972.

One reason "why not" turned out to be finding advertisers who wanted to push their wares in a magazine whose content, as often as not, was written by dreadlocked dirtbags who lived out of army surplus gear and made fun of the expensive stuff in the ads. For most of the 1970s, George Stranahan of Woody Creek near Aspen, was the *Gazette's* "angel" – an interesting man himself, who supported causes ranging from craft beers to Hunter S. Thompson to education reform. But even angels have limits, and Stranahan pulled the plug on the *Gazette* in 1979, concluding that it would never achieve economic independence, let alone profitability.

The *Gazette* had, however, gained a somewhat devoted following among people who hung out in mountain places – including a college student in New Mexico's mountains, M. John Fayhee, who became a writer, reader and, by logical extension, editor himself after college. Fayhee tells his own story about his relationship with the *Gazette* in his "Foreword" here. But I did not realize how much I'd missed the *Gazette* myself, reading it and writing for it, until Fayhee revived it – again with George Stranahan's revitalized assistance – getting the first issue out late in 2000: It was the same black-and-white format on newsprint; the original *Gazette* had ended with issue number 78, and the first issue of the revival was *Mountain Gazette 79.*

It was not, however, just a nostalgic oddity; the "new" *Gazette* just picked up where the original had left off, with many of the same writers (myself among them) and a lot of new ones, all glad for the chance to again "write with the leash off." Fayhee kept the publication going for almost 13 years, under a series of new owners, all imagining that they could solve the old problem of advertising for an unconventional publication. Finally in the spring of 2013, the last owner folded the print version with *Mountain Gazette 193*. The *Gazette* still exists in an online version (www.mountaingazette.com), but Fayhee has left it to pursue his own writing projects.

I loved the *Gazette* in part because the *Gazette* editors, Moore and Fayhee, loved the kinds of things I like to read – and write, and indulged me by publishing just about everything I sent them. "Indulgence" is no exaggeration; neither editor ever complained about length, even though my essays occasionally went to five or six thousand words. Once, Moore gave me 20 magazine pages for an essay that eventually became part of a book. He joked about my occasional burp of guilt at writing so long, leading to my occasional promise to cut something down; "Sibley," he told other writers, "usually cuts a 2,000-word story down to 2,500 words."

One thing I loved about the *Gazette* was its absence of journalistic pretenses toward "objectivity." Their standard was basically "tell your own story," and take the time and space to tell it right with minimum B.S. Their idea of "editing," beyond *ex post facto* correcting of spelling and grammar, was to throw out an idea, either to a specific writer or to the whole stable – setting everyone off on stories for a "bar issue," or a set of essays around "What is a mountain person?" It may have been more "The New Yorker" of the mountain culture than its "Village Voice." Any editor can cut, trim and correct; not all of them can inspire.

What they were doing was giving writers the opportunity, or maybe the challenge, to "essay." Yes – the verb form of the word. We usually use "essay" as a noun, describing a discrete piece of writing – according to my dictionary, "a literary composition on a particular theme or subject, usually in prose and generally analytic, speculative, or interpretative." But a second meaning is "an effort to perform or accomplish something, an attempt." And that leads to a transitive verb, "to essay": "to try, attempt; to put to the test, make trial of."

So the *Gazette* was a publication not so much for "essayists" as for "essayers." Essayers are those for whom E.M. Forster's observation on writing is more of a mandate: "I don't know what I think until I read what I've said." Yes, exactly. Essayers essay forth into their own unknown, the

9

underbrush by the path, the road less traveled, the ignored past, the rejected future, and if you start out knowing where you're going to finish, you're not really essaying.

Myself, I was not in the mountains out of any huge enthusiasm for hiking, biking, boating, floating, skiing, fishing, climbing, camping, or any of those ways of testing oneself against nature, although I engaged in all of that to some degree because, as Hillary (Sir Edmund, not Madame) said, it was there, and it's what others who were there were doing too.

Why was I there then? I was there in retreat, a gradual withdrawal to the edge-zones of a civilization I had grown up enfolded in and nurtured by (Wonder Bread built strong bodies eight ways), but had ceased to really understand.

What I didn't know when I retreated to the upper Upper Gunnison Valley in 1966, is that I was an early participant in a demographic phenomenon: the "nonmetropolitan population turnaround." For the first time since – well, probably the 1830s, more people were moving out of the metropolitan areas seeded by America's great cities than were moving into them. This phenomenon has ebbed and flowed from the late 1960s to the present – fluctuating with a lot of economic variables.

But the most consistent recipients of these "post-urbanites" have been places that have significant recreational components in the local culture – even places where one might hope to re-create oneself. Places like the Upper Gunnison Valley where I landed nearly 50 years ago, and have not since been able to successfully leave for long. I have done many things here and in adjacent valleys over those decades – ski patrolman, newspaper editor, forest-fire fighter, bartender, sawmill operator, academic oddjobber at a small college – but mostly what I've done is essay around a nexus of questions that all seem to be variations on "what are we doing here?" Not just "here in the Upper Gunnison," but here on earth, all of us? What is the human project? *Is* there a human project? And if there isn't, why were we made to be conscious of, and enabled to alter so fumblingly, this incredible mix of beauty, madness, meanness, glory, love and hate, fear and foolishness, strange order and ordinary chaos that is our planet?

Somedays, I get up in the morning and go to work at some mundane business or another. But other days, I get up – or just stop in the middle of the business – and get back to essaying. This book is the tracks of some of that essaying. It's my hope that you will find it interesting and maybe challenging – I like it best when I so irritate or confuse a reader that they look me up for a beer, which I will always gladly buy.

***

While I have your attention, I need to thank a few people: obviously Mike Moore and John Fayhee and their *Mountain Gazette* for giving me permission to go ahead and just write; Ed and Martha Quillen and now Mike Rossi for another often indulgent publication, *Colorado Central* magazine; Sandy Fails of *Crested Butte* magazine who has given me a lot longer leash than that kind of magazine usually does; and Art Norris and Don Bachman who crossed my path the way stars cross and bend the light passing them, and who pushed me from "wanting to be a writer" to "write or else" with the *Crested Butte Chronicle*. (I was a lousy newspaper publisher, a terrible ad salesman, and too undisciplined to be a good reporter, but that experience – four or eight empty pages a week – sure taught me how to be a writer.)

Then there are all the people who have put up with me and my often erratic ways – my partner Maryo Gard with whom the first beer of the evening is often the best part of the day; my first wife Barbara, and our two offspring Sam and Sarah who may change the world as much as they've changed me.

And all the day trippers and campfire sitters and 12-to-2 riders of the night who keep sharpening me up for the work that we're still trying to figure out, the work that's actually worthy of us and this planet we're trying not to destroy before we find out – well, what William Stafford said: "Your job is to find out what the world is trying to be."

At Lake Wallowa
(February 1998)

The writer thinks of songs to write
While walking down the road,
And hears the song the water writes
On the rock in the woods beyond,
And sees on the lake nine ducks write Vs
Across the shimmered Vs of trees grown down,
While above it all on the mountain's ridge
The wind with snow writes something on the sky,
Something too large to read today;
I'll have to come hear it another day.

Writers read what's written there
In flakes and grains and drops that, like the word,
Are nothing till ordered, arranged and heard,
And writers write, it's never done,
And songs are singing, never sung.

Mendicant Mountain

The land was ours before we were the land's....
Something we were withholding made us weak
Until we found that it was ourselves
We were withholding from our land of living,
And forthwith found salvation in surrender.

— Robert Frost
("The Gift Outright")

First published in *Mountain Gazette* 83, Nov.-Dec. 2001; then reprinted in *High Country News*, March 18, 2002 as "How I Lost My Town".

I know I'm starting to lose it. My sense of place. It really hit home the day I didn't stand up for Snow Days.

I had just finished making a presentation about our local economic development corporation to a local leadership-training group. I live in a mountain valley that, like most mountain valleys in the Rockies, has two principal towns, one upvalley and one downvalley. Some mountain valleys have more towns, but they will all sort into "upvalley" and "downvalley" towns – more liberal and industrial upvalley, more conservative and agricultural downvalley. I've lived in both types of mountain valley towns, enough to know that both are a long way from being that "society to match its scenery" that Wallace Stegner talked about in "The Sound of Mountain Water." But we keep trying – and one of the most consistent efforts toward improvement on the part of each town is to try to help the other town improve with frequent criticism.

That is what the leadership meeting that day had devolved to: most of the people in the group were from the downvalley town, so they were providing a critique of the general business practices of the upvalley town, practices they believed were not sufficiently rigorous and disciplined. "You go up there," one person said, "and you never know if you're even going to find a business open." "Yes," chimed in another, "especially if it's snowing."

Well, that jogged a few memories of my own days as a businessman in the upvalley town – to the extent that a very small newspaper is a business. If it was snowing – especially the way it can only snow up in the high mountains, that straight-down drowning thick fall – there was no uncertainty at all about whether a business, including my newspaper office, would be open: it wouldn't. I kept the "Snow Day, back by 5:00" sign taped to the door jamb inside, ready to slap up quickly in a snow emergency. Other days, especially on a Thursday or Friday after the week's paper was out, I might tape up the "Out on a Story " sign and go up for a couple chairlift interviews in the late afternoon. But Snow Days – those were as sacred as Sundays used to be. That was a big piece of why we were there.

But at that leadership meeting that day – I didn't say anything. Save it for a better time, I thought to myself, a better forum. But this was the anointed future leadership of the valley; where would there be a better forum? Nevertheless – I said nothing, and let the criticism roll, and thus am probably becoming part of the problem that is my topic here: sense of place, and the subtle war, usually civil enough, we have over differing senses of place in a generic homogenizing global society.

***

For the past four decades, I've lived in a real estate development called Colorado. Colorado has been a real estate development from the start back in the 1850s: four straight lines laid down on a map, a surveyor's wet dream, unnatural laser lines attached not to geography but to the abstract concept of property, subdivisible with liberty and licenses for all.

Because of this cultural history, Americans today usually talk about "place" and "property" as though they were interchangeable, the same thing. But if you are going to really consider "place," the first thing you have to do is distinguish it from the concept of property. Both place and property are matters of possession, but it's who and what are possessed, and how, that's important. "Property" is a cultural convention whereby a person has the belief, confirmed legally by properly filed papers, that he or she possesses a piece of land by virtue of investing some money or labor in it. "Place," on the other hand, is something related to the land that comes to possess a person.

People in farm communities seem to understand this: in a long-time farm community, when Jones buys Smith's farm, it doesn't automatically become "the Jones place"; it's still "the Smith place (where Jones lives now)." But if Jones works that property long enough and well enough, then it becomes "the Jones place" – even after Jones dies or sells it to Garcia. Your property is not your place until there's more of you than just your money invested there.

Nonetheless, "place" is a concept every bit as anthropocentric as property. "No place is a place," said Stegner, until two things have happened: one, "things that have happened in it are remembered in history, ballads, yarns, legends, or monuments"; and two, "it has had that human attention that at its highest reach we call poetry." So the geography itself is not the place; geography only becomes place when humans become all bound up with it in some way.

***

But one thing that begins to sink in after a while in a "place" is that the "sense of place" people have there doesn't necessarily have much to do with the natural geography or environment in which the place is located. In fact, in the American West, most of the places to which people are attached have a kind of reductive relationship with the natural environment there: a place exists to milk something out of the environment in the most major way possible; the place is a base from which to extract something or otherwise exploit nature in order to trade along the back azimuth with the parent culture. The places we carve out of the natural environment usually have a lot more to do with the baggage we carry from our parent culture than with anything inhering in "the nature of the place" itself.

This is not just true now; it has been true from the time the American West was way back on the East Coast. We say that, to a man with a hammer, everything looks like a nail; well, to a culture with the belief that Jefferson articulated – that "farmers are God's chosen people" – everything in nature looks like an incipient farm. So the people who thought of themselves as "New Englanders" struggled stubbornly for a couple of centuries to convert acidulous coniferous forest land with rocky undeveloped glacier-ground soils into the English farmscape they knew God really meant it to be. Thanks to their stubbornness, they made it work okay (climate notwithstanding) in some of the valleys and on slopes with southern exposure where the great Central Hardwood Forest had invaded and laid down a good leaf-based humus. But it didn't work very well at all where the old conifers held sway, and that has a lot to do with why the "sense of place" one picks up on from multigenerational inhabitants of a lot of New England places has more to do with stubbornness than pride, and a kind of sullen antagonism that comes of generations not quite succeeding in a war against nature.

In the same way, when Brigham Young looked over the gray-green desert lands between the Wasatch Mountains and the Great Salt Lake and said, "This is the place," he wasn't seeing what was there then; he was seeing what would be there as soon as the Mormons earned their "beehive" emblem by irrigating that desert and turning it into Deseret.

And then there are these mountain towns. They were all built in the most vigorous repudiation of local nature imaginable. The false front building – a two- or three-story front backed by a one- or one-and-a-half-story building, or maybe a tent – wasn't built to reflect the mountain environment at all, but to establish a convincing facade of the urbanity the "unsettlers" wanted to transplant there. The first public building (after a dozen bars or so) was not a simple church to celebrate God's grace, but an elaborate hotel replete with wine, women and cigars where the avatars of back-east money, looking for investment opportunities, could be made to feel at home; and the second public building was often enough an opera house built by a *nouveau riche* who hated opera but knew what kind of a place money liked. The mercantile stores offered "the latest Paris fashions" (and still do, in the really toney mountain towns). Most of these towns were founded by megalomanic dreamers envisioning cities, and copying cities, creating places grounded in what all cities are grounded in: the concentration of wealth. A concentration used by most cities to complete the transformation of nature to something more civilized, more controlled, more useful to humans, even more beautiful to some eyes. New York's

Central Park, the first preserved "wild park," probably continues to shape more people's sense of "the natural" than any other single place.

***

The fact that so many people are talking about their "sense of place" today doesn't mean this tendency to recreate geography in our own image is any less ubiquitous. To the contrary, "sense of place" gets manufactured and distributed today just like everything else that can play on desirable (and therefore potentially profitable) feelings and emotions and impressions.

Everyone arrives in the mountains with a pre-packaged "sense of place," thanks to our industrious media and an aggressive culture in general. Everyone arrives with a calendar-art sensibility about "place" grounded in years of exposure to the soft-core airbrushed ecoporn of "place artists" ranging from Currier and Ives to Adams and Fielder; they've all read the Thoreauvian musings on mountain places cranked out by dozens of writers like Abbey, Bass, Ehrlich and the whole bibliography down to yours truly, and of course Thoreau himself. They all know from the calendar they got for their Save-the-Whatever donation almost exactly what to expect to see every month of the year in all the basic mountain settings from alpine tundra to high desert.

More to the point, they all arrive with a well-developed sense of what civilized people do once they get to the place they've chosen. This is more true in direct proportion to the extent they have bought into and succeeded individually in the civilized world. That is to say, the more money they come with, the stronger their sense of place, and what a place should be, and their place in the place and what they want in the place. They have been inundated for decades with images of the right car to take into the scenery with which they have been inundated for decades; they've seen the kind of houses with which we crown our success in everything from the Sunday paper real-estate sections to the house-beautiful magazines devoted to starter castles and menopause manors. Television shows running the gamut from "Northern Exposure" at the low cool end to "Lifestyles of the Rich and Famous" at the high vulgar end are devoted to cultivating the sense-of-place part of our cultural education. And since one major component of that education is the absence in our place of a whole lot of other people (especially people who are "other" from our kind of people), the first thing we do, once we're in place, is become a Friend For the Preservation of the Place, dedicated to making sure that the place continues to match our sense of what the place should be – namely, "the

17

way it was when I got here." Once we've built, we want the building to stop – certainly within our viewshed. We want the historic-looking little old town to continue looking as historic as it did the day we first saw it (although maybe with new paint in authentic neo-Victorian colors), and so we donate to the creation of a historic district; we talk up covenants and architectural reviews; we cultivate the favor of the handful of remaining oldtimers, working as hard to get them to smile on us as we ever worked to win over a customer or employer back in the real world. And we accept, as natural enough, most of the changes that had been wrought on the place before we got there. You mean God didn't put that road there? Those ski runs aren't natural breaks in the mountain forest?

In short, we do what we can to make sure the place matches our sense of what such a place should be, and so do what we are able to do, as mere individuals, to change it for the rest of the cultural age to a more generic representation of what the culture stands for and nurtures. This is what civilization is all about.

***

There is, however, a more subtle "sense of place" that comes to those who inhabit a place long enough. This comes from a growing awareness of things there that just are what they are, and are not going to change to accommodate to our superior civilized sense of what the place ought to be. Thus the North Woods slopes and glacial gravels of New England, once 80 percent cleared for farming, are now about 80 percent forested again. And a lot of impudent "Capital City" type places in the mountains here have melted back into high meadows marked only by the occasional pile of rusty cans. Sometimes retreat, with or without dignity, is the only way. And even where the people stay, they sometimes change their civilized ways – stop building buildings with flat roofs in snow country, for example, or clear-cutting on mountain slopes, or running low-country cattle breeds in high altitude meadows, or a lot of the other things that are "the way we do things."

It stands to reason, common sense, that those who come to a place more or less empty-handed, maybe empty-minded, will more readily sense the innate and intrinsic qualities of a place than will those who come with the full baggage of civilization and a well-developed sense of what a place should be. Over in the Smith Fork valley, north of the Black Canyon of the Gunnison River, there's a beautiful castellated ridge, above the town of Crawford, called Mendicant Ridge. I've never been able to track down the source of that name – and to be honest, haven't tried that hard, for fear that it probably traces back to something totally mundane, like a homestead at its base built by old Fred Mendicant.

Better to think that it is so named because someone came there with a truly mendicant spirit – not poor because of a failure to strike it rich, like those who named all the Poverty Gulches and Busted Flats of the West, but poor on purpose: someone who gave up all that wealth of baggage, that baggage of wealth that even the poorest of Americans carry around on their backs, someone who gave that up in order to better seek out some essential spirit and meaning in life. A true mendicant like St. Francis, coming deliberately uncluttered enough to see what might really be there.

I may just be saying this, however, because I had – not cleanly and deliberately, but through an escalating series of screwups – reduced myself to a kind of a mendicant state when I was possessed by a place in the real estate development called Colorado.

Call the place Mendicant Mountain for our purposes here; that's not its real name, but then we haven't been here long enough to know the place's real name, if it has one. Just say that below the mountain is a typical enough Colorado mountain valley: longer than it is wide, but a little wider than it is tall, beautiful with the orthographic diversity that comes of relentless gains in altitude, and occupied by only a few thousand people in a couple of towns that aren't yet "a society to match the scenery" but are still trying. The people, including me, are occupied in selling a growing variety of mountain experiences, including of course property.

I first came to this valley as an industrial worker in the mountain-experience industry that we call a ski area. At that time in my life, I wasn't expecting or desiring to be possessed by any place or anything. I'd been more or less bumming for the previous couple of years – ski-bumming in the winter, construction bumming in the summer. Prior to that I'd been caught up in the accumulating chaos and disorder of about half a decade of dropping out, without tuning in to anything significant and turning on primarily with excessive quantities of beer. That long quasi-deliberate slide of a fall had culminated in a close encounter of the worst kind with the United States Army over legitimate wars, a situation that had ended in a way that, according to everything I'd been taught about American society, meant that I probably had no future at all and could count on bumming all my life – I was lucky that I hadn't ended up in jail.

But I made the mistake no true bum ever makes; I went back to the same place twice. After ski patrolling for a winter in that mountain valley,

19

I had vacationed around Mexico for a month, then worked construction for a friend in Boston for the summer – then hitched back to the valley, because, well, they'd invited me to come back (bums always say sure, but don't do it), and that place seemed as good as any other (bums know the new place where you've never been is always better).

The ski area took me on early, in September, to putter around the mountain on all the tasks that are part of turning a big slowly eroding hunk of rock into a bourgeoisie adventure not too obviously marred by the general untidiness and casual dangers of nature. Three of us, the ski patrol leader, the mountain manager, and private last class Sibley, wandering all over the mountain, in the ski area's beatup old pickup or afoot, cutting off stumps, blowing up rocks, changing wheels on the lift towers, fixing up the marmot-chewed patrol phone cables, et cetera.

I'd never been that close to a mountain, or anything else that big in the natural world – day after day, wandering over it like a gnat on a pumpkin, seeing something new every day, even in places where we'd been the day before.

It was also my first mountain autumn, and to the best of my knowledge, nature has come up with nothing in the way of sheer overwhelming mindless beauty that quite compares with a Rocky Mountain fall. A "Pacific High" tends to settle in over the Colorado Plateau after the Labor Day doldrums, and when it really settles in, it pushes incoming weather north or south of the Southern Rockies for as much as a month; a day of clouds or rain or snow might sneak around the southern edge of the plateau, or an early front might spend its way down from the Arctic for a day or so, but the High usually prevails, as it did that fall: day after day of pure blue sky, and the mountains going from late summer's heavy somnolent greens to the psychedelic intrusions of yellow among the green, then the yellow aspen regnant, turning the darker greens of spruce and fir almost black in contrast. Then the leaves all fall off and it gets in to the more somber brown beauty of November, with snow starting to creep down the mountains the way the morning sun does in mountains. The Pacific High is less enjoyable then, at a ski resort anyway; people start to get nervous, long for a cloudy dark day, waiting for the fat pregnant clouds to crawl over the jagged horizon – but I'm getting ahead of myself.

The seduction of the mendicant: I remember going back to work at the ski area one day after a two-beer lunch in town, and watching a whirlwind from out of nowhere run up through the aspens on the mountainside, spinning a column of gold maybe a hundred feet above the trees from which it was lifting the leaves.

20

Or sitting up on a lift tower one day checking telephone cable connections, and a bear walked down the service road, right under the tower.

Or sliding and stumbling down a slope, checking the cables for the patrol phones, and seeing a marmot sitting on a rock, and getting into an involved discussion with the patrol leader about whether it would be better to come back in the next life as a marmot, or as the rock a marmot sits on.

Or looking up one day into a sky so clear that we could still see the planet Venus at ten in the morning.

And always there – present in both detail and completeness on the brilliant cloudless days, but somehow both more real and larger on the days when clouds gave only partial views – was the mountain, a jagged hook of a mountain. And it hooked me: daily going into its shadow going to work; clambering over it all day; seeing it over my shoulder going home, and shadowed and ghostlit in moonlight when I came out of the bar late in the evening; I saw those things and can't forget them, and they all changed my life. The place got me, gifted me with a sense of itself.

***

But the mountain's town (the upvalley town, in the cultural geography of the valley) seduced me that fall as much as the mountain. Like all places out on the margins of civilization, that town was (and continues to be) marginal in many ways. Certainly this was the case economically. The town had one small struggling hardrock mine still operating, but its "mining heritage" was pretty clearly not a "mining future." The ski resort was also struggling; it had just been through a foreclosure and "financial reorganization" the year I got there – the reason it was so easy for any bum to get a job there.

But economic marginality is a relative thing that takes its standards from the mainstream economy – which is to say: it was only economically marginal if your "sense of place" and what places should be held that the local economy should offer about the same kind and level of economic activity and rewards as the mainstream offered.

If you came there in retreat from civilization, though, you didn't measure the economy in those civilized terms; the economy went back to its old bio-anthropological definition: whatever the living things in a place did in order to keep living there – the only base standard being better alive than dead, or in lieu of the latter, forced to go elsewhere. Embraced and environed as it was by that brilliant autumn, the whole town felt

21

revolutionary in ways unique to my limited experience. In the larger swirl of things, it was the end of the "Summer of Love," the beginning of the serious anti-war season (of which my inept lonely revolt from the Army had been a kind of a pale confused foreshadowing), on a deeper level the beginning of a serious, if short-lived, re-evaluation of American civilization. And all of that was present in my mountain place, there under Mendicant Mountain.

Rental houses in town were all full that fall, months ahead of the ski season, and the tenants were mostly the spitting image of those San Francisco hippies being portrayed in the national press. What was blowin' in the wind had blown some our way. Dope first hit the valley in a noticeable way that fall; that was when marijuana began to compete with alcohol as the Dionysian drug of choice in the mountain valleys – which of course horrified the old retired miners tanking beer in the bars all afternoon and evening.

But the hippies weren't the only characters stirring the pot, as it were, that fall in Crested Butte. The real ringleaders in fact were as unlikely a motley as you could imagine. A retired Marine officer become jeweler. A couple of professors from a nearby college, both living upvalley rather than downvalley. A midwestern businessman with a latent imagination who found himself running a marginal ski resort. A former government secretary who'd given in to an urge to carve wood. And a brilliant but difficult man who was both a licensed doctor and a licensed lawyer, and who had already set up a summer forensics "academy" in town.

This consortium of individuals , separately, together, and in shifting constellations, held all kinds of open meetings that fall to talk about the future of the place – and in all those meetings the sense that civilization had retreated, abandoned the valley, not only did not feel like a disaster; it felt like a blessing.

The future, it seemed, could be whatever we decided it should be: a little skiing, a little mining, sure. But there was also a lot of support for a lot of education of a certain sort – the retired Marine-become-jeweler had, in an impromptu way that summer, found himself hosting a small jewelry-making class up from a university down in one of the cities of the plains, and they wanted to come back, and surely there were others like them, hundreds, maybe thousands of others like them, looking for a real place for learning: workshops and festivals celebrating art, music, dance, writing, politics, revolution, whatever, all in the shadow and reflected glow of Mendicant Mountain, and all of that art and music and dance and poetry and politics there to celebrate the mountain and the mendicant spirit of the place it created.... We were the people of Mendicant Mountain, surely all possessed by the place, that beautiful brilliant fall, absolutely possessed.

Out of all those meetings came an organization that still exists in an ever-transmogrifying way, and that organization leased an old abandoned school building for a dollar a year, and one translucent Saturday morning everybody – old timers who had gone to school there and didn't want the building to fall down, us hippies who weren't much good for anything but laughs, a few people recruited because they actually knew what to do – everybody turned out to put a new roof on the old building, and that day may have been the high point of my life, roped up on the roof (because I already knew how to use a hammer), people milling around below kidding each other, some hippie chicks in granny dresses lugging a big pot of some kind of healthy goop down the street from the nearest rental house for lunch, and all of it surrounded by this glorious blaze of leaf death, watched over by the mountain – for the first time in my life, I consciously felt something I hadn't even recognized as missing from my life: a sense that there might be hope for the human species. Possessed: we were all possessed by the place that transcendent autumn day.

***

That's so – *naive* – I'm embarrassed to even be trying to describe it. But there it was, and I will have to say that life has never since been any better than that; truth to tell, it has mostly been a downhill trip into what passes for reality in America, an increasingly comfortable subsidence back into "civilization as we know it."

Civilization of course came back. Not charging hard, banners waving, to overwhelm our impertinence: it came back sort of like the Spanish came slinking back into the Southwest after the Indians of the middle Rio Grande had revolted in 1680 and kicked their civilizing baptizing European asses all the way back south of El Paso. The ski resort's financial breakdown had led us to think, naively I now see, that the world of money had abandoned us, that we were actually on our own to do whatever the place seemed to suggest. Now I can see, have seen, that civilization never abandons anything that has any remote possibility of profitability; it just occasionally has to withdraw and regroup for a new assault in the mega-effort to make every place part of its marketplaces, to impose its sense of what a place is supposed to be on every last place on earth where there is some saleable good or service.

23

So before we really knew what it meant, someone with money to invest owned the ski area. The hippies were replaced by (or just became) hipsters selling real estate – some of them a bit apologetically, "but you've gotta do what you've gotta do" – and the cost of renting, investing, living in general began a slow steady rise in a curve that looked like the geometric curve of the slope up to the hooked peak of the mountain (except that that slope ended in a peak and the costs of living in the valley just keeps climbing).

Without ever meaning to, or even realizing it was what I was doing, I contributed to that re-entry of civilization. I bought a newspaper – basically just a masthead, a list of 300 delinquent subscribers and a hand-powered Addressograph machine – for one dollar and a six-month printing contract, from a printer who had inherited the paper for unpaid bills in the ski resort's earlier meltdown (and figured he would probably get it back after six months, but with someone else paying to put it out in the interim).

Why a newspaper? Because the town didn't have one, and my residual sense of what a place ought to be said it should. The damage I could do to the fragile possessed soul of the place with a "media instrument" was limited by my total lack of any meaningful journalistic training, and anything you get into for a dollar, you can afford to play around with, give yourself on-the-job training for whatever you perceive the job to be. So in full violation of the journalistic standards I didn't know, I decided the job of a newspaper in that town was not so much to report the present as to help invent the future, along the lines we'd dreamed that fall, so I was probably guilty on occasion of what one American media historian called the problem of "representing things that had not yet gone through the formality of taking place." But by violating most of the stuffy precepts of civilized journalism, I succeeded in getting enough of my own persisting possession by the place down on paper to make the town and the valley seem really attractive to a lot of people – not all of them, unfortunately, as possessed by the place as we had been. Too many of them people who came knowing what the place should be.

I not only lacked journalistic training in fundamentals like the alleged "objective reporting" on which civilized papers pride themselves, I lacked any modicum of business sense, and wasn't that interested in learning it. I loved writing the paper, but hated selling advertising, keeping the books and keeping regular office hours; so there weren't just Snow Days, there were hiking days, biking days, afternoons instigating old-timer stories down at Starika's, Walt Whitman loaf-and-invite-your-soul days. Still living under Mendicant Mountain. My relationship with the newspaper resolved itself in a kind of accommodation: if the newspaper would support itself financially, through people who wanted ads badly enough to hunt me down, then I would support myself through working construction or tending bar or whatever. I would write the paper so long as I didn't have to work too hard on building it as a business – with a one dollar investment, what did I have to lose?

But the town was changing around me. Businesses were changing hands right and left; instead of more mendicants, the place was attracting the "ground floor people" – the advance guard of civilization looking for good deals, the town-oriented equivalent of the pioneers who cut down all the trees on their homesteads, then sold the treeless places to real farmers who turned them into civilized farms. The ground floor people didn't look any different from the residual mendicants in the place, but they worked harder, and I began to get the feeling that they didn't understand the place in some essential way – weren't as open to it in the mendicant way. The word "quaint" began to be used more and more – and I realized that it wasn't just applied to the ramshackle architecture; it was being applied to the still barely-evolved way of life that included us mendicants and our business practices. I was becoming quaint, in my better newspaper moments.

My own life was changing too; I got married and a family sort of started to happen. The upshot of both sets of changes was a decision to sell the newspaper rather than try to learn how to really run it the way a newspaper more or less demands to be run in a civilized environment. The newspaper had a lot more subscribers than it had when I bought it – mostly out of town subscribers who I suspected were more interested in the real estate ads than my editorials – but other than that, it had not really grown at all, I'm perversely proud to say: it was still basically just a masthead, no building, no printing press; the typewriter was personal property; the only piece of real property owned by the newspaper was still the little hand-powered Addressograph machine.

But instead of selling it forward for the dollar it was certainly still worth, I found I was able to sell it for several thousand dollars, and did. And so committed my first truly civilized act in that place – against the place, I would say. The guy I sold the newspaper to for thousands of dollars eventually resold it for tens of thousands of dollars, and it recently resold for a price somewhere in the low hundreds of thousands.

That same thing, happening with houses and businesses all over town, is the way civilization effectively dispossessed the possessed and repossessed the town and the valley, remaking it in the image of a more civilized "sense of place": an increasingly airbrushed postcard of a place that matches, more or less, the global imagery of what such a place is supposed to be. A "society to match its scenery" in the same way that the expensive color-coordinated paintings match the expensive walls in the big Houses Beautiful in the valley.

And who can afford to close their doors for Snow Days with mortgages like that? I applaud those few who still do (and always call first if I've business upvalley on a snowy day). But basically the valley is now well into a whole different economy, a different world. In this economy, no mendicants need apply.

***

The thing is – it isn't really working. By the standards of American civilization, the standards by which we now measure things around here, Mendicant Mountain and its valley remain a marginal place – indeed it may be getting more marginal as both the skier base and the general economy contract. As success is measured in America, there are successful people here, but many of them brought their success with them; there are not, in fact, very many people succeeding *here*. The saying is, the way to make a small fortune in the mountains is to come with a big fortune.

The general response to this is to try to do things more and more by the forms and formulas of civilization; they don't work the same way here, if at all, but we don't seem to know what to do instead.

I keep getting involved in attempts to try out ideas here in the valley, most of them fragments of the old ideas that seemed so brilliant that first brilliant fall, but something is missing – probably the mendicant attitude. I'm afraid I've gotten pretty civilized myself. After holding out until I was almost fifty, I finally took on a fulltime, year-round job, with salary, benefits, mortgage – "the full catastrophe," as Zorba said. I've gotten involved in "economic development," hoping that someday we will all begin to distinguish between "development" and "growth" – trying something different rather than trying more of the same thing that's already not working that well – but that seems to be a little like Jules Verne's vision of taking a train to the moon: we just don't have the right vehicle.

I go back to the mountain every now and then – Mendicant Mountain, as I still think of it. Steal an hour from my important work – and occasionally get lost for a couple hours. It's hardly what one would call a wilderness, scarred all over as it is with roads and clearcut trails and blasted rocks and stumps, some of which scarring I had a hand in. But it's still a mountain, still bigger than any of the works scratched on it, and still my residual home of hope.

I was up there a couple months ago – on my way to a meeting in the upvalley town but with an hour or so to kill, so I went walking on the lower slopes. I wasn't there long, but long enough to stop just seeing the scenery and to again start picking up on subtle things – like an aspen grove up on a little rise that seemed to summon me. I went up to it, but presumptuously sat down in the middle of it and it shut right up – I should have just stayed on the edge of it.

But getting back down to the trail I'd been on required a detour to get past a soggy willow thicket below the grove, and that led me suddenly into the edge of one of those ageless old residual pockets of really big spruce down in a slightly less soggy hollow. And ringing that pocket of spruce bog, more different kinds of mushrooms than I'd ever seen in one place. I stopped there for a bit (staying on the edge). Stopped looked and listened for a sense of that place I'd never seen before on the mountain, and will probably never find again.

But then I had to get on to town for something I was already late for. So on down off the mountain, back to civilization. But haunted by the feeling that I may be losing this place, that it may be losing me. If there's hope, it's hope that someday I'll again be driven by the growing poverty of our civilization into the mendicant posture, on my knees before the mountain and the universe praying that they will again open up to me.

> *Walk quietly, Coyote,*
> *The practical people are coming now.*
> – Thomas Hornsby Ferril

Hawks and Haying at Clarke's Ranch

They seemed a team, symbiotic:
The quiet man on the John Deere,
The hawk floating along behind
Waiting for something to dart out
Of the over-rolling row of winnowed hay.

With my English major's romantic camera
I put together the pictures and poetry
That showed up in that week's paper.
Clarke chuckled. "You ever buck a day of bales,
You'll see some different pictures."

Next year Clarke was gone, forever.
But I was there again, helping his sons buck the bales.
He was right. Finally they put me up on the wagon;
Arms and knee could no more boost them from the ground
So I just shuffled the bales into place.

Braced against the lurching hay, sweat and bugs
In my eyes nose and crotch, I laughed along
With the kind jokes, kinder than sympathy,
About my puny arms, fit only for typing and beer-bucking —
And glancing up, saw the winglocked hawk loft above us.

Just the hawk, left from last year's team,
Floating over the draw where I'd followed the tractor,
An abrupt upthermal carrying her
Up aslant beyond the aspeny slopes and
On above Round Mountain into the cirrus rivers
Of the sky where she hovered and gyred
And whatever had ever been together there
Felt as together as ever.

Dragons in Paradise:
In the Mean Time, Out in the Edge

First published in *Mountain Gazette* 100, January 2004,
revised in 2004 and 2014.

I started thinking about dragons one Sunday, out doing a little cross-country skiing up toward the edge of the Fossil Ridge So-called Wilderness Area, one of places here in the Upper Gunnison where we go to play. I say "so-called" because the Fossil Ridge Wilderness Area is a beautiful once-wild place that has essentially been either reduced or elevated to just a beautiful place. One could, of course, still die out there, just as one could die in the middle of our so-called civilization by doing something stupid or careless – stepping off the curb at the wrong time in one place, stepping on a loose rock at the wrong time in the other. But out in the so-called wilderness are no longer any of the active threats or promises, real or imagined, that haunted our perception of the unknown wilderness that cartographers used to mark with the words: "here be dragons."

The Fossil Mountains – basically a rocky wrinkle between the more massive Sawatch and Elk Ranges – were never aggressively anti-human; nothing that we called "wilderness" ever actually was. The Fossils simply didn't care one way or the other about us and our survival, and being both conscious of that and insecure about it, we took some affront at that indifference. Now, we and our civilization are the ubiquitous presence here, thoroughly surrounding and permeating the so-called wilderness – the native species all catalogued and under study, non-human predators mostly radio-collared, the Rescue People always poised and ready to run in to rescue us at the drop of a cell phone, and some agency or other prepared to take extreme sanctions against any bear that takes the wilderness boundary too literally and eats a human or two. Even the omnipresence of that natural indifference of the place have receded, although it can still be pretty aggressive on a cold and windy day.

So it's standing up there near the near edge of the Fossil Ridge So-called Wilderness Area, ready for the always exciting run back down to the wilderness parking lot, that this minor epiphany strikes: the realization that I go to this so-called Wilderness Area to escape the more intimidating wildness loosed in the world today. And what, if anything, am I going to do about this bracing, invigorating, aesthetic, healthy cowardice I practice, running away to designated wilderness from the increasingly ugly wildness below?

***

So here we are in the Year of Our Lord 2000-something, but we're counting now from the Year of Our Fear Ground Zero. In the mean time. Maybe the meanest time we've ever had in this country. It is not the first time, of course, that a third of all Americans have been trapped in a grinding kind of genteel poverty, or forty or fifty million people have been a sickness away from bankruptcy with a diminished social safety net, while a few percent have lived in the fat lap of luxury, enjoying the passive support of the brainwashed masses they impoverish. (Because in America, we believe that someday we will all be rich, right?

I do think, however, it might be the first time in recorded history when we've *gone back* to that kind of primitively selfish society, the first time we've allowed the angry old alpha hogs to start reversing a century of serious efforts to implement the kind of universal access to opportunity we've paid lip service to for most of our history – lip service and little more until the 20th century.

Look what was accomplished in the bravest part of that bloody century: we established a common right to a moderately dignified old age; we established basic rights for former chattels like women and racial or ethnic minorities; we established a public commons in air and water, making appropriators from that commons pay for most of what they took; we even established the right for all other forms of life on earth to live protected from our mostly unconscious efforts to make them extinct.

And now, after all that, we are allowing the old medieval forces of fear and greed to undo and dismantle the whole process? To paraphrase Churchill, never have so many allowed so few to take away so much.

Why? Since the Year of Our Fear Ground Zero, it has been fear of *them* – terrorists, fanatics. But that was just the opening the dragons were waiting for. The Big Retrenchment has really been going on since the mid-1970s, when the more subtle fear of ultimate oil depletion began to wake up the dragons; the Year of Our Fear Event just gave them the opening for instituting more extreme means of crowd management and manipulation toward the end of turning us into a frightened, cowed and confused people (shuffling through airports in our stocking feet, holding up our beltless trousers), willing to give away any and all freedom for security – or just the unsupported promise of security.

It makes me to want to just go skiing up in the Fossils, or West Elks, where things make more sense – where we've mostly cleaned up the natural wildness but not let in the cultural wildness to any great degree.

Not yet, anyway. But just wait till the first terrorists – "ecoterrorists" will do – are found hiding out, or are found to have maybe been hiding out, or are suspected of maybe being hiding out, in the so-called wilderness. Or wait till the argument is launched that *eventually* they probably will be hiding out there, therefore necessitating preemptive occupation. What possible argument will then work, here in the Years of Our Fear, to keep the humvees and hoptercopters out?

***

If you are new to the mountain valleys, or any other edge, you probably think of "the edge" like Wisconsin academic Frederick Jackson Turner thought of it a century-plus ago: a "frontier line...at the hither edge of a free land," "the meeting point between savagery and civilization." In its most general sense, the edge is a line between this and that.

But if you have been here in the mountain-valley towns for a while, you have probably developed a more ecological sense of "the edge" as an "ecotone" – not a line at all, but a lively zone between this way of doing things and that way of doing thing, where both ways of doing things are interacting in ways that actually generate new ways of doing things.

Here in the Upper Gunnison River edge zone, for example, we collect our garbage in cans, then the bears and coyotes and coons from over the edge one way compete with men in big trucks from over the edge the other way, to haul our garbage away – while we who are truly at the edge dream of a way of converting that garbage to something useful here in and of the edge. We haul a little wood from beyond the edge one way down into our edge zone to burn in our "aesthetic solid fuel burning devices" (actual term in our Gunnison County Land Use Resolution), but most of our energy for keeping warm comes in a pipe from beyond the edge the other way. What we in the edge dream of, however, is a way of keeping warm and well-lighted from what flows naturally into and through the edge (water, wind, sunlight), without having to physically or economically haul our energy in from over the edge in either direction.

That brings us to the concept of "environment." By circular definition, the environment is that which "environs," encircles, surrounds us, and is there independently of us: it is everything out there that we neither create nor initiate nor directly control, and therefore *have to adapt to*. The environment is everything that lies beyond our edge zone – either way.

Back when we were all relatively isolated hunter-gatherer groups, almost all of our energy and intelligence for adaptation went toward adapting to the natural environment – the weather, the physical geography, watersheds, plant and animal communities. We basically had two options: to adapt to that natural environment or to leave it for something better. We now know that, in this valley, the Upper Gunnison, isolated hunter-gatherer groups adapted reasonably well to this somewhat challenging environment for six or seven thousand years. *Six or seven thousand years* – that's as long as recorded history. Then, about 3,000 years ago (halfway into recorded history elsewhere in the world), something happened – probably a climate change of some sort – and those early people here had to leave or die. They probably left, although we have no way of knowing that for sure – if they all died here, we just haven't found where yet.

But today – today adaptation to environment is different. In an accounting of the things we have to adapt to here, in the Upper Gunnison edge zone, some of them, to be sure, are out there in the same natural environment that the old hunter-gatherers had to adapt to. But those adaptations are all relatively easy compared to the adaptations we have to make to things we cannot create, change or control from the other side of the edge – over the edge in our so-called civilization.

Most of what we need to live today – almost all of our food (including most of the meat we eat, despite all these cows in the valley), most of our energy resources, most of our building materials (even lumber and strawbales), most of our clothing, pretty much everything – comes not from the "natural environment" surrounding us, like it did for the old hunter-gatherers, but from *the cultural environment* downstream and out in the larger world beyond. Even if we decide to get our "energy source" as firewood from the forest, we have to go first to the cultural environment (United States Forest Service) for a firewood permit. And the only thing that works consistently in interactions with that larger world, that cultural environment, is money, so we spend a great deal of our time and energy doing what we can to bring money from that cultural environment into our edge-zone, our ecotone – so we can send it right back out to bring in the things we need to live here in the manner to which we've become accustomed.

But that cultural environment – since it is made up of humans like ourselves, shouldn't it be a friendlier and gentler environment to interact with, adapt to, than that vastly indifferent natural environment out from the other side of our edge zone – that region of hard and beautiful terrain and storms and droughts and great ski slopes and avalanches?

Well – yes, one would think it should be. But don't count on it, especially if you interacting via an 800 number and working your way through a dozen menus, with the first human voice you encounter putting you on hold. Going that direction from the edge, you will speak with professionally nice people, and receive professionally composed answers that may or may not tell you what you need to know, but one thing you will not hear is either confirmation or denial of a suspicion that, as it used to say on the blank spaces on the map: There be dragons.

***

Let's think about dragons for a moment. Like the so-called wilderness, dragons are an idea that has been tamed and civilized. Pete the Dragon,

My Father's Dragon, Puff the Magic Dragon. Most of the modern stories about dragons run parallel to the dominant mythology of mankind as master of nature – stories about dragons being ridden by humans, turned to human purposes, just another conquerable force of nature.

But there are more mythically accurate portrayals of what dragons really were in the human imagination. Novelist John Gardner nailed cold, calculating reptilian dragon nature pretty well in *Grendel*. The "worms" of *Dune* are blind deadly forces. And J.R.R. Tolkein held to the true nature of dragons in *The Hobbit*: a bestial being of immense size and power driven by a brain stripped down to efficient reptilian essence. No evolving neocortical cover on Smaug's brain, capable of abstract thought, of beginning to think, however haltingly and episodically, of the potential to be harvested if we all truly committed ourselves to the idea that we are all in it together. And no cortex either, that best and worst evolvement of the mammalian brain – that overheated seat of the emotions that sorts the world into *us* and *them*, good-for-us and bad-for-us, lust and fear and joy and love, those seeds of the herd, the pack, the church, the squad, the arational community for which the "I" would die since without that community there is no "I" at all.

So no neocortex or cortex in the dragon: just that cold reactive reptilian brainstem which sees nothing but itself against everything else. Tolkein's Smaug knew nothing, respected and acknowledged nothing but Smaug and what Smaug claimed as Smaug's. He did nothing useful or even interesting with what he accumulated; he just sat on it, slept on it, and destroyed anything that came with any idea of retribution or redistribution. There's no heart to the reptilian mind.

Ages ago, we pushed the edge to and beyond the point where we could any longer believe that "there be dragons" out in the natural environment – and we began to miss them; we've gotten nostalgic about them, just as we got nostalgic for wilderness. We hang onto a few longshot hopes – that there might actually be a "Loch Ness monster", that a "Lost World" might still exist in some remote jungle place – or now, in the genetic age, that a "Jurassic Park" might be constructed from preserved DNA. But imagine: if some kind of a saurian throwback were actually to be discovered in Loch Ness, it would immediately be declared an endangered species, a World Heritage Thing; it would be protected like the so-called dragons of Komodo, and what kind of a dragon is that?

But look now the other way from the edge, away from the officially designated wilderness and downstream toward civilization. Is there anything that way that is immensely huge and powerful, that accumulates for the sake of accumulation, that is driven by the cold selfish calculation of the reptilian sensibility, and that overwhelms with a cold ferocity anything that challenges it in any way?

Well – how about your friendly mutual fund, whose managers have been ripping you off for personal gain in timed-trading? How about the big box retailers working to replace your whole local downtown with convenient total one-stop shopping?

Or how about the overseas megacorporation that informs the local mountain-town entrepreneur with his little backpack factory that, since his stuff is now selling so well, they are either going to buy him out cheap, or copy him and undercut him and drive him out of business? Or the megarealty firm – Coldcock Bankwell ReMagnum, whichever – that decides your town is ripe and makes your local realtor an offer she can't refuse to get your town on the global market? Or the "health company" that maintains its chops in the executive-pay game by carefully balancing raised premiums with lowered payouts on claims? Or the big electricity wheeler who chortles about shutting off granny's power to scare California into giving it obscene profits? Or the petroleum company that fights any attempt to address energy or climate issues?

These entities are absolutely reptilian in their calculated self-absorption – and they are blessed in that by our own Supreme Court, literally ordered by the court to make accumulation of money for their stockholders their first priority, above any social responsibility – and then the rest of us are told by the court that money is speech, even if it isn't free (the money that is), so it is okay to expect your money to talk through bought legislators and presidents....

Maybe then there still be dragons, today. Big things that devour everything in their insatiable desire to possess everything. Born, nurtured and legally sanctioned with the full (if passive) complicity of those they devour. The occasional "St. George" emerges – Eliott Spitzer, Bernie Sanders, Bill Moyer – but for the most part we just lie low and hope the dragons miss our town. What can we expect to do against them?

Thinking about that – I think I'd rather just get my skis and go poke about up in the Fossil Ridge So-called Wilderness. Things make more sense up there. No dragons there, yet, again.

***

In addition to edges, environments and dragons, I find myself thinking these days about evil – real old-fashioned malevolent Biblical evil. Look up "dragon" in the dictionary, and one of the definitions is "Satan" – another mythic figure that has lost a lot of his oomph for sophisticated people like us hedonists out here in the edge. But....

I think specifically, from time to time, of the Biblical myth of the "cities of the plain" – Sodom, Gomorrah, Denver, L.A. – wups, getting ahead of myself there. But I wonder – what were they really like, those Biblical cities so evil that the old billygod of the Bible decided he had to destroy them entirely, and lace the land around them with salt so nothing could ever rise up there again? Even more specifically – were *all* the people in those cities consciously, deliberately evil, buggering each other relentlessly in Sodom and doing whatever Gomorrahtites did?

Or was it more like the situation of the "evil Germans" in the middle of the 20th century: a handful of truly evil people manipulating a lot of basically ordinary decent people, people just like the ordinary decent American relatives and descendants of those Germans today – an aggressive and conscienceless minority driving a docile civilized majority by keeping them frightened, alienated from each other, and in the dark about the really evil purposes toward which they were being driven?

The larger question there is – if basically decent people live in a society where evil is being done, and they do nothing about it, either because they are brainwashed to believe that evil is not evil, or because they believe that evil is relative or just misunderstood, or because they are so easily intimidated and brainwashed to fear and hate on command – if that happens, then have those basically decent people who do nothing about evil become evil themselves?

And if one is living in a society, or out in the edge of a society, that preaches the gospel of wealth at any cost, that openly and shamelessly worships Mammon, that aggressively scorns decent people who get impoverished by bad breaks and a heartless economic algebra, that sanctions and even encourages selfishness in its most malignant forms, that persecutes loving and kind gays while openly marketing soft porn and dirty sex to its sons and daughters, that drives out the unique and the diverse with big-box formulae – how can one look at that, from out in the edge, and not see it as evil?

And what of those of us who just go along with it because we have no idea how to take on that whole foul cultural environment?

That was, in a sense, the question that ancient Abraham asked the old billygod about Sodom and Gomorrah, four thousand years or so ago, when history was just starting to unroll this ongoing story – and we haven't improved a bit on Abraham's solution: according to the Bible, he just fled the cities of the plain and went to a town called Zoar, a "little one" (Genesis 19). So – Zoar 4,000 years ago, New England 400 years ago – and most recently, the receding remnants of another America, another Zoar, places like Aspen back in the 1950s, Crested Butte or Moab in the 60s, Driggs in the 80s, some yet undisclosed place today – we've been leaving the cities of the plain for a long time, leaving behind those huddled masses yearning to be safe and cared for; coming out to the edge to do our noisy little democracies, indulge our freedoms and other victimless crimes, all slightly above (we hope) the benevolent radar below that wants to protect us from ourselves, out here now on the edge of whatever it is we humans might become if we finish evolving to become something a little braver and smarter and more altruistic and *more interesting* than we're likely to become in this mean time....

Four thousand years of leaving the city, in quasi-orderly retreat from that which seems to pile up where there are too many people, that garbage-mass of greed, fear, powerlust that cooks in the dark into a money-leavened corruption that subsumes the initiative, inspiration, aspiration, perspiration, opportunity, creativity, hope and all the other qualities of the meaningful life brought by the previous generation of flight from the previous city, before that sanctuary became the new city – or the new terminus of the same old city. One remembers Alexandria's poet, C.V. Cavafy:

> *There's no new land, my friend, no*
> *New sea; for the city will follow you,*
> *In the same streets you'll wander endlessly,*
> *The same mental suburbs slip from youth to age,*
> *In the same house go white at last —*
> *The city is a cage.*

"No ship exists to take you from yourself," Cavafy says later in the same poem, and – speaking only for myself – I've gradually become aware of how unconsciously impure my flight to the mountains was, how uncleansed I was of that which I thought I wanted to escape. I was still at a stage of life where all my material possessions still fit in the trunk and back seat of a car – and the car itself was so decrepit that it broke down on the move – threw a rod – and for my first two winters in Crested Butte I lived (just fine) without a car. But it's only partly the physical stuff one brings ("Up there I might really *need* an SUV"); it's mostly the attitudes, ambitions, conscious and unconscious desires.

I brought here – in my music, books, and mind – the attitude of rebellion, but lacked the discipline of revolution; I was still in Cavafy's cage. There's now enough of the city here so it's hard to tell parts of it from the "same mental suburbs" you'd find in Jefferson or Boulder County down in the metro area. This is not all my doing, of course; but it is a consequence of me and the rest of the refugees with whom I arrived here not being able to get it together to do anything different.

Is it too late? I continue to work on committees and projects and programs committed to the idea that some lines can be drawn, institutions modified, laws and guidelines established, conflicts worked out that will put the dragons in a cage – or more likely, us in a cage like the divers that study sharks, safe from the dragons roaming unchecked everywhere else.

Here in these mountain valleys, where we've got the highest education attainment levels in the nation, and a dominant majority of people who have come to their Zoar like Abraham, asking, what now, what next, O Lord, and bringing wealth with them, not just dollars but experiences good and bad, a wealth of mistakes from which wisdom should come – shouldn't we be able to come up with some better system, some truer America, that might work toward something better than the model of enforced commercial "democracy" we keep trying to impose on Middle Eastern countries?

But all that is just hope, nothing more, nothing less. Keep plugging away and hope. And meanwhile, the dragons slither in. A hardware megastore comes to town where we already have two good hardware stores; one of the "Dollar" stores comes affirming that we are thereby officially economically depressed. The local arts hold their own against the dragons – still getting audiences of 70 or a hundred compared to the three or four thousand who are watching dragonvision on any given night. And it really doesn't matter whether they're watching football or the history channel – they're there, not here, babysat by the dragons.

Keep plugging away and hope.

So how far are we now from the meanest time, a time of real evil? An American president told us early this century, "The American people need to understand that the war in Iraq is about peace." That puts the corruption of meaning about one short step from the ultimate Orwellian generalizations: "War is peace," "Slavery is freedom," *"Arbeit macht frei."* Is that evil, or just good marketing?

But more to the point – what can be done about it? As I write this, there's a national election coming up – there always seems to be an election coming up – and all sides are painting it in the dark tones of

Armageddon. But I don't honestly think the outcome will make all that much difference, at least not at the national level; nothing will happen to change our commitment to a domestic and foreign policy of reliance on force to change hearts and minds, nor to our commitment to the moneyed powers to do nothing about climate change and energy alternatives, nor to our commitment to tax policies too low to rebuild the infrastructure of an increasingly rundown nation.

That noted - do vote anyway, early and often – but with particular attention to the local elections, for county commissioners, school board members, DAs, judges to be retained or dismissed, et cetera. Because from here on out, I think, if anything good happens, it is going to happen here in the edge, in Zoar, where the dragons only occasionally swoop down and stoop to buying the candidates they want.

And that's where we seem to be now. Here in the mean time, in the Years of Our Fear. Out on the edge is a good place to be, even if you aren't doing anything but watching the decline and fall with the morbid fascination we bring to other massive erosions, like the Black Canyon of the Gunnison just downstream here. A lot of people, here in the edge, poopooh my concern: they don't believe in dragons, don't believe in evil; there just aren't those kinds of things in America. Let's go skiing instead.

So we'll see, I guess. And in the mean time – might as well head up into the Fossils, or the West Elks, up beyond the edge into the once wild places where now no dragons be, for the time being, turning our backs again on the rampant wildness of the undisciplined human animal unleashed. When in rout, go higher.

The Keening of Ants

Ants I'm told are social insects and I think of this
As I stand poking the garden hose ever farther down
Into this pustule of busy dirt in this otherwise acceptable
Lawn that makes *me* feel like a social insect.

I know I'm destroying a society as I watch the eggs,
Little white turdlets, begin to float up on the mass
Of dirt and dirty water and swimming ants clutching at
Those eggs as if their very lives depended on it

Which I suppose they do, I think, as I continue
To poke and probe the hose at their deepdown labyrinth
Of intestinal tunnels and hemhorroidal hanging
Eggs in the dark so deep beyond light.

I really hate ants, the way I really hate everything
That submits to the march, that lockstep subsuming
Of self to the society that wants the whole world like itself,
That tolerates nothing that's not its selfish selfless self.

But still I wonder, as the hose wins this small battle
In a war I know I'm losing, know we are losing,
Because the ants are so much better at waging this war
Of social beings against only semi-social beings—

Still I wonder, watching the little white eggs float up
To the light and dry shriveling air, the too deep sky above—
I wonder if ants understand grief, if ants remember, tell stories
Of the last time I destroyed their city: ants who mourn, who keen.

And what it is, the keening of ants, what's the sound to ants
As the old auntie ants wail and sing their history of struggle,
Their stories of heroes and martyrs and the victory to come,
A siren song to stir and move the quadrillion ants struggling
To wrestle our world away from us.

Getting behind the False Fronts

First published in *Colorado Central* magazine, not sure when.

Cripple Creek, one of Colorado's most famous and infamous 19th-century gold towns, has done an interesting new variation on the "false-front building."

Cripple Creek's main street – Bennett Avenue – is lined with what we've come to call "quaint turn-of-the-century mining-town-Victorian architecture." A feature of this architecture is the false front: a fancy brick, stone or wood structure that appears to be the front of a three-story building, although the actual buildings behind the old false fronts were more often two, or even one-and-a-half story buildings, depending on how the roof was built. Bennett Avenue is all brick or stone false fronts because (like Aspen, Telluride and Central City) it was a relatively prosperous gold-and-silver mining town; the brick and stone replaced earlier wood false fronts (usually after a big fire) that were even more poignantly blatant in their falsity, sometimes just fronting a tent pitched over a barrel of whiskey.

The purpose of the false fronts was to make a raw little mining camp look like a big prosperous city. But in Cripple Creek's latest resurrection, as a gambling town since the early 1990s, most of those historic false-front buildings have been bought up by casino operators in blocks of two or three or four adjacent buildings; and the buildings behind the false fronts have, in some cases, been taken down entirely, leaving just the historic false fronts standing propped up. Then big buildings four or five stories tall and three or four "fronts" wide have been built behind the preserved false fronts (the upper stories tastefully set back enough to not be looming above the historic false fronts from the street view).

So what was originally an architectural device designed to make small buildings look large and modern, is now being used to make big modern industrial buildings look small and quaint.

What does this mean? Probably nothing to the gamblers. Blackhawk, Colorado's most successful gambling town last I heard, just went ahead and permitted a lot of big undisguised industrial buildings purely designed for the most efficient vacuuming of the pockets of tourists, and they are doing just fine. Industrial tourism as upfront and undisguised as it gets.

But the Cripple Creek dodge is the more common phenomenon in the urban-industrial West. I've seen the same thing, less expensively, on the edges of western towns where warehouses have been painted with cute street scenes of false-front buildings with stagecoaches and cowboys riding by. I'm told that down in Durango – Colorado, not Mexico – there's a Walmart Supercenter carefully hidden behind a row of small shops, built by Walmart and leased. The parking lot is behind the big box, rather than in front of it – which one hopes is not too confusing to the Walmart tourists in their RVs who seem to just go from one Walmart parking lot to another for their overnight stops.

All this has to do with a traditional American cultural dichotomy that I think we need to re-examine: what sociologists have called "the rural-urban dichotomy," or "the rural-urban continuum," but what I am increasing inclined to call "the rural-urban illusion" or maybe "the rural-urban bait-and-switch." *Caveat emptor.*

By the sociologists' dichotomy, there were rural sociologies and urban sociologies, with schools of sociologists studying each, and another whole school trying to sort out which was which, and what the distinct examinable characteristics of each were. I won't go into a "review of the

42

literature" here – although I did once, in graduate school – but I will just say that first the scientists, then all the governmental programs designed to bolster and help "rural communities," had a difficult time agreeing on a common functional definition of "rural."

What brought this to mind there on Bennett Avenue that day – I was there sitting in on a meeting of the Colorado Rural Development Council. A meeting of a Rural Development Council in an industrial city like Cripple Creek? But rural ain't what it used to be. The first evening there, rather than hitting the casinos like I should have on my Spring Break, I went to their County Building where a panel of local officials told some of those there for the meeting of the problems they were confronting in Cripple Creek and Teller County. Public transportation, public health, affordable housing, useful engagement for local youth – the generic litany of problems common to every urban area in America today.

Oh, and one person did address the problem of keeping agriculture viable in the area – that's rural, right? But even there, in what passes for agriculture in the mountain regions, it is interesting to explore the phenomenon of the "false front."

You drive past a field, and in the field there are cows. Or some kind of crop growing: here in the mountains it is probably hay for cows. That's rural, right? But what do you actually know about that field full of cows? Are the cows owned by a family that lives off of those cows in the most direct way – eating some of them and selling the rest for enough cash for coffee and other things that don't grow in the mountains? Do the people in nearby towns get their meat from those cows? Or do those cows go directly out into a global market? Like they do here where I live in Gunnison, which tends to think of itself as a "rural ranching community", but where the local people buy their meat in plastic wrapped packages at supermarkets just like urban folk?

And are the cows, and the field they're in, owned locally, or owned by a Texican or New Yorker who uses the whole operation as a way of writing off a loss to balance his gains as an investment banker? Is the field under contract for a suburban development once the plan works its way through the hoops of government? Is the rancher selling off 35-acre ranchettes around the edges to make up the difference between his cow-calf expenses and his returns? Or has he received a substantial cash payment for a conservation easement to keep his lands out of development "in perpetuity" – a cash payment partly acquired from the quarters fed by the fistful into the slots in Cripple Creek, and used by the rancher to diversify his income by investing in a franchise business in the strip mall on the edge of town?

So today a field with cows in it can be as much of a "false front" as a three-story brick edifice fronting either a small business trying to look big or a big business trying to look small. And it's all what we call "rural" – from Cripple Creek's Casino Row to the tax shelter vanity ranch to the actual family farm.

Speaking of which – I visited a family farm recently too: in Indiana, where a cousin has married into a longtime farm family. Her husband runs a seed business – wheat, corn and soybeans. He is kind of an "anti-Monsanto": a family business dating back to the 1930s, employing a couple dozen people locally in the niche business of producing seeds genetically designed for the specific glacial soils south of the Great Lakes. But what amazed me, riding around with him, was the extent to which farming has become a scientific process. Space precludes a full description, but it is kind of summed up in the great hulking harvesting combine, a machine as big as a small house, that is linked to GPS satellites and keeps a running computerized record of how much yield is coming out of *each part* of every field – a record that will be used the following year in fertilizing and planting those fields, to minimize waste effort and maximize yield. "The margins are such that you just can't afford to use the old 'broadcast' approach," my cousin-in-law said.

So when even real farmers producing only for their local region are using global positioning systems in computerized combines – what truly does "rural" mean?

I would argue – especially back here in the mountain valleys – that it has become a meaningless term, only used for nostalgic purposes, chief of which is to sell real estate.

Arguably, it has never been anything more than a nostalgic phenomenon in the wet dream we call America. We are a nation of immigrants who almost all came here for one of two reasons: either to escape the unfolding Industrial Revolution and its inevitable urbanizations, or to exploit that urban-industrial Revolution in the new virgin continent. It makes more sense, to me anyway, to think of the American Revolution as a counter-revolution to the Industrial Revolution – which makes most of our westward American history (which began on the East Coast) a long losing retreat of the counter-revolutionaries in the face of the triumphant industrial city. But we keep holding out – although, truth to tell, in the complexities of the human heart, that nexus of hopes and fears, ambition and conscience, it was and still is hard to tell from day to day which side of that revolution any particular individual is really on.

But certainly after the railroads laid their network over the land, the old rural vision of the Jeffersonian village, sufficient unto itself for its necessities and putting out for trade only the surpluses it needed to sell in order to bring in the exotics and luxuries like coffee and Christmas oranges, disappeared – if it had ever really existed as anything other than a dismal subsistence hamlet succumbing to the tyranny of the milk cow and Marx's "idiocy of rural life." After the railroad came, the grain elevators by the tracks topped the local churches as the tallest things in town, and they were the place where the people went to pray for the prices over which they had no more control than they had over the weather they prayed about in church.

Here in the mountains, it was cattle, or maybe potatoes and onions, rather than grains, but the situation was the same; instead of the sufficient-unto-itself agrarian village, it was all production for the railroads to haul to the cities, except for those who raised breeding stock to sell locally, like my cousin-in-law in Indiana producing seed to sell locally.

Duane Smith, historian of the Southern Rockies down at Ft. Lewis College in Durango, calls the Southern Rockies an "urban frontier." He points out the fact that, from the early mountain men trapping fur for city-dwellers' hats to the gold-and-silver boomers, to the ranchers who came in to feed the boomtowns, then began shipping the cattle on the trains to the cities, to the contemporary recreation and tourist industrialists, modern socioeconomic culture in the mountain valleys has always been about supplying the city with its needs and wants. Jane Jacobs, in her great book, *Cities and the Wealth of Nations*, showed how once rural places became the supply regions, hinterlands, for the growing great cities – as did William Cronon in *Nature's Metropolis*, the story of how Chicago "captured" the entire Midwest. This is true of just about every place in America, post-railroad, that we try to call "rural," with all the old Currier and Ives tints; and it might make more sense to just acknowledge the urban foundations and networks that underlie all human culture today.

I'm not sure, however, that it is that romantically hopeless – I hope it isn't, anyway. Out here in the "mental exurbs," it seems to me that there is a continuum with maybe three major benchmarks along it: pre-urban, urban and post-urban places, and I find hope, or at least hope's scent, in the last.

The pre-urban places are Jacobs' supply regions for the cities, the mining, farming and other raw-resource hinterlands that we call "rural"

45

least ambiguously – the places that docilely produce and send off to the cities all the raw materials the city needs, including their children. They sell these raw materials to the city at prices set by the city, then buy back finished goods from the city at prices also set by the city, so they are always poor places, except in the rare times when urban demand exceeds pre-urban supply and prices go way up. But when that happens, the cities find other pre-urban producers to exploit and they eventually succeed in keeping each other poor.

The most heart-wrenching way in which the pre-urban places have impoverished themselves is in building and supporting public schools whose function is to educate their own children to leave for "a better life" in urban places hopefully not so poor. It was not ever so; the old one-room eight-grade schools (watch out now for the slow drip of nostalgia) basically tried to teach what was necessary to run the farm or local business and be a reasonably intelligent citizen. But by the early 20th century, the centralized "county high school" became mandatory rather than optional, and those schools became ever larger, ever more urban-oriented in their curricula and ever more expensive for the pre-urbanites who funded them – moving from the center of town out to empty land between the several towns sending their kids – trying to provide the kind of sophisticated education *cum* swimming pool and football field that would enable the children from the farms and mine towns to fit into the city (and to want to do that).

The urban places of course are the nodes and clots of concentrated humanity that we have always been encouraged (by those who live in the urban places) to think of as the apex of civilized culture. But another way of looking at them is to realize they are just a necessary consequence of the swarming of the species: it has become necessary to figure out how to handle large masses of people as efficiently as possible on a finite planet, and cities are just the best idea we've come up with to date.

Historically, the great cities taken as the mark of great civilizations have been just the bright flare before the burnout of cultures that have outgrown their resource base. And while there have never been cities on the scale of those today, there is no reason to believe that it will be any different this time. George Santayana suggested that "civilization might be taken as a purely descriptive term, like *Kultur*, rather than a eulogistic one; it might simply indicate the possession of instruments, material and social, for accomplishing all sorts of things, whether those things were worth accomplishing or not." Our civilization accomplishes what it does – a great deal of it maybe not worth accomplishing – with "instruments, material and social" that are oil-driven, and shows no indication of being interested in learning how to do these sorts of things with less finite but more difficult resources, so the cataclysmic burnout will probably come with the wars among global city-states at the end of the "Oil Interval." This Armageddon seems to already be heating up in the Middle East, and closer to home in the fracking and pipeline skirmishes.

But – then there are the post-urban places. These are places still designated as "rural" by census counts, but there is a simple test for distinguishing between pre-urban and post-urban places: are they still losing people *to* the cities, or are they gaining people *from* the cities? Is a community still exporting its young generation to the cities? Pre-urban. Or is the community plagued by an invasion of young barbarians and old sybarites who are looking for something "rural"? Post-urban.

I'm not making this up; demographers in the late 1960s began to notice what they called a "nonmetropolitan population turnaround" – more people moving *into* certain "rural" areas than were moving out of those areas in accord with the traditional American demographic pattern. It has flowed and ebbed, along with the economy, over the decades since, but has remained steady in certain places – like the mountain valleys of the Southern Rockies from which, of which, I write. In 2002, a couple of demographers – Calvin Beale of the USDA and Kenneth Johnson of Loyola University – did a study of counties where this post-urban nonmetropolitan population turnaround was most persistent and consistent through the last third of the 20th century, and found that most of them were counties whose economies included a significant "recreation component."

But that doesn't really begin to describe the "post-urban" places. What happens when a lot of people who grew up in cities, but have decided there must be a better way, retreat to small marginal places in the mountains? Well, a number of bad things can happen – depending usually on how much urban wealth they bring with them.

If they come young and poor and generally ignorant, they do less damage, but – especially if the young and poor come in large numbers, like the hippie invasion of the 1970s – they still usually manage to unknowingly trample whatever small flowers of unique culture are blooming in the places they unsettle.

If, on the other hand, the post-urbanites come old and rich and sophisticated, they bring a lot more baggage with them and a highly developed, if unexamined, sense of what they deserve from life in their senior years. Having floated to the top of the urban mass, they are usually

47

more accustomed to being listened to than to listening, and begin to make demands on the place to improve its roads, its appearance, its cultural life, its local services, et cetera, et cetera. They don't want the place "to become another Aspen" – but if Aspen has a music festival, then so, they assume, must their Vail or Keystone or Telluride or Crested Butte.

Rich or poor, though, through both demand and a willingness to pay based on familiarity with city prices, the post-urbanites drive up prices for everything from housing to beer in the bars (although the quality of the beer usually improves).

But good things begin to happen too. Those who stay long enough begin to realize their own footprint on the place (after going through the phase of blaming the footprint on everyone exactly like themselves who came after they did). Once they get beyond the just-say-howdy affectations of presumed rural behavior, they begin to think about what a community really is (a collective of people who have agreed to try to live together whether they really like each other or not), and they begin trying to apply their more cosmopolitan perspectives to both the challenges and opportunities of living on the edge of civilization, spiritually as well as materially.

They begin to sit – and not just sit, but think and talk – on local planning boards and economic development councils and REA co-op boards. They teach evening classes through the local college's extension program, in Alternative Energy and Grant-writing as well as the usual Yoga and Macrame classes. They start to put together, if only in the mind and only in talk, other worlds that might work well enough with less accompanying destruction.

The best of the post-urbanites begin to look behind the false fronts of civilization, to see what kinds of engines and beasts are driving things there. Sometimes they learn to dance, the way you dance when you begin to see that the only alternative is to continue to march for civilized progress, entirely too linear and one-dimensional an agenda. Not, however, to be confused with hiking.

I speak there of course of aimless hiking, as distinguished from the focused hiking that urbanites practice when they come to the mountains with a limited time frame and several hiking objectives to accomplish. Aimless hiking is actually a form of dancing, which you do outdoors alone, when getting somewhere and back suddenly and subtly ceases to be important; you either strike out crosswise from the trail and try to get a little lost, or you might just stop and sit down under a tree, and let your mind begin to dance.

48

I don't know if we post-urbanites will ever create "a better world" than the urban world we left pretends to be, or whether we will just spend ever more time sitting under trees letting our minds do the dancing. That might actually come to be the secret of Life after Oil: how to successfully and maybe somewhat happily do less with less.

It may in fact be, that behind all the false fronts there is nothing but an ephemeral tent city. The whole Judeo-Christian heritage that underlies our opulent civilization began with a people leaving those great doomed desert cities, Sodom and Gomorrah, and retreating to tents without false fronts – bearing a god who *wanted* to live in a tent, and who started to get seriously pissed off at the people when they built him a temple.

Maybe (I think, sitting under a tree) all wealth really is borrowed from tomorrow to finance the excesses of today, and these post-urban places out on the marginal edge of civilization aren't poor because we are failing to make them rich and urbanish; maybe they are poor because that's what life out on the edge is; maybe learning to do less with less is the shape of the future beyond the Oil Interval.

At any rate – forget "rural." "Post-urban" is where it is, where it's going to happen. Whatever it is, or isn't.

Peak Coffee: Is this Cup Half Full or –
Oh, Never Mind

This cup of coffee has outlasted my desire to drink it.
And here I sit with an empty plate, a full mind,
But only a half empty cup.

Roughly half the people in the world, I'm told –
Or maybe it's exactly half – would agree with me
That this is a half empty cup.

The other half – a rougher half for sure, I think –
Would insist (pushing the point toward tedium)
That the cup is still half full.

But now I've taken another sip, and now
The cup is obviously something less than half full –
Or something more than half empty.

Maybe I'll just leave this cup half empty – or,
If you insist, half full – and just take my full mind
On to another part of my life where

Maybe something will be new, something otherwise,
Something different; maybe for the full mind,
A half empty cup is half full of hope.

Skiing with a Shovel:
A Paleotechnician In Paradise

First published in *Colorado Central Magazine*, Dec. 1996

W hen I moved to the mountains, I imagined myself to be in retreat from "urban-industrial America."

I arrived, of course, in an automobile, with the back seat and trunk holding a record player, records, a toaster, boxes of mass-produced books and clothes, and all the other accoutrements of the mass-produced life (Sixties version) – enough to have told me, had I been listening, that maybe I wasn't so much fleeing civilization as advancing it.

But I also arrived in the mountains with a residual 19th-century sense of what "industry" was – a picture shaped not so much by my liberal-arts education as by the backdrop for that education: the city of Pittsburgh. When I attended Andrew Carnegie's temple of learning in the early 1960s, Pittsburgh had cleaned up a lot from its earlier days, but it was still a place of steel foundries that belched huge gasps of sulfur dioxide every Sunday evening, a land of fiery furnaces and fabricating plants and other great industrial hulks whose function I never knew.

So when I hired on at the Crested Butte Ski Area, which didn't look at all like Pittsburgh, I did not immediately realize that I had just

51

arrived at one of industrial America's new frontiers – where industry was moving from the mass-production of goods into the mass-production of good times.

The history of the Industrial Revolution consistently shows, though, that the reorganization of capital, labor, technology and resources into efficient industries does not happen overnight. It takes time to reduce production to a set of discrete mechanical tasks, most to be done by machines, others unfortunately still to be done by less predictable and efficient humans.

Social philosopher Lewis Mumford detailed the process in a book of his: in the process of industrialization, he said, there is a "paleotechnic" stage, in which the discrete tasks have not yet been identified, nor the machines invented which can do those tasks that can be done by machines. Until then, in that developmental stage of industry, humans do all the tasks in a machine-like way, over and over.

Crested Butte had experienced "paleotechnic industry" of the most obvious sort in its early days when it was a coal-mining town. Today coal-mining is still a dangerous sport, but it is highly mechanized: big reamers run along the wall of a seam under a hulking line of hydraulic shields that hunch themselves forward as the coal is ripped off the face and falls onto conveyors that carry it out. The miner has become a machine tender, and hardly has to touch the coal itself. But Crested Butte's paleotechnic miners prior to the 1950s literally clawed away at the coal seams with tools not much advanced beyond the pick and shovel, and every pound of coal that came out of the mine was moved by animal muscle – man and mule.

Ironically, when coal mining moved on into its truly technic era – a seismic change with which I was peripherally connected because my father was Product Engineer for the first commercial "continuous miner" – the machines increased miner productivity about a hundredfold, which means that – despite a booming demand for coal after World War II – lots of mines and their miners were no longer needed, and Crested Butte out on the edge ceased to be a coal mining town at the same time my father's company was achieving that triumph of mechanization.

But – equally ironically, I guess – I had no real understanding of industrialism when I arrived in Crested Butte in the mid-Sixties, so I didn't realize that these mountains with their ski lifts and cut trails were just another Industrial Age industry – in its paleotechnic stage, still getting its mechanization and technology up to speed. Nor did I realize, getting hired onto the Ski Patrol, that I was just repeating the history of the early coal miners in Crested Butte eighty years later, only aboveground: becoming an industrial muscle with a shovel.

Ski Patrollers today are basically paramedics, real professionals: most ski areas require them to have at least emergency medical technician training, some want crowd-management and law-enforcement skills – not to mention superb skiing skills. But when I patrolled at Crested Butte, a Red Cross card was enough, and Crested Butte was so strapped for employees the year I showed up that they just took my word that I could ski. When I think of some of the orthopedic and potential cardiac disasters I hauled off that mountain with no more training than you got for a Red Cross lifesaving card, I break out in a cold sweat. But I was young and stupid then – which left me eminently qualified for the rest of a patrolman's duties in that paleotechnic paradise.

To really understand, it is necessary to think about the nature of the industry – the production of good times. The very nature of skiing seems to make it an unlikely and precarious pursuit on which to try to base a good-time industry, since industries are based on the concept of the mass production of whatever: no mass, no industry. And to try to base a mass industry on something that takes place in the winter when it is cold, and depends on snow, which means that a lot of the time it will (god willing) be snowing – that doesn't automatically sound like a good mass investment. But America, then at least, was still a more Protestant nation than Catholic, and moderate suffering for pleasure was still a cultural value.

If, however, there was to be a successful industry based on creating good times in places where winter maxes out, it would have to eliminate the most predictable elements of serious suffering involved with sliding downhill on skis – and the most predictable and easily eliminated element of suffering there is the trip back uphill to earn the turns downhill. You can't change the weather that might shine or snow on the customer, but you can get him uphill quickly and give him the most pleasant possible trip back down, encouraging going up again. Getting them up the hill safely and down the hill safely – that is the industrial process.

Concerning the uphill part of the process – those of us who lucked into Crested Butte in the 1960s were really lucky. The main lift at Crested Butte while I worked there was an Italian three-passenger gondola –a lift so inefficient at hauling people up the mountain that the Forest Service only required a seven-person Ski Patrol, since it was impossible to put more than a few dozen people on the slopes at a time. Since it is an obvious fact that the greatest danger to people on the ski slopes is other people, we had minimal risk in that respect. The first year I patrolled at Crested Butte – a year for which there had been no marketing at all due to serious financial traumas the year before – there were days when seven patrolmen outnumbered the paying skiers.

But on the downside of that equation – meaning the side of the industry where the skiers were having a pleasant experience going downhill – we ski patrollers also had a major responsibility for keeping the slopes skiable. And our main tool there, in those paleotechnic days, was the Number Two Scoop Shovel – big metal shovels designed for grain but adaptable to snow.

To be sure, we had "snow cats" – tracked vehicles designed to operate over snow. But at that time, the snow cats were the most paleotechnic part of the ski industry, at least in mountain environments. They had been developed for arctic research stations and telephone linemen in places like the plains of north central Canada, where they needed a vehicle that could travel over level wind-crusted snow. They had tracks about two feet wide that worked well enough in any winter conditions except deep soft snow and steep slopes – which of course are the fundamentals of a ski area.

So a lot of our patrol time skiing with a shovel involved getting our snow cats unburied from something they had slid into, or off of. And sometimes, someone had to go down and back up the slow old lift to get a couple other primitive industrial tools, the ax and saw for some unauthorized trail widening when the cat has slid off into the woods.

But most of our other patrol activity in the paleotechnic era was a little more directly oriented to improving the skiing experience. And when you're part of a seven-man patrol (all men at that time, but there were women before and after my years on it) with responsibility for keeping the whole side of a mountain skiable, it gets challenging.

Snow, for instance: until you've lived in a place that gets a real blessing of snow, you can maintain a lot of misconceptions about it – like that it's always soft and fluffy. It is – for a few hours after it falls. But then it settles, and more falls on top of it and settles, and if you've operated a Number Two Scoop Technology in a place that gets three to five hundred inches of snow a winter, then you begin to get a sense of how glaciers could carve big bowls out of granite mountains, or even crack the crust of the earth to create the Great Lakes.

"Moguls" were the main problem. When rugged American individuals ski, most of them don't act very individualistic at all, but go right where others before them have gone, either because the terrain suggests it or just because it is easier to follow a track than to make one. And as a result, snow gets pushed and packed – I emphasize packed – into ever-larger piles between grooves that get cut ever deeper. The result is "moguls," from a Norwegian word, I've been told, that means "bumps in snow."

But "bump" hardly begins to describe a slope after a few days of traffic if the moguls are allowed to persist. Narrow canyons as deep as a person is tall separate carbuncular micro-mountains of hardened snow. Level or even up-sloped on the uphill side but with precipitous cliffs on the downhill side, those "bumps" are unskiable by all but the best skiers with shock-absorber knees for the canyons.

What to do? Well, in the paleotechnic era of the ski industry, we went out in the morning with our Number Two Scoops to attack the moguls, an hour before the lifts opened. But that was of course the time of day when everything is frozen hardest. Some of us worked with the shovels, busting the tops off the moguls; the rest worked with their skis, stomping the lumps tumbled into the canyons into smaller lumps marginally skiable.

Sometimes we got distracted too – snow-wheel competitions. We would cut the biggest round "wheels" we could out of the top of a mogul, then roll them down the slope, see whose went the farthest, or got the biggest air off a mogul, before it eventually crumpled into smaller lumps below.

We did that until the lifts opened, then went to our other duties, like hauling out of sight on our sleds the unfortunate victims of bad encounters between skiers and moguls. But when we'd been too long without new snow to hide or cushion the moguls, we would have to put two or three patrollers on slope maintenance all day. So there we would be, stripped to the waist and sweating like hogs under the Colorado sun, reducing big lumps to little ones while gaily dressed skiers zipped and careened and crashed around us: that was as nakedly paleoindustrial as skiing ever got.

In a kind of rural-agrarian way, we imagined better and tried to realize it. We had an imaginative Mountain Manager and a downvalley rancher's son who could rebuild or reweld anything man had invented. By March of every year, we would have some new contraption to try out for mechanically reducing moguls in a neo-paleoindustrial way. It always involved a patrolman perched precarious on the back to operate some mechanical levers that raised and lowered welded rows of teeth, blades attached to two-by-eights salvaged from the decaying part of the maintenance barn.... And one of us would ride this device – if really balanced and lucky – to the point where it was necessary to step off its transformation to debris that the rest of the patrol would then have to move off into the woods.

But better-trained minds than ours (not necessarily "better," just "better-trained") were working on the problem, and post-paleo solutions began to emerge. Now today, the minute the lifts close, fantastic machines growl to life and emerge from the maintenance sheds – snow cats with tracks four, six feet wide instead of two, hydraulically controlled blades and rollers that make the high places low and the low places skiable, with heated cabs with piped stereo to make the long night hours of creating the perfect recreation experience pass more quickly....

Snowmaking has also relieved ski patrolmen of dealing with the "bald spot" problem. Serious ski areas all have snowmaking potential spread all over their mountains: buried flex-pipe to which special nozzles can be connected when the temperature drops low enough, to convert a little water into a lot of something sort of resembling snow. Back in the paleotechnic era, when the snow cover got thin, ski patrolmen piled into the otherwise useless paleotechnic snow cats and went into the woods far enough to find some snow; we loaded it into the cat and went out and unloaded it onto the bare spots and tromped it down. Today, the snowmaking crew just hooks on the nozzle, points it in the right direction, and next morning the bare spot has a foot or so of something resembling snow.

So do patrolmen ski with shovels today? No. Not very much anyway.

But on the other hand, that's just the good news about the industrialization of skiing; the bad news is that they've also made the uphill movement of skiers a lot more efficient. The old three-passenger gondola that could move about 200 skiers an hour up Crested Butte Mountain has been replaced by a quadruple chair that moves four or five times that many people up the hill, and there are other networks of lifts making sure there are as many people going up as is technologically possible. But this also means four or five times more people coming *down* the slopes, and because accidents on the mountain increase exponentially with any increase in the number of people on the hill, the ski patrol does not get to relax and enjoy its freedom from the shovel. The Ski Patrol at Crested Butte today is five or six times larger than it was when I was on it, and they work harder than I ever did, doing the things that machines can't do, like helping other humans in trouble. There will never be a "robopatrolman" for that.

But I wouldn't trade their job for the one I had – even if I were technically, medically qualified. I haven't skied at an industrial ski area for almost a decade now: it's all too fast, too efficient – speedily up the hill, and either speedily down or you cower on the edges watching them speed past: it's too much like work. I've reverted to pre-industrial skiing, where if you want to go down the hill, you have to trudge up it first, "earn your turns" as the purists put it, and I'm not good enough on the turns to want to go up anything more than the gentle stuff.

It occurs to me that the paleotechnic stage of industrial society might be the only stage I'm psychologically fit for – which means, I guess, that I might be more into retreating from civilization than advancing it.

Winter Solstice

When at the end of a long black night
The far pale sun seems barely able
To reanimate the lazy crystal flicks
Of air beginning to fall out of air

When at the end of the brief blue day
The last lilac light glancing cold off the snow
Is so lovely it makes the heart ache
The way it makes the fingers and toes ache

In all this we can sense if not see
Earth's ponderously stupid tangential urge
To be free from the sun's imposition of order

And in this centrifugal surge we can only pray
That the sun will hold on, reassert order, that our sun
Still wants us, as much as we want our sun.

Summer Solstice

On the day when the sun lingers longest
We want to linger with it, don't want to think
Of the sweet slow retreat of the blessed light,
The aspen's capture in leaves of the leaving light,
The slowing pulse of life, the growth of night
That will lead to the distant short day when
Our prayers and fires are needed to turn again
The earth back toward the light, back from the night,
Back to the slush and flush of life resurgent, back
To this day when the sun lingers longest.

Slouching toward Simpletopia:
Simplicity, Superficiality,
And Other Roads Increasingly Traveled

Once a rustic, always a rustic – the simple life for me.
But living the simple life these days
is a very complicated proposition.
– Ernest C. Steele, 1928

First published in *Mountain Gazette* 79, March-April 2001.

"The simple life" continues to have *cachet*. In fact, it gets worse all the time. Every year we get a fresh crop of simpletopians here in the mountain valleys: people – young and old, rich and poor (usually either young and poor or old and rich) – wanting to "get back to the simple life," as though it were something we all once had but lost. Simpletopia. When I go to a big bookstore now, I find I can peruse whole racks of magazines and long shelves of books about "simplicity." It's become not just a yearning; it's an exploitable yearning: a "lifestyle" to be cultivated for profit.

I'm no pot to be calling the kettle black, of course. I was pretty much a simpletopian when I stumbled into the mountains in 1965, one of the young and poor variety. And I did a lot of things back in the 1970s that could have been construed as simplicity-seeking: after most of a decade at the end of the cultural road in Crested Butte, Colorado, my search for low rents and affordable time for writing led me and my family to a caretaking position six miles beyond the end of the plowed road. Even worse – after that, my lack of imagination and desperation for material led me to write a book in the late 1970s about my "life in the woods"; anyone who didn't read it closely might have put it on the "simplicity" shelf. As it happened, hardly anyone read it at all; it never really even made it onto the big bookstore shelves, which spares me the problem now of having to explain very often why my "life in the woods" really wasn't part of the simplicity movement.

But at any rate, my suspect past notwithstanding, I want to take a closer look at the simplicity movement. With the movement increasing in numbers and visibility about as fast as the pace of life in general is increasing, questions arise. Is "simplicity" real? Is it possible? What does it help? What does it offend?

***

The simplicity movement – the revolution, some call it – is most often described as "voluntary simplicity." As opposed, I guess, to the kind of involuntary simplicity imposed on those who truly have nothing, not even prospects – although such a life is rife with its own complications today. "Voluntary simplicity," according to one of the movement gurus, Linda Breen Pierce, "is not about living on as little as possible or about depriving ourselves. However, it does involve unburdening our lives, living more lightly with fewer distractions."

Pierce – author of *Choosing Simplicity: Real People Finding Peace and Fulfillment in a Complex World* – sees the movement as having two categories, or maybe they are stages. She says in an article in *Simplycity* magazine (September/October 2000): "Some people are interested in simplicity for those values that are primarily self-directed – more time, personal freedom, reduced stress, a slower pace, control of money, less stuff, fulfilling work, passion/purpose in life, joyful relationships, deeper spirituality, better health, and a connection with nature."

Others, she says, "are motivated more by other-directed values – protecting the earth's resources, remedying social injustice, serving the community, and caring for others." She observes that "many people first approach simplicity with an interest in self-directed values and later develop other-directed values. An almost magical transformation takes place (as) people...get acquainted with their true selves, and then naturally become aware of their connection to other life forms – people, plants, and animals.... They discover that their personal fulfillment is intimately connected with serving others."

Based on the evidence presently stacked on my desk, the chief means chosen for serving others, by the people who have discovered this type of "personal fulfillment," is to write a book or two or three to tell everyone else about the joyous virtues, the virtuous joys of the simple life. The shelf of titles is imposing: *Choosing Simplicity, The Circle of Simplicity, Simple Abundance, Return to the Good Life, Inner Simplicity, Living the Simple Life, Simplify Your Life with Kids,* and *Simplify Your Life: 100 Ways to Slow Down and Enjoy the Things That Really Matter.* Many of these are available as books on tape, so you can be inspired as you sit in the traffic on your local Interstate parking lot.

There is also an ever-changing array of magazines with some variation on *Simpl---* in the flags and evocative words like life, home, body, soul, style, et cetera in their subtitles. As is the case with most magazines, the real function of these publications is to bring readers together with advertised products that will realize the yearnings the publications feed on, from the serious hardware of the simple life in *Mother Earth News* to the organic lipsticks and "simple shoes" of *Real Simple* and *Simplycity.* One notes that most of the simplicity hardware is priced to keep the dollar flow up: if people are going to be buying less, then it only makes sense that they should pay more for it, and that's the reality of simplicity buying and selling.

Beyond the magazines are a host of catalog companies that feed, or feed on, the simplicity movement. At the origin of this species one suspects a December-May coupling of the grumpy old *L. L. Bean* catalog and the flower children's *Whole Earth Catalog*; the growing progeny from that union of ideas now also runs from serious hardware to a host of austere looking catalogs offering simple fashions that require complicated financing for all but the really wealthy.

The extent to which this is a modern growth industry is indicated not just by the product lines it has launched, but by the real and virtual webs of workshops, seminars and information sites spreading across the

61

nation, and the globe. You can keep up with the movement, and your manifold options for buying into it with all the websites that will pop up with a simple browse of "simple."

So what's really going on here?

Some of this stuff is so thoroughly precious as to be terminally irritating. There is a line of journaling guides and workbooks that holds the pole position at the "self-directed" end of the simplicity spectrum. These are written, I think, for women of vaporous spirit, women perhaps a little too sensitive for a testosterone-driven world; to such women is offered a sanitized and scented "inner journey" that will, if successful, leave them safely cocooned in – quoting from one of them – a "tapestry of contentment that wraps us in inner peace, well-being, happiness, and a sense of security." Important to this journey is finding one's "authentic self," the "woman we were meant to be," the inner woman who for decades has offered "overtures" that have been ignored: "Wear red...Cut your hair...Study art in Paris...Learn the tango."

These books are for women so I'm not going to go overboard in turning them into locker room humor. But despite a New Agey tone, this simpletopia seems to be solidly grounded in an earlier age, an almost Victorian sensibility. Reading in them, I began to think of "Mother," the central woman in E. L. Doctorow's *Ragtime,* the industrialist's wife who had grown up cocooned in a Victorian "tapestry of contentment," and spent most of her time trying to avoid suffocating in its folds, and in her own indulged and somewhat enforced uselessness – especially after she became more intimately aware of the extent to which her bourgeoisie tapestry of contentment was woven for the lucky few by the many laboring in industrial hell.

It's no great leap at all from that version of simplicity to the more commercial simplicity fashion magazines. Yes: wear red (here's two pages of simple red outfits), get that haircut (here's a list of salons that understand simplicitous style). This isn't voluntary simplicity; it's voluntary Victorian superficiality, for those who can afford the time and money. The real man who secretly longs for the end of feminism and a return to the time when women were ladies might try giving each new squeeze one of those kind of books: if she doesn't laugh out loud or throw it at you, you might have yourself a good Victorian keeper that you can get up and out of the way on a pedestal until you need her.

Almost as irritating, to me anyway, is the helpful hints literature, the seven or seventy or seven times seventy habits of simplicitous people. This is, however, probably the most American part of the genre because we Americans have always been suckers for someone stating the obvious to us in a numbered list. This represents an almost mystical faith in the power of books: I think we acquire them in the naive hope that, if we have them on our shelves, or maybe under our pillows as we sleep, we will never have to actually read them; the obvious good sense they represent will just seep into our lives the way a potpourri or a fart permeates our air. I read enough of one of these listing books to know that there is nothing there but pretty obvious common sense. "Drop call waiting." "Reduce your needs for goods and services." "Make water your drink of choice." "Do what you want to do." Okay. Sure. Makes sense to me.

But does anyone who is seriously moved to change his or her life really need this kind of advice? If you can't figure out your own "hundred ways to slow down and enjoy what really matters," you might as well save your energy and not start, because you're not going to be able figure out what to with all the time you save when you get there – although probably someone has a sequel in the works for that stage.

Once past these kinds of irritants, and the didactic, earnest and tendentious zeal that infuses it all, there is some reasonable stuff in the simpletopian literature – mostly because some of the books get past the "self-directed" level of indulgence in bourgeoisie superficiality, and on into the "other-directed" realms in which there is at least some examinable political and socioeconomic purpose driving the urge to simplify. Simplicity for some of its acolytes becomes a way of life in the world, not just an individual's commoditized "lifestyle."

Some of these books are worth mentioning by name. Linda Breen Pierce's book, *Choosing Simplicity: Real People Finding Peace and Fulfillment in a Complex World*, is her effort to find out if all this good formulaic advice actually works for people. "Most of the simplicity books I read told me *why* or *how* to simplify my life," she said, "but I found little written about real people who had actually tried it." (Pierce 18) She was curious about "the thin note of loneliness weaving through many of these stories" of people who had "simplified." (Pierce 14) The stories in her book seem to be upbeat but generally honest accounts of people fumbling along the path to simpletopia.

She herself admits, "When I look at my own life, I see that I have a long way to go before I can truly walk my talk. Even though I have reduced my dependence on material possessions and cut back on my utilization of earth's resources, I still consume more resources than four-fifths of the world's population.... (But) before a child runs, she must walk. Before she walks, she must crawl. I am at the crawling stage." (Pierce 38)

63

A nice disclaimer that should be more prominent in this literature – but might also leave one wondering if instruction in the early stages of crawling is really going to be worth the price and time.

Cecile Andrews, author of *The Circle of Simplicity: Return to the Good Life*, plows a lot of the same old terrain in the same old earnest way, but her real contribution to the movement is the idea of "simplicity circles," which are a close variation on the Swedish "study circles" that are credited with helping to shape modern Swedish democracy. And the Swedes in turn borrowed the idea from the "learning circles" of the American Chautauqua movement in the late 19th century, a kind of early "distance learning" program that filled a big gap in higher and adult education in the Midwest until it got co-opted by the pre-electronic entertainment industry. And the whole idea probably has its richest tradition in the Jewish Torah study groups that gave depth and meaning to the Jewish experience through many a diaspora (for men only, of course).

Essentially, "simplicity circles" are people gathering in living rooms, libraries or bars to discuss their progress in simplifying their lives, the problems they are encountering, and new ideas for new efforts. Who knows, all kinds of weird ideas, like democracy and social justice, might emerge out of such homely structures; when the corporate masters catch on, they will probably have them outlawed (although I guess turning them into Tupperware and Mary Kay circles has been a good way of co-opting or pre-empting the phenomenon). But however minute such phenomena might seem in terms of developing meaningful social or political or economic change, they are sure a lot more on track than cocooning oneself into a tapestry of personal comfort.

A big question lurks, however: is this kind of thing really "simplifying" life? Is getting together with a roomful of other people for serious discussion really a "simplification" of anything? Is democracy simple? Duane Elgin, in his book *Voluntary Simplicity: Toward a Way of Life that is Outwardly Simple, Inwardly Rich*, attempts to address this kind of paradox. For Elgin, living "more voluntarily" – more deliberately, intentionally, purposefully, consciously – is as important as living "more simply"; we live more *simply* mostly to remove the distractions that keep us from living more *voluntarily*, with "a more direct, unpretentious, and unencumbered relationship with all aspects of our lives: the things that we consume, the work that we do, our relationships with others, our connections with nature and the cosmos, and more." (Elgin 25)

Nowhere in his book does Elgin make what I think is the mistake of proclaiming that a life of "voluntary simplicity " is a *return* to anything

– bourgeoisie Victorianism, or the even more naive Currier and Ives ruralism. He begins in fact by saying he is not talking about living in poverty ("involuntary and debilitating"), not talking about turning away from economic progress (not "no growth" but "new growth"), not talking about embracing rural living ("rural living does not fit the modern reality"), and not talking about denying beauty ("rather than involving a denial of beauty, simplicity liberates the aesthetic sense").

Rather than a "return to the good life," Elgin calls for a movement – not just a solitary ambling by individuals out to save themselves, but a movement – *toward a way of life* that is somewhere we presumably haven't been yet. So doing, he kind of links this end of the simplicity shelf to the shelf of global economic alternative thinking that includes names like E. F. Shumacher, Herman Daly, Mary Clark and Hazel Henderson. He cites frequently from this shelf – drawing, for example, on Dana Meadows' analysis in *Beyond the Limits*: "If the human family sets a goal for itself of achieving a moderate standard of living for everyone, computer projections suggest that the world could reach a sustainable level of economic activity that is roughly 'equivalent in material comforts to the average level in Europe in 1990.'"

But what's so "simple" about all this? Elgin is pretty honest about that: "When we combine these two ideas (living more simply and living more voluntarily) for integrating the inner and outer aspects of our lives," Elgin says, "we can describe *voluntary simplicity* as a manner of living that is outwardly more simple and inwardly more rich, a way of being in which our most authentic and live self is brought into direct and conscious contact with living. This way of life is not a static condition to be achieved, but an ever-changing balance that must be continuously and consciously made real. *Simplicity in this sense is not simple.*" (Elgin 25, final italics added)

Ah.

Now maybe we're getting down to it.

***

I want to propose that there is a massive and unfortunate muddiness at the heart of all this "simplicity" discourse. We are, as usual, using words badly, trying to peg down good intuitions with sloppy articulations that we then commit to, as though some god had carved it out in stone for us; and the end result is a lot of misconceptions built on misconceptions that ultimately offend the original unarticulated intuition.

65

In the particular instance of this "simplicity" thing, I think the problem – in America at least – starts with Thoreau. That old cultural enigma, Henry. All of the simpletopians acknowledge him as the demigod who carved out "simplicity, simplicity, simplicity!" for us all, or found it carved in stone on Mt. Katahdin perhaps. Because we have made him a demigod, there's a general presumption that he must have known what he was talking about, and so we continue to perpetuate what may have just been Henry's massive misinterpretation of all his carefully collected data from nature.

Walden, or, Life in the Woods is one of my favorite books, but I don't like all of it. It's a Jekyll-and-Hyde book, exhibiting two Henrys: one is a classic old-school naturalist "observing Nature," looking for its "sermons in stone, books in the running brooks." But the other Henry is a preacher, a New World Jeremiah looking at a cultural landscape which I don't think he fit into, or liked enough to even understand in an empathetic way. In the long run of the book, I think the naturalist is a stronger and steadier presence than the preacher – but the preacher seems to have captured the imagination of modern America better.

To see the two Henrys at their close-woven best and worst, consider what may be the most famous passage from *Walden*. When Duane Elgin says "to live voluntarily is to live more deliberately, intentionally, and purposefully – in short, it is to live more consciously," we're just getting a typically earnest and pretty pedestrian paraphrase of the beginning of Henry's famous "simplicity" rant:

"I went to the woods because I wished to live deliberately, to front only the essential facts of life, and see if I could learn what it had to teach, and not, when I came to die, discover that I had not lived. I did not wish to live what was not life, living is so dear; nor did I wish to practice resignation, unless it was quite necessary. I wanted to live deep and suck out all the marrow of life, to live so sturdily and Spartanlike as to put to rout all that was not life, to cut a broad swath and shave close, to drive life into a corner, and reduce it to its lowest terms, and, if it proved to be mean, why then to get the whole and genuine meanness of it, and publish its meanness to the world; or if it were sublime, to know it by experience, and be able to give a true account of it in my next excursion." (66)

Well, that's good stuff; no one has ever better expressed that yearning to live "as deliberately as Nature," learning what life had to teach, and when Henry was focusing on that, he was as good it gets. But Henry's problem was that he could hardly go a page without having to look back over his shoulder at the village of Concord, at which point the naturalist immediately succumbs to the preacher. So he downshifts directly from that wonderful passage above into the rant that launched a thousand simplicity books:

"Still we live meanly, like ants; though the fable tells us that we were long ago changed into men; like pygmies we fight with cranes; it is error upon error, and clout upon clout, and our best virtue has for its occasion a superfluous and inevitable wretchedness. Our life is frittered away by detail. An honest man has hardly need to count more than his ten fingers, or in extreme cases he may add his ten toes, and lump the rest. Simplicity, simplicity, simplicity!"

And he's off and running.

It's not always easy to tell exactly what it was about antebellum Concord that Henry found to be so un-simple, so meanly detailed, so complicated – or why he found it so much more complicated than the profound complexity of the great hardwood forest communities that throve on the south slopes of New England. Henry the preacher was never so descriptive as Henry the naturalist. But I have to say that his diatribes don't fit my own experience.

I started this unfinished argument with Henry quite a few years ago, when I found myself out in the woods for a spell – winter caretaker for a summer biological field station up in the spruce and aspen about six miles north of Crested Butte. I'd like to be able to write as nobly as Henry wrote about my reasons for being there, an hour or four by ski beyond civilization, depending on the weather; but the truth is that I was there for the rent-free living, and the fact that, at a time when I needed a little drying out, it kept me out of the bars except for the weekly ski to town. I was there to see if I could make the big step from journalism to writing, and have to admit that the results are still mixed.

I also wasn't there under Henry's condition of solitude either; I lived in a sixteen-by-twenty cabin with my wife and son, who was six months old when we went there and a five-year-old when we left – by which time we also had a daughter. So my "life in the woods" wasn't very uncluttered, and it wasn't solitude – except when you stepped outside the door, into the whispering silent realm of all possibility that Henry called Nature.

And was there simplicity there, in "Nature"? Only if you didn't look very closely. Outside the cabin there was momentary relief from the clutter of culture inside the cabin; it was quieter outside my head than it was inside it. But to sit in it for longer than a minute just looking and listening – in our fine south-facing outhouse, or up on the edge of the springbox with the water dipper – was to begin to see and hear (even in the depths of winter) the rustle and rush of life, the grand fractal exfoliation of size and type and texture and color and scent that is nature. Nothing is simple there.

What I brought back from the woods, after four years of watching the ebb and flow of life there in the woods and floodplains of the East River valley – the mix of elbowing and collaborating, competing and cooperating that goes into the annual recycling of a plant community; the play of eagles on the mountain updraft and the badgering of skunks by badgers; the sad beautiful withdrawal of life into itself as our slightly wobbly planet tilts toward the long night, and then the soggy green explosion as the planet tilts back toward sun – what I brought back from all that was a rough measure of the magnificent *complexity* of real life, of "nature." And a sense of the extent to which civilization as we know it is just a great (one might say gross) set of *oversimplifications* imposed against nature.

This over-simplification is undeniable: in the conversion of the wild prairie to vast monocultures of wheat and corn, the conversion of mature multi-storied mixed forests to even-aged pine or Doug fir plantations, the replacement of a natural mix of animals with herds of inbred cows, the conversion of the mountain valleys first to timothy hay and now to monocultural expensive suburbs and golf courses – it's as if our ancestors, and now we ourselves, had looked at that random and rampant multiplication of diversity we call nature, and said: "Simplify, simplify!" Who wants all that motley of life? Who needs it, who can really bear it? How can we assert any economic order if we have to carry along the useless with the useful, the fiscally worthless with the worth more?

Our global civilization is probably different from the swarming of every other successful species – lemmings, army ants, whatever – mostly in the success we've had in extending our swarming phase through our technological adaptation to our needs and desires of all earth environments. We're working on simplifying the whole planet into a set of vast monocultures designed to serve just one single globally ubiquitous species. Even most of our efforts to slow or halt this process – the efforts we call "environmentalism" – have a kind of freeze-frame simplification to them: let's go back to the moment just before us, and make it mandatory.

When we stand back and take a look at this massive project of global simplification humankind is embarked on, solid science confirms what intuition suggests: it's a risky business. The more we simplify the planet in order to supply the swarm's needs, the more vulnerable we become to the kinds of changes that we can't control – the planet's wobble around the sun, the eruptions of tectonic activity in the restless crust of the earth, the vagaries of wind and water in the global climate. Not to mention the human-induced changes we probably could control if we wanted, like the buildup of human-generated greenhouse gases that exacerbates those vagaries, or our slow poisoning of air, earth and water.

The Mr. Hyde who urged us to "simplify, simplify" was also the Dr. Jekyll who observed that "in wildness is the preservation of life," and therein lies the two-faced paradox of Thoreau's message. If there were a "vast eternal plan" to the evolution of life on earth, which I doubt, then it would be the all-contingency type of plan evident in "wildness": basically, a plan to put out such a proliferation of interwoven, variant and redundant systems of life that there will always be something that will keep the life force churning along no matter what challenges and opportunities universal chance imposes on the planet, short of a direct hit by a bigger lump of galactic matter that knocks us out to somewhere west of cold dead Mars.

So in his lauding of wildness Henry the naturalist saw the need, or at least the incipient rationale, for a diverse complexity of systems. But Henry the preacher didn't seem to pay much attention to Henry the naturalist. So the naturalist's insight gets lost in the preacher's message, because the preacher's message seems to be just to do what we're inclined to do anyway: simplify, simplify our blue-green jewel of a planet down to our own comprehensible little anthropocentric tapestry of contentment.

As usual, irony treads on the heels of earnestness. Look at a couple of our greatest simplifications. The automobile, for example, which we tell ourselves is transportation. And indeed, it does transport us from one place to another: usually, eventually. But the automobile is primarily an instrument of convenience and insulation – simplification. Convenience because it enables us to just get in and go, rather than having to know a bus or subway schedule and having to organize our day around such schedules; and insulation because it enables us to move around without having to interact with all those idiots and assholes out there (except maybe occasionally flipping someone the bird through our protective wind-and-people-shield).

In short, it simplifies our lives – or seems to, until we start factoring in the cost of keeping one running, the cost of paying one off, the time lost in traffic jams, and so on – not to mention the externalized costs of all those by-products going up into the air, the replacement cost of fuel, and the eventual clutter of the landscape with its wornout hulk. When we look at all that stuff, an automobile starts to look a little less convenient. In exchange for a little simplifying of the immediate complexity of dealing with mass transportation and the masses, we pay through the nose and pile up an incredible clutter of complex problems for our kids to solve. But we allow ourselves to be persuaded by four-color ads that those costs are more than balanced by the gain in convenience and insulation – and we are easily persuaded to buy ever more massive and convenience-laden automobiles that lead to ever more massive traffic jams that make a mockery of "transportation." But transportation is not what the automobile is really about; it's about simplifying.

Consider too the simplification represented by "screens" in our lives. As in movie screens, television screens, computer screens, the windshields the British call "windscreens". We are a species that probably survived to the sticking point by telling each other stories. Colorado scientist R. Igor Gamow suggested that "being able to tell a story is perhaps humans' most distinguishing feature. . . . Storytelling was a means of holding early groups together and thus, since this was an advantage, was selected for."

But sitting around in a circle with a bunch of other people, some of whom are hard to like in spite of or on account of their stories: this is...well, it's not simple. Often it's inconvenient. Sometimes embarrassing. So a whole lot of culture has come to be about screening ourselves and those like us from the sometimes uncomfortably rich mix of all the rest of us. We go to great and expensive lengths to simplify our contacts; we no longer want to huddle around the fire with the rest of the tribe, telling and singing and dancing our stories, because the tribe is too big; we've swarmed; the stories have gone exponential. So we put more and more "screens" between ourselves and the swarm, screens that only let through the sad sweet funny songs of humanity in carefully measured doses, professionally filtered doses, with audience-tested stories, in the private comfort of our living rooms – with laugh tracks to tell us what is and isn't funny since we no longer have the rest of the sweating, smelly, milling mass right there to clue us. Simplify, simplify.

All of these efforts to simplify our lives are, of course, expensive in a number of ways, and they lead directly to a lot of clutter in our lives and throughout our world – mountains of clutter, vast landfills of it, barges circling the seas looking for new places to pile the clutter. But all of it: what is it but the consequence of a lot of efforts to buy our way out of the complexity of life, into a misbegotten vision of simple, insulated grace?

***

Some of us do get bored enough, stifled enough, in the clutter of small, screened, insulated tapestries of simplification we've woven around ourselves, to actually want to seek out the complexity of the larger world, and a lot of us instinctively come to the mountains for that, for a couple of reasons: first, because the gross monocultural simplifications of civilization have not taken so well in the more rigorous mountain environments, so the natural complexity of life is still residual. And second, mountain environments have kept the human swarm from arriving in its full strength. A city of millions just isn't possible in a high mountain valley – at least not without levels of organization way beyond our current capabilities.

But once here, we most of us do some variation on the Henry dance, imagining that complexity lies behind in the city and simpletopia lies here in these "quaint Victorian mining towns." But it's just the opposite: you've come from a massive but ultimately simple brontosaurus of a culture, a big but pretty straightforward eating machine that consumes the diversity of the earth and converts it to monocultural appetancy – and you've come to a place (if you were lucky enough to get there early enough) where there's little insulation, no cocoons, and the rich yuppie retiree with his 5,000 square-foot menopause manor ends up on the town council with the dreadlocked hippie Marxist freestore saint. And all of us who can afford it of course bring the baggage of the old urbanized simpletopia with us, and eventually recreate a lot of the old insulations and conveniences we thought we wanted to leave behind, because the real complexity of living together in small places, with large mountains watching, is – well, it's complex.

"This (voluntary) way of life is not a static condition to be achieved," said Duane Elgin, "but an ever-changing balance that must be continuously and consciously made real. Simplicity in this sense is not simple."

Well, then, let's come up with a better word for it than "simplicity." How about "complexity"? As in "the true complexity of life"? Then we might begin to develop a willingness, however cautious, to grow into the reality of life – to complexify, complexify, complexify! Make life interesting again! Even if it occasionally hurts a little! Throw off those Victorian tapestries and middle-class cocoons!

A quarter century ago, I resolved my one-sided argument with Henry – more or less – by suggesting that what he *really meant* (this is

71

easier to do when your proponent is a century or two dead) was that we should unclutter our lives of all those expensive simplifications piled up around us, in order to clear the decks of our consciousness to be able to truly embrace the real and important complexity of life that is going to impress itself on us (or our children) in the long run anyway.

In *The Golden Day*, a book about American culture in the 19th century, Lewis Mumford came to about the same conclusion about Henry Thoreau: "Thoreau was not a penurious fanatic, who sought to practice bare living merely as a moral exercise: he wanted to obey Emerson's dictum to save on the low levels and spend on the high ones. It is this that distinguishes him from the tedious people whose whole existence is absorbed in the practice of living on beans, or breathing deeply, or wearing clothes of a vegetable origin: simplification did not lead in Thoreau to the cult of simplicity: it led to a higher civilization."

But one has to overlook a lot of Henry the preacher to come to that conclusion – like Henry's assertion that "in proportion as (one) simplifies (one's) life, the laws of the universe will appear less complex...." Why do we always have to seek this kind of illusion? Why aren't we capable, as Keats begged, "of being in uncertainties, Mysteries, doubts," without having to look for 100 easy ways to make it simple? Why can't we turn around in Plato's cave and just squint into the sun, and say, *Goddam! How magnificently intricate, interwoven and complex this all is! How can we make ourselves worthy of our limited comprehension of such magnificence?*

To just acknowledge ourselves for what we really are would be a first step in answering that question, for of all the complexity that's woven into the tapestry of life on earth, we are probably the most complex thing so far – a form of life blessed, or maybe cursed, with the capability of being aware of it all, and of making choices about how to proceed further in the life project. But weighing the fruits of our consciousness so far, it's a little discouraging: on the one hand, a lot of good science, some good poetry, and a few exemplary lives like Gandhi's, all actively embracing the complexity of life; but on the other hand, hundreds of religions, political ideologies, socioeconomic theories, and cult movements all bent on pushing some particular brand of simpletopia in which 100 simple formulas rule and everyone is promised a tapestry of contentment (in heaven if not on earth) unilluminated by any troubling reminders of our true and truly difficult nature.

But see, I begin to rant on like Henry the preacher, and the first thing you know, I will be making notes for a book to launch a new cult:

100 Quick Ways to Begin Appreciating Life's True Complexity. Forget it.
But also forget simplicity. Go ahead and unclutter your life of some of
those things that were supposed to make life simpler now, at whatever cost
to the future, because they don't really work anyway – but then, buckle on
your cross-country boards, ski up a valley, and try to really look at the
fractal history unfolding all around you. Or just go to the local public
hearing on the latest subdivision proposal. Complexity, complexity,
complexity! Rejoice in it when you can, suffer it the rest of the time. But
what the hell: face up to it, and get beyond all this children's literature
about escaping it. Life is our destiny if we'll embrace it; it's us; and it's
not simple.

That Virtual Lake

Because he loved the dawn and the dusk
And all that was there between and before
(Except for the hard light of noon when
Life sleeps in the death of its shadows) –
Because of all this he thought he might be a poet.

Because he loved the women as they were
All that he saw and more imagined,
And loved the men the same only different
And wanted to see them all large as life –
Because of all this he thought he might be a poet.

Because all this pooled into a large lake
Beyond the green streams and rapids
Of his riverent soul, and he wanted
Wanted to share that lake with them all –
Because of this he hoped he might be a poet.

But as he practiced the long slow drain
Of that great lovely lake from deep in his mind
But could only do a pale wordatatime drip
Soaked up, blotted by the cold and white real –
Because of this he despaired of being the poet
He needed to be, to be that poet.

Remembering the Bots

Mostly from the *Crested Butte Chronicle and Pilot*, December 9, 1994, on the occasion of the death of Rudolph "Botsie" Spritzer, a Crested Butte native.

See you this coming fall, Captain.

The Bots said that a lot – I never figured out what it had to do with anything, but that's what he would say, instead of a simple goodbye: "So long, Captain. See you this coming fall." He called everyone "Captain" because he knew everyone and it saved trying to remember names.

Rudolph Spritzer, Botsie, the Bots, was a Crested Butte native; he was born at home in Crested Butte in 1915 and he lived there all his life until a couple years before his death in 1994, when he moved to an independent-living place for seniors down in Gunnison. Until the move to Gunnison, he had never moved farther from his place of birth than across the street, to the living quarters behind the ramshackle old saloon building a block off the main street where he let me locate the *Crested Butte Chronicle* in the late 1960s.

I encountered the Bots my first winter in Crested Butte – everybody did. A short, stocky little man with a nose even bigger than mine and a damaged arm, he was always out and about in town, and in the bars and restaurants, along with a lot of other old men from the time before

75

Crested Butte was a ski town. I was usually out in the bars for about the same reasons they were – bachelors looking for human companionship, or just looking.

There was something of a "Greek chorus" about the row of old men you'd find lining the bar in Franks's or Tony's in the afternoons, talking to each other through the mirror in the back bar – a gathering that kind of sat in judgment on everything that was going on around town. They were not unfriendly to us new people, just a little distant until we'd "lasted the winter," a fairly objective and reasonable criterion for evaluation.

But Botsie was a little more gregarious than most of the others. A born *bon vivant* and schmoozer – not to mention an aggressive flirt with an absolutely democratic approach to any and all women – he was kind of a one-man welcome wagon downtown. If he didn't know for sure whatever it was the inquiring stranger wanted to know – and he usually did – he made up something that worked well enough.

Botsie was also the town's resident accordionist; he played for dances nearly every week through the winter, and pretty often in the summer. Botsie and his "stomach Steinway" at the Grubstake or Frank and Gal's were my introduction to the union of polka and beer as something beyond the shuffling high-schoolish mating ritual that had always been dancing in my whitebread background – dancing instead as pure transcendent celebration of just being alive and, at least for the moment, loving it. Botsie was self-taught on the accordion; we were mostly self-taught on the dance floor: the best way to learn.

The Bots had entered the world in about the middle of the big family of Martin and Appolonia Spritzer – seven boys and two girls. Martin and Appolonia were both immigrants from the Croatian part of what we know as Yugoslavia. Their story was pretty standard: Martin came first to the United States; he got to Glenwood Springs and the mines there, and despite abysmal wages, got far enough ahead financially to bring over Appolonia, who Botsie said was the daughter of a *tsar*, a kind of tribal or village leader. They eventually made their way to Crested Butte around 1890.

Martin himself had something of the *tsar* or tribal "big man" about him. He was physically a big man, outgoing, generous, gregarious, and because of those traits destined to get by okay but not get rich in a commercial culture that respects but doesn't reward generosity and just tolerates gregarity. He was a good enough miner and politician to work his way into a foreman's position, and the family (with the help of a few sons bringing home most of their wages) eventually managed to get enough ahead to get out of the mines entirely and purchase the business building across the street – a rambling story-and-a-half false-front saloon building with maybe a thousand feet of living space behind the saloon room. That was where Botsie and his siblings grew up, and where the Bots lived almost all his life, eventually alone as everyone gradually left home, one way or the other.

I batched there with the Bots for a year or so, and it seemed a little small at times for only two of us. I tried to imagine the seven brothers sleeping up in the little upstairs room and frankly, couldn't. That kind of a concentration of adolescent dreams and nightmares, midnight mumblings, arms and legs flopping around, beer sweats and sauerkraut farts – it's not in the suburban American cultural imagination to even conceive of it.

It was Martin Spritzer's bad luck to buy a saloon just in time for America's Noble Experiment with Prohibition. That was, however, only a minor setback for saloonkeepers in immigrant towns like Crested Butte where tradition and culture were stronger forces than puritan morality. Botsie and the other old men told of the freight car of grapes that showed up in town every fall, the grapes efficiently and untraceably distributed throughout the town by the following morning. There was a reasonably well-disguised cellar under Spritzer's saloon with several barrels of wine. There were also local purveyors of popskull whiskey and beer – about all Prohibition seems to have done was to remove any quality controls from the production and distribution of alcoholic beverages.

What was always of both quantity and quality in Spritzer's saloon was the music. Martin himself played a variety of instruments – the tamburitsa (a Yugoslavian stringed instrument that came in sizes from mandolin-size to string-bass-size), the violin and the clarinet. Some of the older Spritzer sons played the accordion and whatever Dad wasn't playing. And among the regulars at the bar were a saxophonist, more accordionists and tamburitsa players, somebody who played another Yugoslavian instrument called the berda – and if you didn't play an instrument, you played your feet. You danced.

There were a lot of kids growing up in Crested Butte in the 1920s and 30s, despite the odds against it which were large. The normal coal dust and smoke that infiltrated the whole town, not just from the mining but from everybody burning coal for heat in mostly uninsulated buildings, was bad enough, but on top of that there were 80 coke ovens cooking the impurities out of coal and emptying it into the air, and all this in a valley prone to inversions – it's a tribute to human adaptability and durability that anyone survived there at all. And a stroll through the cemetery shows that a lot of kids from those years didn't survive. Two of Botsie's siblings didn't.

But a lot of them did survive; the Bots did (if not unscathed), and like all kids, found it a good place to grow up in because it was what he knew. According to the Bots, there were idyllic days, up Coal Creek fishing or playing "William S. Hart" cowboy games. Evenings there were neighborhood games of "Run sheep run" and "Hide'n seek" – but only till 8:00: that was the town curfew for kids. It was a town that took seriously the idea that it takes a village to raise a child.

But the flip side of that was the xenophobic nature of the Old World cultures that made up the reluctant melting-pot amalgam of the village. It's the village culture to take care of your own kind but to be wary of everyone else, and ethnic and cultural differences were made a big deal, distinctions that trickled down to the kids. If you were from the "roundhead" (Yugoslavian) part of town, you didn't go to the "dago" or "pollack" or "yaicher" parts of town without a small army, and if you went with your small army – the Coal Mine Gang, the First Street Gang, or the Yaichers from north of Elk Avenue around the Congregational Church – then you went looking for trouble. A lot of it was just name-calling and rock-throwing across the well-drawn borders, but there were occasional matchups of the strong man from one gang against the strong man from another. Basically the same story that was being played out in all the industrial cities of America – but a little more concentrated in the physical space, and without the huge inertial masses of people.

In one or another of those games, Botsie took a bad fall and hurt his left arm. Everybody thought it was just a sprain, but it was actually a break of the big bone. Untreated and uncoddled, a bone infection developed, and most of the bone had to be removed, which left the Bots with what was a serious disability for a working man in an industrial society – assuming one wanted to be an industrial worker, which the Bots actually didn't.

His lack of enthusiasm for what passes for work in an industrial society manifested itself early, in our American indoctrination into industrial behavior: school. Botsie hated school. "Why did they want to take my life away and put me in prison?" he asked with typical passionate purple rhetoric.

He claimed to have gone to school for 12 years without getting out of grade school. I found that hard to believe; he was so sharp and quick that I couldn't believe – even in the days before the "social pass" – that anyone as smart as the Bots could manage such discipline and creativity in acting dumb. But when I asked other members of the Greek chorus if that was true, I would get the kind of vague answers that suggest a myth in the making: some stories sound so good that, even if they aren't true, it's a more enjoyable and interesting world if you allow them to be thought so.

His long tenure in some of the elementary grades he attributed to a preternatural affection for some of the single women teachers who came to town (back when women could only teach until they married). "If she was pretty and had a four-year contract in fourth grade," said the Bots, "so did I."

He said that in his 12th year, the school gave him what he thought might be a graduation certificate, but when he opened it up, he found an eviction notice. It may be true – and may have been directly related to something like the time he claims to have performed a bathroom act on a hot radiator to generate a day off.

But if he didn't show much interest in school learning, he certainly had a penchant for learning the kinds of things he saw as important. Hunting, fishing, and making music were three of those. Growing up in his father's house, he taught himself to play the accordion as soon as he could hold it. Nobody encouraged him, which probably helped.

But his real developed art was in fishing, and maybe to a lesser extent, hunting. Basically, I think the Bots was a hangover from the Paleolithic, one of those in whom our residual hunter-gatherer hard-wiring was still strong. He could get by in the Neolithic when he had to – working off and on at a variety of jobs, from surveyor's rodman to camp cook to whatever, to all of which jobs he brought a basic field intelligence, sense of humor and fast talk that enabled him to get by. But he was only truly inspired by work when he was either on the hunt (and fishing is hunting, just different tools) or cooking up the results of the hunt.

Summer was his season – summer and fall, and even the mess of melt mud and late snow called spring in the high valleys. Winters he kind of hibernated – I remember working in the office one afternoon around dusk, and the Bots kind of stumbling out of the living quarters in the back; he asked me what time it was. "6:00," I said. "That A.M. or P.M.?" he wanted to know.

But in the summer, he was up early, no matter when the night before had ended, and ready to go. He ran an unofficial and probably slightly illegal guide service out of the bars. He'd be dressed and waiting when some hungover tourist from the cities of the plain, someone he'd met the night before, would come weaving down the street, maybe with a family in the car, and off they'd head for some stream or river.

The Bots was a fantastic fisherman. I'm a lousy fisherman, but know the real thing when I see it. I go out with the attitude that anything stupid enough to be fooled by whatever's disguising my hook probably deserves to die, and the fish, I think, sense that grumpy attitude. But people like the Bots – and his godson, my son, is another – they seem to surround themselves and their hook with the aura of feast, a party to which they are inviting the fish to take a central role, and the fish all but line up to be part of it all.

I remember fishing with the Bots up at a local reservoir one nasty spring day before the streams were clear enough to fish there. To make lake fishing interesting enough, Botsie put two hooks on his line, and three times he hauled in two fish at a time while I was still waiting for something to at least steal my bait. So I accused the Bots of taking the good spot since he knew the lake.

"So let's trade," he said, and we did – and he started pulling out matched pairs from where I'd been standing. I can't explain it.

I actually saw this mystery enacted in detail, once up in the West Elk Wilderness with my son, Botsie's godson, who was about nine at the time. We were fishing some little willow-bound creek up there, where the willows were too thick for throwing a line around on a long pole, so we'd rigged up a little two-foot willow stick with about eight-feet of line and a little hook on it with salmon-egg bait, trying for little six or eight inch native cutthroat. Actually Sam was fishing, I was just watching over his shoulder: he would creep through the willows to the bank, and hand toss the line into a pool where we could see the fish swimming around.

One fish in particular – I knew the fish must have seen us, and he wasn't even coming by to look at the salmon egg anymore. "C'mon, Sam," I said; "he's seen us, let's move on."

"No," Sam said, "he's going to come." And sure enough – a few flips more and the fish just gave up, gave in, joined the feast. That's the kind of fisherman the Bots was, and I'm glad it rubbed off on my son, if not on me. I don't fish anymore, but I appreciate someone who does it well.

The fact of the matter was, most of the fish the Bots caught did get to participate in a feast, at least if he was doing the cooking. He had no patience for Neolithic chores like coal-mining or any other day-in, day-out work, but he made a seamless flow of stream-to-table work that seemed –

to me at any rate, frequent beneficiary of such work – to bless the whole process.

One of the *holiest* meals I've ever eaten was late one October night, when he and Fritz Kochevar and a bunch of their interrelated nephews and cousins from all over the state celebrated a big elk one of them had shot that day by cooking up his liver and heart. All my life I had hated liver, mostly because it usually came to the plate just a little more tender than fillet of sole – shoesole. But the way the Bots cooked it – and I've tried a lot to replicate it for my family, but with only middling success at best – it was food from a better world.

There was nothing sanctimonious about that evening; it was just a big raucous celebration of the sort that beer ads try to imitate – but that liver sat in the middle of the table like a great dark flower till the Bots sliced it up and turned it into food for gods, and it touched the night with grace. No gods there, just us; but it made me want to live a better life, live up to that elk.

One of the only really smart things I did as a newspaper editor in Crested Butte was to "hire" Botsie to write a column, which he wanted to call – naively or knowingly, I didn't know – "The Sporting Life." A lot of local history got into his column, which had been my first thought on asking him, but the Bots had no real sense of history; he was a true Paleolith in that all time was always present, and the stories he told always had the pedigree of people and place attached that kept them living.

He was a lot better at telling stories than writing them down, truth to tell. Sober, he wrote like a guy who had spent a lot of time hating school. A couple beers into a story, there was a point when he would start writing like he talked, but that point passed pretty quickly, and inspiration began to run away with the pencil; the writing became a wavy line that flowed like a river and was about as readable. So we resolved it by me becoming Boswell to his Johnson: Monday evenings, I hunted him down wherever he was, and he dictated what he'd been thinking about. It worked better if I got him earlier in the evening rather than later – but not always. I remember one cold winter night when I found him later rather than earlier, and he had to interrupt his rambling dictation to go relieve himself. Coming back looking for his fly, he said it was sure a lot better than having to use the outhouse and "backing away from the icicle." That observation launched a column that got more letters of outrage and approval than any of my great editorials.

Having the Bots on the side of the newspaper was sound from the business side too. He averaged about a subscription a night through the summer and fall – he'd find me the morning after and give me a wad of dollar bills with a couple bar napkins that either had addresses on them or what looked like spider squashmarks.... Sometimes I'd get a note mid-fall from somebody down in the cities of the plain saying they thought they'd subscribed to Botsie's newspaper. I'd send a fast note in response thanking them for solving yet another mystery, and add a six-month bonus on their subscription. He also got the occasional ad – like the time he met a Jeep dealer from Montrose and talked him into doing an ad with his Jeep up on the bluff west of town and I had to go up and take the kind of an ad picture I fundamentally hate.

When the newspaper got evicted by a pizza oven from the back room of Tony's Tavern, where I was working off the rent bartending a couple of hours so the owner could go eat dinner, Botsie said I could come use the old saloon area if I could figure out how to keep it warm – and he knew where we could get a stove just for picking it up. I told him I couldn't really pay much rent until I figured out how to run a newspaper. That's okay, he said. We'll get by.

So we got by, for a time, until the get-ahead philosophy dominant in the 20th century kind of rolled over the get-by philosophy.

As we newcomers worked, kind of mindlessly, to re-industrialize the town around tourism rather than mining (a different kind of mining), there was a tendency to make the old timers from the mining era a kind of living furniture for our "quaint turn-of-the-century Victorian mining town," as the brochures put it. That was about the point where the Bots would either get really grumpy and drunk, or would maybe (actual event) just grab the breasts of the nearest woman who thought he was quaint Victorian furniture and say, "How are you captains!" The Bots wasn't furniture to be taken for granted in anyone's world.

The Bots turned me around in a lot of ways. Took a once well-trained but confused kid and taught me how to dance and at least understand why I couldn't fish, and introduced me to the Paleolithic philosophy that worked for our first three or four million years: we'll get by.

Somebody (not the Bots) told me once that "botsie" – or (phonetic spellings) "botsa" or maybe "batza" – was a Slavic-root word for "the old people" or "earlier people" – maybe like what the Celts called the "Tuatha du Daneen," the people from before who were there first but whose time had passed.

It had happened to the Bots' people in the valley of the Upper Gunnison; when the Crested Butte mines closed in the early 1950s his brothers and sister had to leave to find work, most of them down to Colorado's Front Range cities. But they came back every summer – usually around the Fourth of July: an occasion that caused the Bots great stress in its anticipation but joy in its execution. They still come back every summer – no longer to Crested Butte *per se*, but to the valley, all converging with tents and trailers and campers on an aspeny place up one of the valleys not far from town. Botsie's brother Emil brings his accordion; his son Dennis his guitar (an American tamburitsa); brother John's son Marty another accordion – et cetera: it has all changed, and it is all the same.

And a growing number of the Bots' nephews and nieces and grand-nephews and nieces have made their way back to the valley, to work at this and that in the local economy.

So we'll get by. And with their help, someday maybe even begin to rediscover what it is to live here without needing to get ahead, to improve ourselves, to make things better, to do well by doing good, to get rich – we'll learn again to just get by, captains, and our gain will be nobody else's loss.

See you this coming fall, captain.

My Church

My church is the church of
The resurrection through rot,
My faith is my belief in the law
The universal I hope immutable law of
The conservation of matter and energy.

The despair that drives me to prayer,
The dark vision that fires my fear and outrage
Is the gray night at the entropic end
Of all that was, is and will be in
A universal dispersal of waste,
All that was, is and will be then become
A spread of spent gas and molecular dust,
A dark dust cloud with no points of fire,
No sparks of new starts,
The heat death of the universe.

That's the despair that drives me to prayer,
To the resurrection through rot,
To my faith my belief in the law
The universal I hope immutable law of
The conservation of matter and energy.

The Trouble with Money: Mountain Town Economics

*For Mike, Cazoo, Denny, Tom and all us other Crested Butte
Idea Capitalists, this past half century.*

First published in *Crested Butte Magazine*, Winter 1992-93, revised June 2004.

T he purpose of this piece is to arouse awareness about the most addictive, most culturally destructive, and most abused substance known to humankind: money.

Some conventional Christian capitalists might want to gently correct that, and suggest that "love of money," or maybe "lust for money," is what is destructive, but the same can be said of all the other drugs this society wars against, and in all those instances, we are expected to believe that stomping the addictive substances out of existence will eliminate the "love of substance" problem. I've always thought this dubious, given our desperate creativity in always being able to find something with which to mangle our minds. But where money and its corruptive effects are concerned – far more pervasive and pernicious than all the opiate and coca derivatives put together – we hardly even have a guerilla war going on; as a society we've surrendered completely to the predations of money.

Until I came to the mountains, I thought that money was good because we were a capitalist society, and I thought, or had been generally encouraged to think, that money and capital were one and the same. This was because I'd grown up in a mostly decadent capitalist society where money had already driven out or destroyed all the higher forms of capital.

But coming to the mountains in the mid-1960s – and especially to Crested Butte – I was coming to a region that was mostly lagging behind the rest of America in decadent capitalistic institutions; money had not yet driven out all of the higher forms of capital. The forces of money-driven capitalism had, in fact, already failed twice in Crested Butte: once around 1950 when Colorado's steel industry had found itself overextended and closed down its more remote fuel mines, and again just before I got there in 1966, when the first assault on converting the local economy to a resort industry had failed, due to too much arrogance trying to cover for too little money spread too thin.

So when I arrived in Crested Butte in November 1966, shortly after the forces of money capitalism had had to retreat for a financial reorganization that most locals mistook (unfortunately) for the rout of bankruptcy, there was very little money around town. The historic mining economy was all but dead, no coal-mining at all and nothing but a little R&D work going on up at the hardrock Keystone Mine; and the financial reorganization at the ski area didn't get sorted out until a month before the ski season, which pretty much precluded advance marketing, even if the "reorganized" owners could have afforded any.

But bad as that was for those with money-capital investments in the valley, it was a good time for moneyless capitalists like myself to come into the place. Ultimately, it enabled me to witness firsthand that process of money driving out higher forms of capital. I am embarrassed to say I even helped it along.

I did not, of course, think of myself as a capitalist at that time; I thought of myself more romantically than that – proud rebel above material concerns, follower of as yet unidentified impossible dreams, the postmodern Promethean English Major Unbound. Or, reflected in the eyes of locals who had seen me before: Ski Bum.

But I also started to learn some basic capitalist economics that winter, although it took a while for it to settle in that that was what I was learning. That learning mostly took place down at a local economic exchange called the Grubstake Bar and Restaurant. "Grubstake" is, of course, a respectable capital concept: a "grubstake" is money capital that someone who has money but no ideas advances to someone who has ideas but no money, on the gamble that the grubstaked's idea will reap enough reward to return the grubstaker's money with a dividend.

Well, we are all accustomed, or more probably indoctrinated, to recognize the grubstaker's money as capital. But what would the money do with itself if it didn't have an idea to latch onto?

I looked it up in one of those serious books I've accumulated over the years, either from college or my post-graduate yard-sale education: Robert Heilbroner's *The Economic Problem* – a book I still keep around because Heilbroner occasionally shows signs of a sense of humor, usually coinciding with something in the text I can actually understand. But Heilbroner defined capital as "anything which can enhance man's power to perform economically useful work" – and "economically useful work" had earlier been discussed as the production and distribution of the goods and services necessary for the society to – well, for the society to continue producing and distributing the goods and services necessary for the society to continue producing and distributing – et cetera.

But anyway – money wasn't just automatically capital; it only became capital when invested in useful work, the production of goods and services for the society. And if the person with money didn't have any real ideas for the production of goods and services for the society, and needed to link up with someone who had ideas – then who had the real capital?

More recently, a much more comprehensive definition of capital has emerged from the mountain region – from the Rocky Mountain Institute over in the Snowmass valley. Amory Lovins, Hunter Lovins and Paul Hawken have published a Big Book called *Natural Capitalism* (on my shelf now with the old Heilbroner) that gives a four-part description of "capital":

- *human capital*, in the form of labor and intelligence, culture, and organization
- *financial capital*, consisting of cash, investments, and monetary instruments
- *manufactured capital*, including infrastructure, machines, tools, and factories
- *natural capital*, made up of resources, living systems, and ecosystem services

That kind of thinking – which was probably partially hatched in some Roaring Fork version of our Grubstake Bar and Exchange – would

87

have elevated the discourse a lot in Crested Butte's Grubstake, where the human capital sat around trying to ignite out of alcohol's blue brainflames some larger illumination of the situation; instead, the conversation usually got doused at some pregnant pause as some stupid son of convention would say something disgustingly trite like, "Well, when you come down to it, money talks," as if he was being profound, was putting the period on a life sentence.

But back to Heilbroner – for those of us without money, in a town without money, he had a wonderful footnote on the section about capital (and where else but in footnotes would people on the margin of the mainstream expect to find hope?): "Is money capital?" he asks. "It certainly is to the individual who possesses it. But it is not capital for society as a whole. For money only represents *claims* to society's real wealth, which is its goods and services. If an individual's money disappears, he loses his claim to those goods and services, and we can indeed say he has lost his 'capital.' But if *all* money disappeared, we could not say that society had lost its claim to its own wealth. It would only have to devise another system of tickets."

Whew! Is revolution writ there or what? Just devise another system of tickets! That footnote, unarticulated at the time, hovered over the meetings at the Grubstake those moneyless years like a murky will-o'-the-wisp that nobody could quite figure out how to catch – but efforts were made, and we did learn something about what human capital, investing in idea capital, can do without much money capital.

Consider, for example, the story I think of as "Portrait of an Artist with One Thousand Railroad Ties." This artist was one of the twenty-somethings who came out of nowhere in particular those years with a modest wad of money, the provenance of which we were all too polite to ask. There were lots of little pots of money like that floating around town in those days – the convention came to be to conjure up an indulgent and recently dead grandmother and call her alleged benefactor a "trustfunder." Most of them invested in something entirely conventional like a house. But not this artist.

In the summer of 1971, he invested a piece of his stash in a truckload of railroad ties. Why? Well – why not? Because they were there. But the challenge was to find some way to use them, and he and another artist-capitalist decided that Crested Butte should have an Arts Festival, which could take place in a structure made mostly of railroad ties. Why not?

They cornered me, as editor of the local newspaper, in the Grubstake Bar and Exchange one day, and laid out the idea. The artist-capitalist with the railroad ties happened to have some connections with the Austin music scene – then just cranking up – and Crested Butte had quite a few pretty good artists and craftsmen, of the year-round as well as the summer sort. So why not have an Arts Festival? Well, it sounded to me like news, something that could actually happen, more interesting than what was actually happening: why not?

So I became an investor with my media capital. I didn't, of course, know at the time that that was what I had, in having a newspaper with which I could do anything that didn't offend the subscribers and advertisers too badly. And certainly espousing an Arts Festival that might actually happen – an event that might bring a few dozen curious potential customers to town – didn't offend anyone, and even recouped the favor of a few who had been offended before.

It should be noted here, and now, that arts festivals have matured a lot since 1971. Matured, aged like fine wine, gained a self-satisfied middle-aged spread, et cetera. Crested Butte's Arts Festival today has evolved as a lovely, juried exhibit of beautiful expensive stuff by a couple hundred artists from all over the West. But in 1971, there weren't many good examples to learn from – and Crested Butteans then, myself included, weren't much into learning from examples elsewhere anyway. Arrogant hippies is what we basically were, destined to learn the hard way. What the Artist with A Thousand Railroad Ties and his partner had in mind was not what has emerged as the "Beautiful-Stuff-for-Sale" Arts Festival, but more of a "Community-as-Art" Festival – people putting something together according to a plan that would more or less emerge out of the effort of putting it together. Communal art in its most fumbling primitive essence.

The "something" that got put together in this case was a kind of rustic, rambling, shady pavilion, built in an empty lot (now the parking lot for Crested Butte's Post Office): it had a foundation of (you guessed it) railroad ties laid on the ground in patterns like big parquet tiles, posts borrowed from someone's firewood pile (the ties were narrow-gauge, too short for roof posts), raftered and roofed with wood from a big old outbuilding that got recycled that summer. (We weren't yet a Historical District, where recycling the past to create the future is heresy).

The capital invested here? Mostly muscle and blood, as the song says, with a little on-site brainpower deciding which direction the structure should ramble next. A couple dozen woodhippies and roadfreaks and established locals (been in town two weeks or more) worked on this erection for two weeks, for beer and occasionally food and, more rarely, surreptitious uncontrolled substances – actually finishing it in time for it to be decorated with the work of Crested Butte's semi-permanent and visiting artists and craftspersons (more capital investment), while a bunch of visiting Texas musicians, led by the then-unknown Michael Martin Murphy, sang in the vacant lot across the street.

All skeptical predictions to the contrary, it was a lovely mellow weekend – and the loveliest thing about it was that strange pavilion, cool and dusky and smelling of creosote. Was it a safe structure? It never occurred to us to ask, or worry – I don't remember whether there was even a building permit. Crested Butte was a lot more relaxed about that kind of thing then. But it didn't matter; it didn't cave in, and a week later, it was gone – the ties reloaded on a truck and moved somewhere, the posts returned to the lender's firewood pile, the recycled barnwood moldering in the vacant lot until mid-fall when a town councilman lined up the town dump truck, a crew from Starika's bar next door (the town bought a round), and hauled it to the dump, where it got accidentally incinerated in an illegal fire a few days later.

But the capitalist idea of the Community-as-Art Festival had been planted and nourished, and the next summer, 1972, there was some new capital invested, very little of it money either.

That was the year after I'd sold the newspaper and moved out to the biological field station as caretaker and unofficial writer in residence. When the road was open late May and I came into town to work construction, I found myself on a crew with one of the Vietnam vets that were then using the town as a kind of sanitarium for trying to rebuild their sanity. In after-work discourse at the Grubstake Exchange, it came out that he knew theater – had in fact been trained and even employed in the art and craft of theater in Chicago before his draft number came up. He didn't just know theater, he loved theater and wanted to do theater, and (being without suitable evening employment, no longer having a newspaper calling) I wanted something to do that would keep me from turning into a total barfly. And I wasn't alone there; quite a few people in town were looking for something to make the beers they were going to drink anyway at least a celebration of some achievement, starting later in the evening.

So we had another big moneyless capital investment, in conjunction with the Second Annual Crested Butte Arts Festival: the investing of the Crested Butte Mountain Theater. The Vietnam vet invested the idea capital and the knowledge capital, and the Grubstake

Exchange provided the energy capital. That original summer production – "Dark of the Moon," an old hillbilly version of the Barbara Allen legend – had a cast of dozens; the vet and I rewrote the script a little to make room for more, and threw in some more song and dance.

It wasn't a startup entirely devoid of money capital; we needed a few hundred dollars worth of wood and Romex cable and the like to build and light a stage out in the schoolyard, and the vet and I put that in upfront out of our paychecks, certain that it would come back after the show, which it did. We also needed a form of human capital that can be as good as money, which is local knowledge, and I had that: I knew whom to talk to get the use of the schoolyard and the gym for rehearsals, whom to talk to at the college to borrow some lights, whom to talk to at the Electric Association to get a slightly illegal line and some help in the touchy task of splitting 220 volts into 110 volt lines, et cetera. And a lot of townspeople invested human capital – muscle power, music power, the brain power necessary to not just learn lines but to learn how to deliver lines from an exacting and often hard-driving Vietnam vet who turned out to take theater so seriously that he infected us all with a sense of a higher calling that was absolutely new for a lot of us.

It was another successful investment in the Community-as-Art Festival. We got our $500 back – and could have taken a return on the investment, but left it in the company.

There is a misconception in Crested Butte today – a lot of it spread by the current generation of Mountain Theatre and Arts Festival organizers: the misconception that the founders of their organizations were brave aesthetic pioneers, bringing culture in, gently raining it down on the unwashed. Nothing could be farther from the truth; we early organizers just looked around ourselves, at the people flocking to the edge, the margins of civilization, and realized that this was where the creativity was, just needing a little capital organization. We didn't want to bring in art, theater; we wanted to develop what was waiting for release there. The Crested Butte Mountain Theater – in its origins – never wanted to be the theatre version of the Aspen Music Festival, importing great musicians for imported audiences; we wanted people to come see something homegrown but unique and good, something that for better or worse could only have happened there, through us.

There were, of course, other more conventional ideas around town, and this all kind of came to the fore the next year – 1973 – when we began to move into a new era of capitalism locally. The Community-as-Art people should have seen it coming because there had been mutterings at the 1972 Arts Festival about "quality" in the arts on display, although there weren't a lot of specifics – which is probably why we didn't see it coming.

But that winter, when we were beginning to think about beginning to commence to proceed to start planning for the summer, a schism emerged. Some of us wanted to move on even deeper into the celebration of the Community-as-Art. After a couple of really interesting winter productions, the Mountain Theater was envisioning the World's Highest Ever production of "The Persecution and Assassination of Jean-Paul Marat as Performed by the Inmates of the Asylum of Charenton under the Direction of the Marquis de Sade." And a wood butcher who had been skeptical about the whole business had said in a bar one afternoon, in front of witnesses, that he thought a real example of community art would be a 50-foot totem pole chain-sawed by local artists, and the tree for that, to his surprise and maybe chagrin, was quickly on order with logger Joe Rozman. Et cetera – ideas all over the floor, piling up in the corners.

But there were other people in town who thought it should be more about "quality." Essentially, they wanted a juried art show, with recognized artists selling their wares to a clientele lured there by the promise of quality, to spend on quality.

Is it just coincidence that this was a time when a lot of the businesses in town were being sold by people who couldn't make a go of it on their mortgages, to new people like themselves at even higher new mortgages? People like themselves who'd never run a restaurant, but wanted a simpler quieter life and imagined running a restaurant was easy enough? No, I would not say this was just coincidence. I myself had sold a newspaper for which I had paid a dollar, to a guy as naive as I'd been, for several thousand dollars. So there is no wonder that these people were interested in doing something that might lure people with money to town, not just another wave of admiring hippies who would then move there and start another wave of candle and macramé shops that wouldn't last the winter. Money capital was starting to challenge the other forms of capital – which, to be honest, weren't always as much cow as hat.

But 1972 was still closer to the 1960s than the 1980s, and the Community-as-Art people carried the day that year. As spring swung into summer, the Mountain Theater people built a huge stage up in a meadow on the ridge – a cold windy ridge, as it turned out – and prepared what was arguably the greatest Mountain Theater production ever, a company supplemented that summer by a cadre of semi-pros who were old friends of the director and didn't have anything better to do that summer. The Artist of the Thousand Railroad Ties outdid himself in luring his then-unknown Austin friends and their friends to town, bringing in names – Doc Whosis, Bonnie Whatsername – that I've since forgotten, to a big stage built down in the Town Park, where a local pickup band also began developing the town's first – maybe only – open invitational bring-your-own-words-and-music vocal-and-instrumental rock-and-roll band, a jam group named Jelly (get it?). And down where Third Street deadended at Coal Creek, Joe Rozman had delivered a fifty-foot spruce log, and the wood butcher and friends were circling it with chain saws and chisels, mapping out lengths and ideas.

It all came together in a weekend you either loved or hated. Elk Avenue filled up with artists and would-be artists and don't-try-to-tell-us-we're-not artists, and it also filled up with tourists. Those who were looking for high quality found it; those who were there to be offended by low quality weren't disappointed. You could, in fact, find about anything you wanted, including a masseuse who was asked by the Marshal to pack up her mattress and leave, or at least move to a side street.

A few things didn't work out very well. The Mountain Theater learned that you could go a little too high and far, aesthetically as well as physically, for Colorado audiences, no matter how good the show was. The painters that we'd put upstairs in Frank Starika's building to get them out of potential rain weren't happy because not enough people found their way up there. Et cetera. But in the overall most everyone seemed to be enjoying most everything.

But as the Saturday sun sank and the Jelly concert and other big musical offerings approached, the crowd began to gather in a way that even I found a little ominous. The people that began to pour into town toward dusk were not art lovers; most of them were the neo-barbarians of the late 20th century, with their life philosophies on their T-shirts and their Bud twelves in their hands. By nightfall they had jammed the town and more were parking down along the highway. There weren't enough restaurant seats in town to feed everyone; Stefanic's Grocery sold out everything that didn't require cooking; the liquor stores ran out of beer.

The concert? The Austin musicians were models of professional decorum, knowing how to move a crowd without agitating it. But Jelly, that local concatenation of gifted amateurs, knew no such fine distinctions. I liked most of what they did, and could stand most of the rest, but was a little dismayed when their best and longest number had a chorus whose main lyric was "F--- you," which the crowd, that near-mob, learned quickly and made to ring out over the whole valley, probably audible in Gunnison 30 miles away.

Did anything bad happen? Late that night, a young woman tripped over a guy rope holding up one of the festival booths and broke her arm, but luckily she was too drunk to think of suing. The trash generated by the crowd vastly overtaxed the town's trashcans, and I participated in a hasty cleanup crew early Sunday morning that filled up a couple of commandeered pickups.

But the sun rose that Sunday morning to find the town intact and pleasantly quiet, and we moved into the last day's events, which culminated in the Erection of the Totem Pole that the five wood butchers with chain saws had miraculously completed without any serious injuries. This was a surprisingly moving event. It was done with equipment no Indians ever had (a backhoe, mainly) but standing it up – a fifty-foot spruce log, small end down – was one of those quiet serious operations fraught with potential disaster, when even the people who know what they are doing have never done anything exactly like it before. But by late afternoon, the sculpture was up, oiled, its base solidly packed and tamped, and it was actually kind of a momentous moment, seeing it towering forty feet above us, with a weathervane on top trying to find the wind. A moment out of time, when one feels things ending, or beginning, or just pausing in transit for a moment, in appreciation.

Things were, of course, both ending and beginning. It was the end of the Community-as-Art Festival, and given the edge-of-chaos aspect of much of the weekend, maybe that was appropriate. I didn't even stay around to defend the idea; Montana and Idaho caught fire that next week, and I left with the second crew of Crested Butte Hotshots (one of our best economic development schemes those years) for two weeks of running away from forest fires at six bucks an hour, and when I got back I never did finish my final report for the Colorado Council on the Arts.

But that third Community-as-Art Festival had been a traumatic enough weekend for many people so that, the next year, there was no Arts Festival at all. When it started up again, it was a juried invitational exhibit of beautiful stuff for purchase, and I was no longer on the committee. No particular animosity, just a tacit agreement to try something else. We were basically in transition from a brief period of time when we had a lot of idea capital operating with very little money capital, to a more conventional situation where the money capital was increasing, but wanting to work (as money tends to) by money's relatively conservative proven formulae.

It's important to avoid stereotypes there – it wasn't at all a bunch of "business suits" bringing in big time big-money capitalism that began to degrade the capital environment. It was a whole lot of really pretty nice people coming to town with little wads of money – they'd sold a house in some appreciating suburb because they wanted to get back to what they imagined to be the simple life, or had a small inheritance and thought they could finally afford the simple life, or had a graduation present and wanted to ski and party for a winter before getting serious about life, or had made a careful transcontinental trip with something in their trunk. But just those people, over a five-year period, nudged rents and real estate prices up a couple hundred percent, and as the prices of businesses increased, so did the price of their goods and services – no more $1.29 Dinner Special at the Grubstake Exchange, no more dime drafts at Tony's Tavern.

And as this happened, our idea capitalists drifted away – no mass exodus, just one by one leaving. The Vietnam vet who started the Mountain Theater went to a college teaching job up in Seattle. The Artist with a Thousand Railroad Ties went back to Minnesota to stop drinking – I don't know where the railroad ties went. The wood carver who masterminded the totem pole went down to Denver for affordable work. I retreated to Gothic most of the time to try to write something for – well, for money. When that wasn't working very well, I went back to school thinking to learn enough to teach something.

The problem was fairly obvious: without much money, it was harder and harder to nourish oneself, let alone oneself and one's idea capital. And if all you could afford to support in Crested Butte was yourself, then, the scenery aside, Crested Butte was just like anywhere else, and you might as well go somewhere else where wages were more in line with rents and everything else. Ultimately, the old-timers were right: you can't eat scenery, however much it inspires you.

Trying to think through all that was when I started reading Heilbroner on *The Economic Problem*. And Heilbroner passed along a little of Karl Marx's critique of capital – which Marx basically equated with money capital, living as he did in a decadent capitalist society where money had driven out all the higher forms of human capital.

Capital has to grow, according to Marx – "M" capital has to become "M(1)" capital or it isn't happy. "M" standing for "money" or maybe "more" but at any rate indicative of what capital was in his world. Capital is basically lost if it doesn't grow because the capitalist needs to skim off some of its growth in order to live to keep investing in growth.

But wasn't the same true of the "idea capital" that got invested in Crested Butte those years? The dusty turnaround where the totem pole was planted is now Totem Pole Park, a lovely little spot of grass and trees and shade around the totem pole, a great place to take a takeout lunch from the main drag a block away. Isn't that a kind of capital growth? But while the town benefits, did the initial investors ever get a transactable return on their physical and metaphysical investment in its creation?

Or consider the Mountain Theater: it's now in its fourth decade of producing theater for the valley, and it has arrived at the point where the Theater can pay a manager (not a lot but something) and occasionally a director. But did the original investors ever get a return on their investment? Well – here one begins to get into the strangeness of "systems of tickets" for claims on Heilbroner's "real wealth of the society." Twenty years after I invested a lot of time and energy and a little money in creating the Mountain Theater, my son and daughter were both in a wonderful summer production of "Midsummer Night's Dream" that was transformative for at least my son, who not long afterward went on to the performing arts college where the Vietnam Vet had gone to teach when Crested Butte gave no living return on his investment. "Return on investment" becomes a complex concept when you try to break out of the heavy gravity of money as the measure of all. But don't try to live without the money.

That, however, just eggs me on to thinking, driven by Heilbroner's great footnote about "systems of tickets" – suppose we had had the imagination and initiative in 1970 to try to institute a "system of tickets" in Crested Butte that rewarded the investment of ideas and other forms of capital with negotiable returns on investment? The entire "system of tickets" we have now is set up by and for the money investors, as though that were the only meaningful form of capital, which is probably why money eventually always drives out the higher forms of capital. Or more accurately: why money co-opts and "disciplines" all the more fragile but more "natural" forms of capital, bringing them into line with the particular and peculiar constraints and imaginative limits of "M" growing to "M(1)." On payday, if the successful idea capitalist is working for the money capitalists, he gets paid; but if she is just working for a stronger community, or for one of those larger communities we call ecosystems, she needs a job (working for money) or a trust fund on the side to get by.

So what would a system of tickets look like that gave negotiable "return on investment" to all our capitalists rather than just the money capitalists? Well, it would certainly be complex – but that's no big deal, for a society capable of coming up with the current tax code, which shows breathtaking imagination in not just dealing with complexity, but in creating it – but all directed toward the parting out and privatization of what Heilbroner called "the society's real wealth." Couldn't we do as well at complexly redirecting a little of the society's real wealth toward the care, feeding and recharging of natural, communal and human capital?

The models for a society that would distribute its "real wealth" that way are probably mostly found, ironically, in what we tend to call "primitive" societies: small societies without money whose economics are probably much more complex than our huge modern money-driven mass societies. Goods and services in those primitive societies get distributed according to a whole lot of criteria involving age, occupation within the community (services), clan relations, congeniality, and a lot of other things we moneybound peoples would regard as hopelessly subjective. Easier to just stick the dollar sign on everything. Simplify, simplify, simplify, Thoreau said – and we have.

Actually, many mountain communities are starting to think constructively about this. The efforts to address the problem of "affordable housing" are at least a start. In effect, affordable housing projects give "community credit" for people who have shown a desire to stay around and work in the community if they can afford to. In places where so-called real estate has gone over the past century from acre measures to square foot measures with the dollar figure per measure remaining basically the same, community credit for housing is powerful.

But the affordable housing programs are a kind of one-tool approach that seem more concerned (overtly at least) with maintaining a workforce in service to money capital than with building up the creative community that ultimately even money capital needs – not that money would ever admit that. Money's biggest challenge – one that requires to the controlled cooperation of all the other cultural "media of exchange" like the major media, the federal and state legislators and agencies – is to maintain the strange notion that money should be the major, if not the only, measure of cultural value – and that the money capitalist is therefore the only logical recipient of return on capital investment. And any money "taken" from the money capitalist to maintain or increase the social and economic stability and vitality – the community, basically – on which all investment depends is a "tax" to be grudgingly given, rather than an investment to be gladly given. Whether the moneyed people actually believe that thoroughly inconsistent ideology, or just pass it off on the rest of us out some perverse convenience escapes me, but it is about as undemocratic and un-Christian as ideology can get.

But there it is. Affordable housing is a start, but now how about an honest health-care insurance program grounded in the principle of all true "insurance" – that everyone pays in a little to cover the misfortunes that will happen randomly but not universally, and eschewing the strange notion that the program will be best managed if some corporation is taking 20-30 percent off the top? If it is going to happen, it is going to have to happen locally, since money has so effectively co-opted our state and federal governments. At some point some county government is going to get brave enough to launch a truly public single-payer health care plan for everyone in the county. And then how about subsidized restaurant chits for everyone who invests a little of himself or herself in some community-building activity, as a way to bring the idea capitalists together evenings for the equivalent of the Grubstake's long-gone $1.29 Dinner Special? Or beer chits? Fight addictive money with other more enjoyable addictive substances. A pub in Ouray gave two-for-the-price-of-one Thursday nights for anyone with a Ouray County address on their ID, which might bring enough idea capital into proximity for a flash point to occur, creating something else that will have the side effect of making more money for the money capitalists.

And how do we pay for all this? Through an equitable distribution, via local government, of the negotiable fruits of all this investment – idea capital, natural capital, money capital – in a vital, interesting and stable place to live and work and play. An honest and just system of tickets from the start, rather than giving it all to the money capitalists to parcel out in wages and whatever niggardly taxes they can be forced to pay.

Idealistic? You damn betcha. A hopeless dream? You damn betcha. But why else come out to the margins, the edge of the big fat lazy and corrupted civilization if not to dream hopeless dreams? Especially if you were lucky enough to land a place where, for a brief period of time, the lesson to be learned was that ideas will get you through times of no money better than money will get you through times of no ideas.

**

In Crested Butte in the 1970s, we were always saying we "don't want to become another Aspen," but the fact is, we kind of secretly lusted for things like the Music Festival and the Aspen Institute that Aspen had – all because one man, Walter Paepke, had come to town in the 1950s with *both* money and ideas. All we had coming to town were ideas.

But there was an important distinction between the way Walter Paepke went about realizing his ideas, and the way we went about realizing ours. Because Paepke had money, he could afford to bring in the best people and experts from elsewhere to realize his ideas. But because we had very little money, we had to figure out how to realize things ourselves. "Real-ize." Interesting word that has nothing at all to do with "real estate" or "reality TV." "Real-izing" at the local level involves the process that efficiency experts eschew, the process of "reinventing the wheel." But cultures aren't industries, and for a culture, inventing the wheels it rolls on might be the key to that "cultural diversity" we claim to need, but get farther and farther from because everyone is using the same old wheel – on which I think Walmart now holds the patent. Not to mention the fact that we are all using the same old generic $y$tem of $impli$tic ticket$.

Today, Crested Butte has a Music Festival not too unlike Aspen's – not yet so world-renowned, of course, but we're only a decade into it – and as upscale and classy and pricey an Arts Festival as you will find anywhere. It is all the best that money can buy or bring in. Get more money behind it, and we'll be able to bring in even more quality from everywhere else. But it isn't –....

Oh well. Most of us moneyless idea capitalists trading at the Grubstake Exchange those years were drinking too much or, after 1967, abusing other substances too much. I know I was, but it was the only way I could seem to pry my mind open enough to realize that what we had to do was to figure out how to "just say no" to money. With a snootful, I could say that – still can – without feeling embarrassed or idiotic or somehow sacrilegious. Sometimes without even feeling my nose or fingertips.

That's how messed up an American usually has to be to get up the gumption to just say no to money, the most un-American thing in the environment, the most addictive substance that we humans have ever invented to divert ourselves from the difficult challenges of discovering intelligent life on earth. We need a better system of tickets for distributing the real wealth of society.

But meanwhile – I guess I hope you bought this book and didn't borrow or steal it since I still can't seem to escape the gravity of our corrupted $y$tem of ticket$ either.

The Eagle's Story

The eagles and cranes have always told it,
But we're just beginning to hear their story.
A story from back when the lizards ruled the world,
And bigger was known to be better,
Bigger and tougher and more armored toward life.

That was their story, the lizard story,
And those were their standards: Might made right,
Until something happened and they all
Disappeared. Just perished from the earth.

But the eagle's story about that is different.
The way the eagles tell it, some of the littler lizards,
Strong in their own way, began to change:
Their claws grew long and light and fragile,
And their scales became long, soft and fractaled.

How the big strong lizards laughed!
Har! Har! thundered the thunder-lizards,
As the soft little lizards hopped and flapped
Along in front of them, little soaring leaps
Before being clawed and bashed out of the air.

But the webbed claws and feathery scales
Continued to lengthen and lighten as the thunder lizards
Continued to laugh their hard and heavy laugh,
Continued to say, might is right, bigger is better,
Bigger claws, thicker armor, more mass, more and more —

Think of that now, said the eagle, as you watch me ride
The shatter of light up the face of the mountain,
Or wonder at the swoop, dive and rise of the swallow,
Or strain to see the cranes a mile above
With their great transcontinental wingbeat.
Think of that as you look for a way toward life in a world
Gone crazy with bigger, tougher and armored against life.

Crows in the Snow

A *Colorado Central Magazine* "Down on the Ground" Column, circa 2000

I'm sitting here trying to think about water, thinking I ought to be writing something about water, but I'm being distracted by a murder of crows.

They're in the yard across the street, about forty of them, some in a tree but most on the ground, pecking at the snow – drinking maybe. A study in black and white because it is a gray morning outside for a change with just enough new snow to cover the grass. It might snow more.

In the mean time, these crows are distracting. Some of them are announcing something to the world in their aggressive New Yorkish way – warning or threatening life in general about something. I could never figure how Poe heard "Nevermore" from his raven (that's just a crow in the mountains). What I hear from crows is "Rack! Rack!"

Or these days, I imagine: "Iraq! Iraq!" They're that kind of bird.

I'm not the kind of nature lover who mistakes birds for sweet and loving beings, the kind of beings I wish people were. I like to wake up on a summer morning to the sound of birds, and the pleasure isn't diminished by knowing those melodious songs are basically the birds' version of the "Trespassers will be violated!" signs that humans use for the same purpose. That's okay – maybe it would help us put private property in perspective if we made all property owners sing their property lines rather than signing them. But when crows do their "Iraq! Iraq!" it is easier to see the "No Trespassing" signs than when it's the robins on guard.

And all those little birds that flock around the winter feeder outside the kitchen window – the sparrows, the pine siskins, the finches: you wouldn't want impressionable school kids learning cafeteria behavior from those cute little birds. Pine siskins especially: some of them will all but starve themselves keeping other siskins away from a feeder that really has enough for all. Cooperation doesn't seem to be a dependable feature of even those birds of a feather that flock together.

Nonetheless, there is an ingratiating combination of pertness, swiftness, agility, gumption and song to the little birds that makes it easy to like their ornery little souls. The really big birds are something else again, the hawks and owls and eagles. They are what you might call "big enough to know better." They keep their distance from us, for the most part, like most of the big mammals, and try to do their thing where people aren't – which of course is increasingly difficult for them.

But crows – crows are big birds with a little bird mentality. They have decided, like the little birds, to coexist with humans rather than grant us our space and seek their separate peace like the really big birds. And they take up an increasing amount of our space – so it seems so to me.

Last summer two crows nested in a big spruce in front of our house, and raised the most noisily dysfunctional family in the neighborhood. I saw the neighbor across the street one morning looking up at their aerie, more easily heard than seen; she saw me and shook her head: "There goes the neighborhood."

Crows are smart too – but in an amoral kind of way, smart like Sarah Palin, or the Koch Brothers, that ilk: single-minded intelligences reducing everything to some lowest common denominator – money, edibles, something material. Maybe there are such qualities as beauty, dignity, honor, altruism in the crows' world, or in Sarah Palin's for that matter, but their lives an102d actions don't express it.

Those determined to apologize for all forms of life not human will remind me that crows do a service in cleaning up garbage and the carrion that sleeps by our highways. But I also see them carrying to the nest baby birds that hadn't yet become carrion and other equally discouraging prizes. Seen up close, those powerful dark bills give me a shudder – make me suspect why their collective term is "a murder of crows," without necessarily wanting to know the whole story.

I know, I know: we humans also eat the young of other life, and are usually about as noisily and aggressively dysfunctional in the world. That's what's most depressing about watching crows: the sneaking awareness that we probably deserve each other – both represent a reductive coarsening in the spread of life. We spread such a feast of carrion before them that I think we give them an edge over the rest of the birds; if they are crowding out the little birds, it is at least partially our doing.

In the mean time here, the crows in the yard across the street have gone off somewhere else on crow business, and the study in black and white is now just the whites and soft grays of a day that looks like it might snow.

Someone told me once that, where crows gather, there's a door open between worlds. Maybe that's where they went, but I doubt it – and if it is, it's not a door I want to use.

I know if I go outdoors and listen for just a few minutes, I'll hear one even if I don't see it, somewhere in the distance; they're ubiquitous, this murder that haunts our town. Iraq! Iraq! Here in the mean time – are there more crows than there used to be? Seems that way to me.

On Driving Past the 100,000th Roadkill

These animals who sleep by the road:
One day they will all wake
Rise up and take back the roads.
The fish flushed in turbines will
Run up the rubble of dams coming down;
New feathers will grow through thick black death
And a million white birds will take back the air.

And seeing that happen, some more complex
And beautiful thing may even emerge from us:
Something capable of sitting still,
Of inviting the now unimaginable emptying of mind
For the inflight and upwheel of those millions of birds.

The Ongoing Search for
The Bird Is Dead Bar and Grill

Originally published in the *Mountain Gazette,* November 2004.

The first time I saw The Bird Is Dead Bar and Grill sign, there was an inch of slushy water on the floor, but it was only early April and we knew there would be more. There's a pump, the realtor said.

I was there with Weird Harold; we were contemplating buying the place. It was the basement of a big old building in Crested Butte that had once been the company store for the Colorado Fuel and Iron Company that had squeezed the hell out of the biggest coal mine, the miners and most of the town. Weird Harold was a jeweler with a tenuous relationship to a little money somewhere behind him; I was a local booster-press newspaper publisher who had been reading too much of my own stuff. A visit to the SBA down in Denver sobered us up pretty well – I can still hear his laugh.

105

Crested Butte then was a town where, if you wanted to make a small fortune, you'd better bring a large one. Which people did, still do.

But there it was, painted on the wall in a small room in the flooding basement of the former company store in Crested Butte, a quality illuminated graffiti: The Bird Is Dead Bar and Grill.

I commenced investigative journalism. The best I could do was to trace it back to the very beginning of Crested Butte's long slide into resortism. Circa 1961, an Aspen refugee – one of those retreating souls who would have had the grace to stop and think, if asked: are you fleeing the empire or advancing it – had collected a lot of stuff from around town and opened up a junk store posing as an antique shoppe.

Among the treasures he'd accumulated was an ornate bird cage, with a well-preserved air-dried dead bird in it. He was too much of an aesthete to do the proper thing; instead, he kept cage and bird intact. And people would come in, and they would admire the cage – then do a double-take. Uh.... they would start, looking toward him with raised brows.

Yes, he would say. The bird is dead.

That of course does nothing to explain why there was a grafitti painting on the wall of a cell down in the basement of the old company store: The Bird Is Dead Bar and Grill.

But it all continues to resonate in the labyrinths of randomness loitering in the nexus of my mind. Hemingway talked about "the moveable feast"; for me, the feast moves on with The Bird Is Dead Bar and Grill – the place where I find myself from time to time remembering what life might be trying to be. The last time I was in The Bird Is Dead Bar and Grill was last spring in the Eldo at Crested Butte's annual end-of-winter Flauschink Ball, which usually ascends or descends to The Bird Is Dead Bar and Grill around eleven p.m.

There have been other episodes in recent years – the night at the Gunnison Brewery when brewmeister Kevin Alexander introduced me to C.S. Derrick, Crested Butte's first master brewer, from whom I got on a set of napkins the whole modern history of good beer in Colorado. And another night there when El Chino was playing with one of his many bands and I got to dance with the Silver City masseuses. And an entirely different kind of evening there with a very cross-disciplinary agglomeration of academics from the college: all these diverse occasions ascended at some point to The Bird Is Dead Bar and Grill.

That basement in Crested Butte's Company Store eventually became The Bird Is Dead Bar and Grill on occasion. A couple guys who could actually afford that kind of mistake bought the building, and (after turning on the pumps) turned the basement into a bar. Their name for the place was The Tailings, which was a clever enough name for a basement bar in a former mine town. I thought at first they should have taken the name on the wall back in the little basement room, but I came to realize that it takes more than a name change to vivify a myth.

One of the times when The Tailings became The Bird Is Dead Bar and Grill was Thanksgiving, circa 1970. It was one of those maddening years when the snow didn't come and didn't come – six or eight years before the ski area installed snowmaking stuff – and Thanksgiving was basically dry. There's nothing in the mountains so depressing as a sunny Thanksgiving morning with no snow below 10,000 feet. If you've lived in a mountain town long enough, you've been there; you know that November is the cruelest month.

Anyway, since we couldn't go to work and/or go skiing, which was all we wanted to do at that point, we had a big hippie potluck down in The Tailings to which even some of the hippie-hating pilgrims came; everybody brought something along with their usual insatiable appetite for everything, and we all got roaring fed and drunk, and danced to the jukebox, and at some point, like the dove descending, the lark ascending, The Tailings became The Bird Is Dead Bar and Grill.

Then someone who had left the party had the good grace to come back in to tell us it was snowing upstairs, outside. So we all ran up the stairs, out into the night, to find about six inches on the ground, feeling it snowing on us as though we had never felt it before, mouths open and tongues out like drowning turkeys, throwing it around and rolling in it, making angels; Murray cranked up the volume on the juker downstairs and The Bird Is Dead Bar and Grill moved out into the street. That night and the next day it snowed about 18 inches. Too late of course to salvage Thanksgiving weekend but what the hell. A typical night in The Bird Is Dead Bar and Grill.

It doesn't even have to be a place which you know, where you are known. Up on a tour of the Olympic Peninsula once with my partner Maryo, we stopped in Everett, Washington, which had an interesting history for anyone who has done time in a sawmill; I wanted to try to talk my way into a tour of the big Simpson mill there the next day, so we found ourselves in some bar for a hamburger that night where we discovered Full Sail Ale. It was a friendly place or at least tolerant, and it was also karaoke night, an event I usually try to avoid, but that night, blessed by the veil of anonymity and the snap and flap of the Full Sail catching wind, I fulfilled a lifelong secret desire to be Grace Slick singing "White Rabbit." I will not call it a success because in The Bird Is Dead Bar and Grill, success is irrelevant. Don't ask, don't tell.

Between those blessed events of course are always the usual run-of-the-mill bar non-events. Nine times out of ten – no, 99 times out of 100, when you walk into a bar, it's just a bar and stays that way, a convocation of semi-sodden mendicants sitting in the church of their choice waiting for the species to evolve. That's okay: a lot of life is putting in time waiting for the species to evolve. But one continues to go in – I continue to go in with the hope that at any moment the right person or persons will walk in, sit down on the next stool or stools, the right thing or things will be said or done, the right spirits invoked or provoked in the right proportions, and all those devout gathered alcohol burners will sputter, hiss and flare, and like the dove descending, the lark ascending, we will all upshift into the overdrive of The Bird Is Dead Bar and Grill.

A lot of people actually turn into drunks nurturing that hope – thinking that somehow The Bird Is Dead Bar and Grill comes from the alcohol and not the burners. I just read a good book about life in an Appalachian coal town – "Coal Run," by a woman purportedly named Tawni O'Dell, who nevertheless has to have grown up in a place like Crested Butte when it was still a coal town, and who must have hung out with older brothers and uncles in the kinds of places where The Bird Is Dead Bar and Grill was truly dying but not yet dead. She made a distinction between drunks and hard drinkers: "A hard drinker is a man who drinks to help him cope. A drunk is a man who drinks because he can't cope." A pretty sexist statement from Tawni – some of the best and worst hard drinkers and drunks I've known have been women.

Myself, I'm neither a hard drinker nor a drunk, not yet anyway; I'm just a mendicant out on the prowl for The Bird Is Dead Bar and Grill because it helps me cope – the memory, promise and hope of it helps me cope.

A night – or an afternoon, for that matter – in the Bird Is Dead Bar and Grill is like a good wake: a not entirely conscious but thoroughly conscientious effort to begin remaking history as it should have been – a time to start roughing out the legends behind the mere stories, roughing them out not just in word but deed, dancing deed, as well. A time when memory serves, but isn't allowed to dictate.

Afternoons are actually often best for seeking The Bird Is Dead Bar and Grill – if you can get in and out with some semblance of grace, and don't try to hang onto the moment so long that they have to mop you up at closing. Between the closed blue of the day sky and the pin-pricked black of night, when the sky goes translucent just after sunset – that's the time to leave after the afternoon, to go out into that time between day and night when the sky is open to forever.

I don't cry much, or easily, but when tears come it is usually in that time that opens up between day and night, like after an afternoon in the Grubstake with Big Al in Crested Butte, or in the Boardwalk in Crawford with Pete Wiebe, or Kochevar's in Crested Butte after the Flauschink parade and I've just had a perfect and fulfilling dance with a woman whose name I didn't even ask, the ultimate rock-jazz-polka fusion, and I'm leaving The Bird Is Dead Bar and Grill and spiraling my way toward home weeping for what we all could be, might be, should be, maybe eventually will be. Rejoicers, celebrants, mendicants finding our real wealth in each other, each remembered (think of that word: re-membered) as we would be.

Then I say, like anyone in a similar moment might say, like they used to say back before we got rid of kings: "Yes! The bird is dead! Long live the bird!"

Thinking About Writing

There's a thickening cast to the personal sky
And the way the thoughts are piling so high
I think there'll be rain
In the back of my brain
I look for a storm in my head

Why write
if you can't find the words
that will make even your own world
slow, the way the creek there
slows, spreads and deepens
in the bank shade
where the great trout waits

Abbey:
A Legend in His Own Time,
Doing Time In His Own Legend

Essay requested for the *Mountain Gazette,* for an issue about
Edward Abbey that didn't happen.

NOTE: *Get your copy of **Desert Solitaire** out before you start reading this.
If you don't have one, go get one.*

"Abbey the man aside for the moment, is his work important? Will people be reading him in a hundred years?"

There it was, a great steaming download on my virtual desktop: *Gazette* editor Fayhee's question designed to occupy vast areas of brain space I might otherwise use for making a living or whatever. An editor who knows how to pull my chain.

I don't know who else he sent this question to, but I guess he thought I'd be a good one to address it to because, a) unlike almost everyone else in the literate West, I had never actually met Edward Abbey in person (close but not quite), and b) I was a literature major in another life who now teaches (not literature) in a college.

The closest I came to actually meeting Abbey was passing through Arizona in 1977. I wanted to thank him: not knowing me from Adam, but at the request of Mike Moore, *Mountain Gazette* editor its first life, he had written introductory letters for me to three of his editors. A generous thing for an established writer to do for an unknown.

He had sent me a number to call, up on a mountain somewhere beyond Phoenix where he was watching for forest fires, but when I called a woman's voice told me that he was away for a couple of days, so that was that – and I was secretly relieved. I had read most of what Abbey had written to that point, and knew he was becoming a little larger than life, something of a living legend – with me as well as most of the rest of us hanging out in the outer edges of civilization. *The Monkeywrench Gang* had been out for a year or so by then, and the rich mixture of fame and notoriety, adulation and loathing, with which he was regarded was reaching its iconic plateau, and I didn't really want to meet an icon, a legend. He'd probably have known how to act, but I wouldn't have.

But back to the question, which I can address untainted one way or the other by personal acquaintance – Is *Abbey's work* itself important, from a literary, or cultural, or whatever perspective we bring to bear on such a question? Will people be reading him in a hundred years?

My immediate response is to refer anyone who actually takes that question seriously to a collection of critical essays, *Coyote in the Maze: tracking Edward Abbey in a world of words* (University of Utah Press, 1998), edited by Peter Quigley, Chair of Humanities and Social Science at – Embry-Riddle Aeronautical University? Well, where else.... At any rate, this is a collection of essays by Abbey *afficianados* who apply the disciplines of literary and cultural criticism to his works, with the isms of anarchy, green and postmodern slathered all over it.

But – what the hell: despite my astonishing lack of credentials for someone who teaches in a college, I want to weigh in on the question too. What makes a writer's work "important"? Never mind "good" – in this age of disposable literature, there are lots of good writers whose work is still pretty disposable. And never mind "controversial" – who is going to be reading this year's political commentators even next year, let alone a century from now?

No, "important" is something more than "good" or "controversial," or maybe just something different. I have a small section of books on my shelves that I think are important – partly because I was told in college that some of them were important, but more because, after my required reading of them, and my re-reading since (no longer required)

I realized they were important in documenting the evolution of this mad dream called America. Or, at least they were important *to me*. (And what else counts in the dream of America but me.) And I've since added a couple to that shelf because they were important to me in the same way, among them one by Abbey.

I call this section of shelf "Ralph Waldo and Sons." All of them are pretty well-used paperbacks, and most of them – I just realized, looking at them again – are those "Signet Classics" paperbacks that you used to be able to buy for (looking at the cover of my *Walden*) as little as fifty cents. Back, of course, when fifty cents was fifty cents. They aren't much for durability, and a couple now need rubber bands, but sizewise they are great for the last 20 cubic inches or so of a pack. On that short section of shelf are:

- *The Selected Writings of Ralph Waldo Emerson* (Signet Classic)
- *Walden (and "Civil Disobedience")* by Henry Thoreau (Signet Classic)
- *Leaves of Grass* by Walt Whitman (Signet Classic)
- *Moby Dick* by Herman Melville (Signet Classic)
- *On the Road* by Jack Kerouac (Signet but not "Signet Classic")
- *Desert Solitaire* by Edward Abbey (not a Signet book at all)

I've thought a better name for that bunch, minus Ralph Waldo, would be "the Ishmael Brotherhood," except today most people would probably think of the wrong Ishmael. "The Ishmael Brotherhood" because they were all – except for Ralph Waldo – guys who got the "hypos" so bad that they required "a strong moral principle to prevent (them) from deliberately stepping into the street, and methodically knocking people's hats off."

Some of them in fact lacked the strong moral principle, and just went ahead with the hat-knocking. But they all self-treated their "hypos" by going off into some wilder unpeopled part of the world – the "watery part" for that first Ishmael, but other wilds for the other brethren – to seek their "strong moral principle" in a wilder nature. They also all—except for Ralph Waldo, who may have had strong moral principles to a fault—they all did spend a lot of their writing time knocking people's hats off.

But you're probably thinking—isn't that shelf of books pretty short? What about Robert Frost? Robinson Jeffers? John Nichols? Henry Miller? Barry Lopez? John Muir? (Aldo Leopold is easy: he was never a

113

son, always an uncle, in this weird extended family.) And what about all the daughters? Annie Dillard? Ann Zwinger? Rachel Carson?

Okay, okay. So my shelf is incomplete. I'm not done reading and thinking yet either. I'm not Allan Bloom; I don't pretend to know the whole canon. And I'm not wanting to turn this into a defensible doctoral dissertation. I just brought it all up in an effort to answer the question: is Abbey an important enough writer so people will still be reading him a century from now, as we are still reading (or at least shelving) those others? Does he belong on my shelf with the others?

And looking at that lineage, I say a qualified yes. Maybe not all his writings, but certainly *Desert Solitaire:* if there are still Americans trying to figure out what America was trying to become before it got so rudely interrupted by corporate personhood, if there are still Americans trying to figure out what the academic critic/synthesist Perry Miller was trying to say when he called us "nature's nation," if there are still Americans who truly believe that creation is fundamentally democratic and creative rather than monotheistically authoritarian... then, yes, Abbey will still be important.

Abbey's link to Emerson is the same as with the others: the literary paternity rap. (I wish we knew more about the mothers of all his sons.) Emerson predicted these sons, literally (or anyway literarily) invited them into existence, and was, even in his own lifetime, occasionally embarrassed by them – as when he went by the jail to visit Thoreau and was chastised by Henry for not being there in jail with him. Or when he sent a simple congratulatory note to Walt Whitman and had it turned into an unauthorized endorsement on the second edition of *Leaves of Grass.* God knows what he would have thought of Kerouac. Or Abbey.

But Emerson brought it on himself, and America. He was a preacher who preached freedom, then had to grin and bear the consequences of his sons practicing it. But that might be selling the old man short too; it might be a better analogy to think of him as a Moses pointing out a promised land he couldn't quite get into himself, but into which he sent his all his spiritual sons.

This can be said about Emerson: he was the first American to look thoughtfully – and publicly – at the world beyond town and farm and see more than Cotton Mather's howling waste, a vacant repository of evil to be civilized into profitable submission. He may have done us and our environments no favor when he carried forward the Christian division of everything into "Nature and the Soul"—the notion that everything is either Nature ("essences unchanged by man; space, the air, the river, the leaf") or

Art ("the mixture of man's will with the same things, as in a house, a canal, a statue, a picture").

But if he lugged forward that unfortunate piece of Judeo-Christian-Cartesian baggage, he also initiated, or at least popularized, the idea that drives all his sons – and daughters too (whose move up from chattels to members of the human race he would probably have aided, had he lived half a century longer). That idea was the belief that humankind has more to learn from nature – or "Nature" as he tended to spell it – than just how to exploit it for human utility.

He addressed this educative challenge best in two essays, from different perspectives – in one called "Nature," and another called "The Poet." These are typical Emerson essays – more assaults than essays, waged the way Europeans were still waging war then: mass the words, fix bayonets, and charge, ten thousand across the front; his essays build like Wagnerian operas, slow, stately, dense and a little eternal in a manner occasionally indistinguishable from tedious. It is hard to believe, today, that most of these essays were essayed forth as orations, talks to people who actually sat still and listened for the two hours or so it took to erect these verbal cathedrals. With citizens capable of that attention span, no wonder there was a conviction back then that democracy might actually work.

But the charge that Emerson laid out for his sons – and the daughters he didn't even suspect the existence of – can be summarized, if not distilled, from the chapters of "Nature": he laid out four stages through which nature will reveal itself to anyone with the perseverance to pursue it: "Commodity; Beauty; Language; and Discipline."

Commodity and Beauty are pretty easy to understand: we convert enough of nature to profitable commodity to make ourselves reasonably comfortable; then we sit back and notice, or acknowledge, that nature (what's left of it) is also pretty. Basic Maslow – although much more eloquently and of course lengthily said.

But – the "Language" and "Discipline" of nature? or Nature? Begin with "Language": Emerson tries hard, but he is really essaying out into the willow thickets of how we articulate how we articulate. "Words are signs of natural facts," he says at the beginning of the "Language" chapter of "Nature." And then: "particular natural facts are symbols of particular spiritual facts." And then – well, those two a-to-b statements alone have probably launched a thousand doctoral ships in philosophy and communications theory without even getting to his leapfrog-logic conclusion, that "Nature is the symbol of spirit" which enables us to use "natural objects in expression of particular meanings"—having said which, he is almost embarrassed at the obviousness of it: "how great a language to convey such pepper-corn informations!" Does the "language of Nature" leave us with nothing more than parables like "a rolling stone gathers no moss"?

And that doesn't begin to touch the monumental mental entanglements that emerge as he tries to rationalize the "discipline of nature."

But there is an intuitive sense to it all that drives – no, inspires – his arrogant, unappreciative sons and daughters. They—we—know or sense that there is a language and a discipline to nature, something from which we are either alienated by *human* nature, or by culture (more likely, arrogant asses that we are), and we will, or might, or could, be better off when or if we are better able to comprehend that language and discipline. So Melville's Ishmael goes to sea in search of the language and discipline of that "moral principle"; Thoreau goes all the way out to the edge of town; Whitman goes off in all directions; Kerouac goes on the road; and Abbey goes to the desert – all of them more or less solitary in those essays.

And finally, in the chapter of "Nature" on "Discipline," Emerson imagines a point at which "the spirit" of the writer/poet comes to a kind of transcending place where it can say, "From such as this have I drawn joy and knowledge; in such as this have I found and beheld myself; I will speak to it; it can speak again; it can yield me thought already formed and alive."

Ralph Waldo delves deeper into this transcendent state in his essay into "The Poet." He speaks of a "secret which every intellectual man quickly learns" (and for all his redneckishness, Abbey was an intellectual man, usually letting us know from whom he was borrowing). Emerson's secret? That "beyond the energy of his possessed and conscious intellect, (the Poet) is capable of a new energy" –

"...that, beside his privacy of power as an individual man, there is a great public power, on which he can draw, by unlocking, at all risks, his human doors, and suffering the ethereal tides to roll and circulate through him: then he is caught up into the life of the Universe, his speech is thunder, his thought is law, and his words are [as] universally intelligible as the plants and animals. The poet knows that he speaks adequately, then, only when he speaks somewhat wildly, or, 'with the flower of the mind'; not with the intellect used as an organ, but with the intellect released from all service, and suffered to take its direction from its celestial life...."

116

Henry Miller eventually expressed it, in "The Angel is My Watermark," a lot more succinctly, as a state where the writer is "taking dictation" from the universe ("The Angel Is My Watermark").

But anyone who has tried knows you don't just sit there and wait for the universe, or nature, to speak. Wordsworth spoke about "the passionate moment recollected in tranquility," but I think he misspoke; I've never had the passionate moment recollected in tranquility; it is always, at best, retrieved (and sometimes, I suspect, partly invented) in desperation, out of the soul's confusion about what really happened that made the moment passionate, intense, memorable and worth trying to write about.

As one who has tried, I can imagine Abbey in his trailer at Arches, working by the difficult light of the candle or the bright confusion of the generator – or more likely, back in the desperate well-lighted anomy of Newark in the winter – trying to pursue his personal essay into the language and discipline of nature. And he gets us there, quite a few times, in *Desert Solitaire*, where he is, in Emerson's words, "caught up into the life of the Universe, his speech is thunder, his thought is law, and his words are [as] universally intelligible as the plants and animals."

It's never when he is looking back at the civilization with that smoggy love-hate, looking for hats to knock off; it's always when he is looking out into nature's landscape, nature's nation, the America that should have been, could – one imagines when transported by such work – could still be. Standing outside the trailer ("Cliffrose and Bayonets") at Arches and doing the slow scan around himself – especially looking at the juniper tree. Or engaged in his staring match with the moon-eyed horse, the only other thing in the landscape as wild as he.

And it's never better than in his picaresque essay, "Down the River," that last long and longing look at Glen Canyon even as the big dam was under construction. It is a trip beyond Commodity, washed in Beauty – but toward the end, hauling himself up somebody else's abandoned rope out of the canyons, he takes it beyond Beauty to a new level, to the Language and Discipline out of Ralph Waldo's "great public power."

So stop reading this right now, and pick up your copy of *Desert Solitaire*. Go to a couple pages before the end of "Down the River" (page 242 in the Ballantine paperback); he has hiked up to visit Rainbow Bridge, and is about to head back down to the river and his friend Ralph who he hopes has some catfish cooking, but a "faint pathway" catches his eye.... Start with the paragraph that begins, "The heat is stunning." Read to the end.

117

(Read)

Okay? That is an example of why we'll still be reading Abbey in a hundred years – along with all the other sons and daughters of Ralph Waldo. If we aren't, the judgment is on America, not on Abbey.

El Camino Popé

For John Nichols

Stopping at Embudo Station on the road to Taos, Spring 2001, thinking of the Indian Popé who had come that way in 1680, instigating the Pueblo Revolt against the Spanish.

El Camino Real, El Camino Popé
The royal road, the real road –
He came this way an age ago, on his way
To rise like these black rocks through earth,
Rise like the river here rises in spring
By El Camino Real, El Camino Popé.

Did Popé really believe for more
Than that first blinding flash of hope
That his people could turn large enough
To drive out the dream – not the dreamers but the dream –
That came with the golden virgin
And her bloody bastard son?

Popé came this way town by town, cried:
Rise up like the river swollen with spring,
Rise up like the flame cleaning death from the forest,
Rise up like the cold wind from mad El Norte,
Rise up like these black rocks blasting through earth:
Drive out the dream that the mad dreamers bring.

But did Popé really believe for sure
That his little people could turn so large?
Already they bred with the dreamers
To get the dreamers' blood in their sons;
Conquered, they only dreamed of becoming
Their conquerors, dreaming the conqueror's dream.

Popé came this way town by town, prayed:
Rise up, as if to the occasion of life,
And his people did, for a moment: rose like the river,
Blew like the wind, ran like the fire, rose like rock
And drove out the dreamers, drove them back –
But not the dream, already red in their sons.

Did Popé really think they wouldn't turn,
His people, turn on him and turn him in?
The dream unleashed, already racing in their sons,
Did he really think they could all just go back
To dreams gone quiet, quiescent, unhorsed dreams
Of people at peace, more or less, the fruit so ripe?

El Camino Real, El Camino Popé
The royal road, the real road.
Black blasted rock burnt under the sun, river
Rising with spring, wind moving down the canyon.
El Camino Real, El Camino Popé
The royal road, the real road.

Friends to Cross Passes With

Published in *Mountain Gazette*, February 2006.

It was getting dark, and snowing harder, and I was wondering if they were actually crazy enough to have come out on this fool's adventure. Was I going to get to the cabin and find out that they'd done what I'd seriously considered – looked at the thickening sky that afternoon, felt it get still and warmish the way it gets when it's going to snow, and done the only intelligent thing and stayed home?

This was well before the cell phone era; I had no way of contacting them. Should I turn around, go back home while there was still a little light and what was left of my disappearing track to follow....

But I didn't. I operated on past experience indicating that they were as stupid or crazy as I was, and so I plowed on across the divide between the East River and Washington Gulch to where I thought Frame's cabin was – the historic old Elkton cabin that a skier eventually accidentally burned down.

And sure enough: right at dusk, I saw a light below and ahead, a lantern in a window; and there they were, just as I'd figured, out on a night when no one in their right mind would be out. And after a moment of hooting and moaning outside the window, playing the Elkton ghost so they'd be glad to find it was just me, I went into the warm, and they were no more surprised, nor less relieved, to see me than I was to see them, and

Benjamin held out the schnapps and asked what kind of a fool I was, to be out skiing in the dark in a snowstorm.

***

This essay should actually have been in the first edition of *Dragons in Paradise,* as explanation for the cover photo of that edition – a picture that was actually misleading for most of the content of the book: it suggested a book about rugged mountain types out challenging nature, doing dangerous treks, and all of that, and I'm not really that kind of person at all most of the time – although one does find oneself in all kinds of strange situations if one lets oneself, and this story is about that.

A lot of places in the West, including most of our mountain towns, have been terminals as much as towns, especially for the people in the 20-to-30 age range that populate the West of the imagination. Etymologically, "terminal" sounds like a place where something ends, but in common usage, a terminal – as in bus terminal, airport terminal – a terminal is a place people are passing through on their way somewhere else, and a lot of people have passed through these western mountain valley towns on their way somewhere else. Even when the towns are at the end of the road, the edge of civilization. Here, we're like spaghetti thrown against the wall: some of us stick but most of us slide off to somewhere else, even if it's only, or finally or at last, back to our past. Some people go back to their past without leaving these towns.

But as a consequence of all this transience, coupled with the human need for human companionship, we find ourselves forming quick, intense, here-and-now friendships with people who are often gone the next year, or the next week. And because we're at the edge of civilization here, with the realm of all possibility on beyond that edge, and because we're usually here because we're intrigued with what's beyond that edge, we often find ourselves out in that realm of all possibility, doing strange things with near-strangers, literally putting our lives in the hands of people we didn't even know a year or a month ago.

Westerners had a term for the kind of person with whom you would place that kind of trust: "a man to cross rivers with." That's sort of sexist, or at least 19th-century; I've crossed rivers and a lot of other divides and edges with women too, some of them better qualified to be there than I, and I think it's more real to just say "friends to cross rivers with." Rivers, passes, divides of any kind. And you do these intense and sometimes naive and stupid things with people in whom you've placed this absolute trust, and maybe in a year they're gone elsewhere, or you're gone elsewhere, and you may never see them again after that last maudlin going-away party where you cry in each other's beer and promise you will never, ever lose touch.

So this is a story about people who passed through my life, intensely enough to warp my course, the way light bends in passing a star. If we live well, which means enough on the edge to stay awake to what's going on around us, and what could or should be going on around us, then we'll find people with whom, together, we'll find the gumption to carry out grand plans, hatched out of that edge-zone mix of boredom, genius, naivete, intuition and maybe an uncontrollable substance or two.

I don't want to unduly incriminate people who might not want to be incriminated, so I will just call my two companions in these follies Frame and Benjamin.

Frame and Benjamin were two people, like myself, who were in Crested Butte on our way somewhere else. For me, somewhere else turned out to be pretty close to Crested Butte, on one side or the other, but not for them; I honestly don't know exactly where they are now, and am probably never going to make any serious effort to find out. They've passed back through the valley occasionally; sometimes I've had coffee with one or the other, but less and less frequently. If we should ever find ourselves in one place together again, I think it would be fine, and we might successfully enough bury ourselves in the past to prevent any fresh outbursts of the kind of creative imagination for which we're probably all getting too old.

Benjamin and Frame had both come to town in 1970; I'd been there a few years already. Benjamin came with a partner and a little money from elsewhere; they'd bought the old Colorado Fuel and Iron company store on Elk Avenue and reopened it as "The Company Store," with a kind of enclosed mini-mall upstairs, and they'd re-opened the old "Bird Is Dead Bar and Grill" downstairs, dba "The Tailings."

Frame was the guy who brought cross-country skiing to Crested Butte. Modern hip high-tech cross-country skiing, I guess I should say, since there were cross-country skiers in the valley long before there was a Nordic ski shop; Al Johnson who took the mail from Crested Butte over Schofield and down the Crystal Canyon to Aspen in the 1880s was a cross-country skier; and from 1949 on, Sven Wiik, Western State Colorado University's legendary ski coach, had some cross-country gear available out of the back room at The Toggery in Gunnison, and he annually led cross-country treks from Crested Butte to Aspen.

But Frame started the modern revival of cross-country skiing in 1970 when he opened up "The Alpineer," a cross-country skiing emporium in the front window-space part of The Company Store, with Benjamin as his landlord.

Frame didn't have any idea what he was doing; he'd never cross-country skied in his life, but he had an instinct for the coming thing. I was an early sucker, trading some advertising in the newspaper I mismanaged for a get-up that included wooden Bonna skis (with pressed-wood edges) and a pair of flat-track Finnish boots that were like winter tennis shoes and had no business at all in the mountains.

A few days after getting geared up, Frame and I skied a little ways up Washington Gulch – then unplowed and uninhabited. Those wooden skis had to be waxed, so Frame measured the temperature of the snow with a fancy skier's thermometer from his shop, and the temperature seemed to correlate with what was on the red wax container, so we smeared a coat of red wax all over our skis, started out – and proceeded to get taller as the snow bonded with that wax and packed up on our skis. We walked up the slopes, then walked back down the slopes, and it was a lot like hiking with really awkward and heavy shoes on. An inauspicious start.

A few weeks later, he got Lars Larsen over from Aspen for a "cross-country clinic" – basically a way to sell more gear to more people. Lars was an authentic Nord who was part of the Nordic revival over in the Roaring Fork, and he taught us the art of intelligent waxing and a few other tricks as well, and by the end of that season, we were slipping and sliding up and down all the local valleys.

So by the next season, we were looking for new worlds to conquer, and thus it developed, late one January night in The Tailings, Benjamin's bar, that we were going to ski to Aspen and back: Frame, Benjamin and me. From the end of the road by the Crested Butte Ski Area up to Gothic and over East Maroon Pass to Aspen one day, then up to the Taggart Hut above Ashcroft the next day, and back to Crested Butte over Pearl Pass and down Brush Creek the third day. The Pearl Pass route is basically the route that serious skinny-skiers today do in something like eight hours in the Crested Butte to Aspen Grand Traverse Race every winter. It wasn't even an extreme idea in 1970; Sven Wiik had taken tours over East Maroon to Aspen regularly from the 1950s on, and Lars Larsen occasionally brought a van-load of paying customers over to party Saturday night in Crested Butte and ski back to Aspen on Sunday. But it was not just a walk in the park either, and not many people were doing it.

We did it Frame's way, which was to just go out and do it; planning was for wusses. Which is partly why we found ourselves, on a moonless night, literally feeling our way down the last mile or two to the Thundermug Lodge or whatever it was, the nearest phone to where the East Maroon Trail comes out onto the Maroon Creek Road. On a truly dark night, down in a narrow forested valley, it's amazing how even the white of snow can disappear.

Part of our problem that day was the fact that, despite a lot of congeniality and good pacing when seated on barstools, we all went at very different speeds when moving. Frame moved through life at a kind of warp speed, while Benjamin was the kind of person for whom the word "deliberate" had been invented. Very deliberate. So for most of that day, I found myself somewhere between the two of them, hollering uptrail, "Hey Frame! Slow it down a little!" and then hollering back downtrail, "Benjamin! You still coming?"

The snow was deep and soft and fun on the Aspen side of East Maroon Pass – not that we really knew what to do with it, especially with big awkward packs on our backs. No graceful telemark turns; that skill hadn't even been rediscovered, let alone mastered. No, it was big long traverses working up the nerve for a careening screaming stem turn into the fall line; if we survived that turn, another big traverse (be still, my pounding heart) working up the nerve for another turn. If we fell, it was five minutes of trying, first, to get the backpack down from up around our ears, then figuring out which way was up in our bottomless pit of shifting snow.

There was apparently no avalanche danger that day, since we experienced no avalanches, however deserving we might have been of one.

Once we finally got down off the pass into the valley the snow was still deep and soft but less fun, as we noted the disappearing light and tried to pick up the pace as much as Benjamin permitted.

The slog down the valley was complicated when we stopped to put on a kicker wax and, for some reason, the bale that holds the ski onto the boot fell off of one of Benjamin's skis, into deep snow. We pawed around for it, but couldn't find it, so I got out the baling wire I always ski with and wired him into his ski in a way that sort of worked.

But time had been lost, and very quickly, it seemed, all the light disappeared, and that was when we realized that no one had brought a flashlight. Fortunately, someone had skied up the trail a ways, so there was a track to follow – and there were places where we were following it like Braille, literally feeling our way till we got to the road. An interesting day.

The next day – after a long sleep – we went to Aspen's equivalent of Frame's Crested Butte outdoor shop, where Benjamin got his ski fitted with a new bale and we linked up with Lars Larsen to get the key to the Taggart Hut. That was our easy day, just skiing up the Pearl Pass road, from Ashcroft where Lars left us off, to the Taggart Hut; there we evicted a pine marten, or something long and dark and slinky, and had the kind of fitful night one has in a strange place at altitude with attitude.

The next morning we set out to try to find Pearl Pass, the pass over into the Brush Creek drainage and home. And that, I think, was where and when we all began to realize how truly stupid or crazy we were to be out there with our wood-edge skis and Finnish flat-track tennis shoes. The sky was clear, but the January sun gave no heat and it was a gusty windy morning, wind packing the snow and engraving it with all manner of weird beautiful abstract designs which I'd have appreciated more if I hadn't been more or less thoroughly terrified and cowed by the terrible grandeur of that place that day.

We went uphill, downhill, across flat places with rises all around. Three times we ascended the low places in ridges only to find ourselves looking out over another great bowl that was pretty clearly in the same drainage we'd been in, with high barrier ridges toward the way we knew we needed to be going. And the wind blew and the sun burned without heat, and I had the sense of being in a war zone that wasn't even my war.

I remember traversing – creeping across – a long steep sidehill that was so solidly windpacked (no avalanche danger there) that we could scarcely poke a pole into it, let alone really set an edge with those tennis-shoe boots. A misstep there would have resulted in a quick journey of five hundred feet on cold sandpaper ending abruptly in the rocky upper edge of the spruce-fir below. A really interesting day.

Finally, we found a low place in a ridge that led into a bowl that went down the way we thought we wanted to be going, and after another thrill-packed descent to timberline, we eventually saw Crested Butte Mountain off in the distance, and had a long quiet – and eventually windless – run out to Frame's car at the end of the plowed road, and we were back at the Tailings in time for the tail end of Happy Hour.

A little bragging there, to be sure – but accompanied with the kind of sidelong glances to each other that let us each know we each knew how lucky we were to still be alive. To be alive is lucky; to know it – moreso. An adventure is something you survive whether you deserve to or not.

***

We were marginally smarter that other time, when we came from two different directions to meet at Frame's cabin up Washington Gulch on a night when it was stupid to be out at all. Our plan that time had been to do a winter assault on Gothic Mountain the next day, with somewhat better equipment but basically knowing no more about winter mountaineering than we'd known the day we wandered around looking for Pearl Pass. But when we woke up in the morning and it was still snowing, we were smart enough to abandon that plan and we just went out and played around for a while in the more or less safe places, then went our separate ways home.

And now – as I said, I really don't know for sure where either of them is, Frame or Benjamin. Frame eventually directed his energies into heavy equipment and construction. Benjamin sold most of his interests in Crested Butte, bought a little farm over in the North Fork valley and started doing decorative stonework, then moved back to his roots in the Hudson River valley. I haven't seen either of them in years.

And I miss them – or maybe not them so much as I miss what we did together in passing through each other's lives. And I wonder if I will ever again be so stupid or crazy as to do something like skiing off alone into a gathering storm because I'm going to rendezvous somewhere out in the wilds with two friends I didn't even know two years before, confident that they will be stupid or crazy enough to be there because they'd said they would be. Friends with whom to cross rivers, passes, or whatever's out there.

La Madre del Agua
(aka Headwaters Hill)

Out along sky's ridge we went
In search of the source of life,
And finally found – almost missed –
An humble roundbacked mother
Whose lap begat three errant offspring.

Her first child left for the sunrise
Ran off to the broad blessed bowl
Of a rich vast land now all drained
To feed the growing confusing hordes
Clustering in miraginous floating cities.

Her second child left for the sunset
Ran off to the dry ripped skin
Of a spare red land all bled bare
By the wet dreams of restless people
Trying again in the ancient desert sinks.

Her third child left for *el sol real*,
Ran off to the rippled hot mirage
Of a larger leaner land made waste
By the revolutions of the running blood
Calling from the once and future Cibolas.

But the mother stays where she is
Cumbent in the cool rise and fall
Of our jumbled mountain hope,
And sends only tears down after her lost,
Weeping life for those in the dry lands below.

Thanks to the efforts of students at Western State College, "Headwaters Hill" is now the official designation for a modest hill south of Marshall Pass on the Continental Divide, where small tributaries for three great American rivers originate – the Arkansas, Rio Grande, and Colorado Rivers – and trickle off to those rivers' distinct destinies.

Partnering with a Border Collie

Anthologized in *Colorado Mountain Dogs*, by M. John Fayhee,
Westwinds Press, 2014.

Barring strange accidents or chance, I've partnered with my last dog –
mostly because my last dog was such a superior partner.

She was a border collie, Zoe; and Zoe was actually the only dog
I've ever really been invited to partner with, however unworthy I was at it.
There were a couple other dogs in my life when I was a kid, but they were
just family pets. Bred for petdom. Border collies aren't bred to be pets;
they are bred for intelligence and bred for work, and they more or less
insist on – I would say, deserve – a working partnership. And my
partnership with Zoe was not really a "fulfilled" partnership because I
didn't really have any work for her to do that was worthy of her skills and
willingness.

Our daughter brought her into our lives; Zoe was a gift from her
godfather, Steve Allen, a rancher over in the valley of the North Fork of
the Gunnison who, for a time, raised and trained border collies on the side.
Then Sarah went away to college three years later, and my (human)
partner and I inherited Zoe, for what turned out to be the rest of Zoe's life
(14 years total).

What border collies can do in a working situation is impressive.
"Sheep dog trials" are held around the country, to show off the skills and

129

intelligence of these dogs. My (human) partner and I once went to the trials up in Meeker, Colorado, to watch the human-and-dog teams work through an almost fiendish set of challenges, that begins with sending the dog out full speed on a quarter-mile circling run, to move a small herd of semi-wild sheep down through some slalom-like gates, and ends with some really complex penning challenges involving splitting the flock to separate out some with colored bandannas.

The champion dogs at the Meeker trials are often older females: they can still turn on the "berserker" look that gets the sheep in gear – wild-eyed, teeth bared and panting like a furnace, moving in a crouch as if about to spring – but they've matured like a certain kind of no-nonsense woman, the kind of woman you just don't mess with, and those gal dogs have worked so long with their human partner (often enough exactly that kind of woman) that one could swear they are reading each other's minds. And that may not be too far from the truth. Steve Allen said the biggest challenge for the dog's partner is not distracting the dog with too much instruction.

We of course had nothing in our towny lives to provide any comparable work for Zoe. Not that moving stock is the only kind of work they find acceptable: border collies can be good baby-sitters; they are used in search and rescue work; they are good in hunting; they are great Frisbee-catchers; and they will keep your yard cat-free. They've been recruited for therapy and assistance work for people with disabilities; one border collie became the "hearing-ear dog" for a woman with severe hearing loss.

But the best tasks we could come up with for Zoe were little things, like the human partner sending her downstairs in the morning, if I was up early, to let me know it was coffee time. Out hiking, Zoe took it upon herself to scout out the trail ahead, stopping at trail forks to consult on which to take. There was also a lot of ball-playing, and she invented tasks for herself, like patrolling the fence out front, tearing along it to keep the cars moving on, but jumping up on it to welcome pedestrians. Neighbors on both sides of us eventually got border collies themselves after daily exchanges with Zoe at the fence.

What really got me about Zoe was her eyes. She would come sit on the floor in front of me and stare at me – not the berserker look she would have used on the sheep, but neither that sappy look of adoration and submission we tend to associate with dogs. A look more like a question: "Hello? Are you there? Isn't it time?" It was as though she had something to tell me that required me to be able to converse in her way.

It got to me: "What, Zoe?" I would say. Sometimes she would actually lead me off, maybe to the door, or her food dish, but sometimes to some place with no point at all that I could see. "*What?*" I would ask, and she would just stand there looking at me, tail in a slow swish, tongue out in a thinking-mode pant, waiting for me to get smart enough to understand.

Zoe made me think a lot about the "interspecies contract" whereby some of the wolves long ago decided to throw in with humans, to start collaborating with us rather than competing. Genetic analysis proves pretty conclusively that all dogs – even little Chihuahuas – are "wolves in dog clothing." There's a lot of speculation on when some of the wolves, coyotes and foxes might have decided to switch rather than fight. Most guesses place it around the time, 10,000-30,000 years ago, when most humans left off their hunter-gatherer lives and began to settle into agricultural and pastoral villages – farming where farming was possible, and herding the big herbivore herds where farming was marginal.

Both farming and herding should probably be viewed not just as "advances" in human culture, but as defensive measures brought about by the population increases that accompanied the mellowing of the climate with the retreat of the last glacial epoch. Gatherers started planting seeds in centralized watered places they could protect as pressure grew from other gatherers; hunters found themselves having to protect the herds they had always hunted from the growing populations of other human hunters as well as from the growing populations of non-human predators. It was not an easy time; open free-for-all turf war often resulted between bands of humans, and between packs of predators – and between the bands and packs, for that matter.

It was in that time of transition that the contract between wolves and humans was presumably born, at the edge of the firelight. Those who say "the leopard can't change its spots" have no answer for why the wolves were able to transcend their "instinct" to run down, harass and kill the big herbivores, and perform the contradictory act of protecting them – even from their own kind who'd stayed beyond the firelight. My feeling (mostly from having known Zoe) is that it had to have been an act of reasoning, the kind of thinking that we humans are supposed to have a sole proprietorship on, however little we seem to employ it.

Which party initiated the contract? I'm inclined to think it was probably the humans, with an offer of food. But that may just be because I am a human. And even though it is on the surface a "will work for food" contract, I think it has to have involved an offer of respect too. A dog like Zoe doesn't work *only* for food.

131

Like most things through time, the relationship has been corrupted in many ways; it's often considered to be a master-slave relationship – not really a contract at all – with the dogs being forced into situations in which no dog would willingly participate. Dogs get turned into attackers and killers; female dogs get bred to death in puppy mills; dogs get bred into genetic disasters. Decide for yourself which party is more bestial.

An engaging and haunting novel about dogs and humans is "The Story of Edgar Sawtelle," by David Wroblewski, a story of three generations of dog breeders in upper Wisconsin who were trying to breed a strain of super-smart, empathetic dogs. The book included a correspondence between the Edgar's grandfather and another dog-breeder, who skeptically observed that the only way we're going to get better dogs than we have now is to become better humans.

Having known Zoe, I can only agree.

> She may have forgiven me
> For never finding the time to learn
> To talk to her with my eyes.
> I'd proclaim her intelligence
> Was limited by the lack of vocal cords,
> Opposable thumbs, et cetera, and
> All the while she's standing there,
> Her eloquent eyes exposing my limits.
>
> That's not all she forgave:
> I couldn't match the unconditional
> Commitment she brought to our life
> Together, her bottomless capacity for
> Forgiving our slights – our forgetting
> To let her in, to let her out, to feed her,
> To meet her eye, to hear what she wanted
> To give us through those great brown eyes.
>
> She was probably still wild enough
> To be useful – not crazy wild, just wild
> Enough to see and hear and feel everything
> You need to see and hear and feel around;
> Out on hikes she went ahead, she led
> Even though she didn't know where
> We were going; she'd check back: I'll lead you,
> She'd say (her eyes), wherever you want to go.

She's gone on now – eyes gone, hearing gone,
Joints gone, kidneys going, we let her go.
It ceased to be a life when she couldn't go
Ranging out ahead where she belonged,
Turning back to see if we were still coming,
To say, as I'm sure she will (me finally able to hear)
If we should meet again on some other side:
"Come on, I'll lead you, wherever you want to go."

Ghosts and Growing Up
In the Mountains

First published in *Mountain Gazette* 78, December 2000 – the first issue
of the "resurrected" magazine.

I'm haunted by a nearby ghost town. Ghost towns are pretty common in
the Colorado mountains, and there are a lot of them here in the Upper
Gunnison River valley where I live – most of them going back to the gold
and silver booms and busts of the last third of the 19th century: towns that
came into being over a summer, peaked with populations in the thousands,
even tens of thousands, and generally disappeared in a decade, often less.

But the ghost town that coyotes around the margins of my mind
was not like those towns. This one probably never had a population larger
than a few dozen people at any one time. But it was inhabited more or less
continuously for around 5,000 years. Five thousand! And it became a
ghost town some 3,000 years ago, long before America was even a gleam
in Europe's eye, even before Christianity began wreaking its blessings on
the world.

This old town lay just south of the present-day city of Gunnison:
across the runway and the Tomichi Creek floodplain, up on a brushy knoll
visible from the west end of today's town. Except to the practiced

archeologist's eye, little remains of that old town – some subtle firepits, some postholes marking out the tentsized brush-and-mud shelters that were the homes in that village, and tens of thousands of rock flakes, bits of bone and the other indicators of thousands of years of local survival. That's all – a disappointment to students I take out there, students maybe too stripped by television of the ability to construct large pictures from small evidence.

Most of what does remain of that much older town has been put in thousands of plastic baggies and stored in Western State Colorado University's Anthropology Department, for this ancient place has become an important archaeological site that is changing our understanding of the prehistoric occupation of the Rocky Mountains. Most of the paleontologists and archaeologists working in the West have believed that Stone Age people did not live year-round in the mountains because the climate was too harsh in the winter – this despite the fact that even in historical times peoples like the Inuit Indians in far northern Alaska have lived for eons in much more forbidding climates.

Nonetheless, it couldn't have been any real picnic out there across the runway, three thousand, six thousand years ago. I think about the town across the runway, across the creek when I'm leaving the college on a winter evening, walking home. When the sky at dusk is in its sherbet mode, lemon on the southwestern horizon up through deep blackberry overhead, with the temperature passing through zero on its way to Gunnison's usual winter 15-25 below, me quickstepping it eight blocks home.

I think: it's going to be a cold night in the town across the runway, across the creek; it's going to be a long, cold, long night. And I reach home, thinking of that, and come into this bubble of warmth and light here at the bottom of that deep cold brilliant night, and I know, quite literally, I may be one of the most undeservingly lucky humans who ever lived.

***

Archaeologists, paleontologists, people who study prehistoric people, call the people who lived in that older town Archaics. They weren't the oldest humans to inhabit the continent; they were the second wave of really old peoples, the ones who were no longer the hunters of woolly mammoths and other mega-mega-fauna because the mega-mega-fauna were all gone by nine or ten thousand years ago. The Archaic people had become, through necessity, foragers as well as hunters – or maybe more forager

136

than hunter: animal, plant, fungus or whatever, large or small, if it was
edible, they figured out how to eat it. Buffalo, deer, frogs, herons, snakes,
sage hens, roots and tubers, and anything else that moved or just grew and
was humanly digestible.

The evidence from their Upper Gunnison firepits and trash heaps
indicates that they also ate a whole lot of piñon nuts, as well as depending
on piñon pine for their chief energy source – the more interesting now
because today piñon trees don't grow in the Upper Gunnison valley.
There's no real reason why piñon pines don't grow here today, but around
3,000 years ago, the trees must have been killed off by cold, or drought, or
both, and when the pines left, the people apparently had to leave too.

Whatever the physical evidence tells us, however, there's one
thing we probably won't be able to extrapolate from it, and that's why
these Archaic people were here at all. Why had they come way up in a
mountain valley dominated by winter? Even if it was a warmer valley
then, it couldn't have been as mild as, say, the lower Uncompahgre valley,
down by present-day Montrose and Delta, where in much more recent
times the Ute Indians hung out during the winter, just coming to the upper
valleys in the summer.

Why come up into the mountains? Maybe there was nowhere else
to go – maybe everywhere else was already full. Hunters and foragers need
a lot more room per capita than do agricultural people – more even than
the modern posturban 35-acre rancherettes think they need. So the early
people of the Upper Gunnison valley may have been an offshoot of
another group downvalley – sent out to find a new place because the old
place was getting too crowded.

I have to wonder, though, if they came to the mountains for any of
the reasons that people today come to the mountains. Their lives, so far as
we can tell, were so precarious and perilous by nature that it is hard to
imagine them going to difficult places in search of adventure, beauty,
Maslow's "higher needs" that bring a lot of people to the mountains today
– although that might just show my limited imagination.

Did the Archaics seek out, appreciate beauty? Enjoy it when they
were in its presence? Down in the Cochetopa Hills near here – a low green
place on the Continental Divide that was a veritable interstate for
migrating animals, including humans – there's a little grassy flat hilltop
that must have been close to a source of good tool rock because there are
little piles of chips all over the hilltop. A little tool factory. But off to the
west and south rise the LaPlatas and the San Juans, and I can't imagine

any reason for lugging the tool stones up there to work them other than because you could look up and there were the mountains.

***

If asked why, when I came to the Upper Gunnison valley four decades ago, I would have said I came for the skiing, but that was only partially – or superficially – true. The deeper truth was that I was in the fourth or fifth year of a long disorderly retreat from civilization. From America's version of civilization: I was a civilization drop-out. I'd made it through high school without dropping out, and college (mostly), but I didn't make it through the last and highest level of civilizing indoctrination: I became a military dropout. And since all my prior indoctrinations had led me to believe that getting kicked out of the Army was only second worse to being a convicted felon, I assumed I was destined for a marginal life in America, so I headed for the margins; I came to the mountains.

I'd like to say I wasn't slinking – that I came in the spirit in which Castro had gone to the mountains, Che had gone to the mountains, Sandino had gone to the mountains, Ethan Allen and the Green Mountain Boys had gone to the mountains, the Galilean Judas and his Zealots had gone to Masada. I'd like to say I came to this valley as a son of our mad old poet, Robinson Jeffers:

...For my children, I would have them keep their distance
from the thickening center; corruption Never has been compulsory,
when the cities lie at the monster's feet there are left the mountains.

But I wasn't really thinking like that at the time. I wasn't in fact really thinking at all. Despite some reactive antipathies, I was basically an American: not thinking and proud of it; that was my bred way of life. And the corruption oozing out from the thickening center was so gooily pervasive and diffidently omnipresent, that it was hard to figure out exactly what to react to or even think of rising against. If I thought something was wrong, then it was far easier to believe that it was probably me. So I was here for the skiing, and whatever work I had to do to support that, and for a while, that's what I did.

As for the mountains, I just knew they were beautiful, whatever that meant – something I knew in about the same way I knew I didn't have a future: somebody'd probably told me so. It wasn't until I was here a while that they started to alter the landscape of my mind.

***

138

Walking home on a cold night from the college where I worked in my post-skiing years, I think of the Archaics in the town across the runway, across the creek. How did they get through these nights 5,000 years ago? Nothing but those little firepits for heat – those and, I suppose, each other, sleeping in people-piles in brush-and-pole shelters about the size of the "family tents" you can buy from one of the Mallwarts for car camping. No lights, no books, no television, no videos; nothing but each other for whatever it takes to get through the night.

Walking home fast in the cold, I imagine what it would be for our two towns to fall into some kind of a time warp that made them co-existent. I imagine the Archaics wandering across the geometric expanse of the runway – itself a strange miracle, a runway for 737s serving a valley of 14,000, a runway longer than the main street of Gunnison itself, probably more runway per capita than anywhere else in America.

The whole population of that Archaic village at any point in its five or six thousand year history could probably fit comfortably (for them) into my 1,600-square-foot house – and imagine their awe at the electric lights, the diffused heat from the furnace, the refrigerator (the extra-vagance of bringing a cold place into a warm place built against the cold).

But before they even got to my house, they would pass – be unable to pass – the Safeway. Imagine them there: foragers and hunters confronted with cases upon cases of produce, even in the dead of winter; meat strangely displayed but still obviously enough meat. Most of it would probably not even register as food – the canned goods, packaged prepared foods, frozen pizzas. But the produce, the meat – they would think they had died and gone to whatever their idea of an afterlife was.

Harder to imagine, however, is the thought of me crossing the runway and those three or five thousand years to do time in their town. I am adept enough at using the myriad mundane tools and technologies that underlie modern life in the Upper Gunnison valley, but I could not create any bit of it myself from raw resources. Build my own car from scratch? A computer? Even a good hammer with a handle, from scratch, or a workable cutter or scraper, given nothing but found materials around me – that may be beyond my basic skills. But judging from the number of flakes found around that older townsite – upwards of 60,000 "artifacts" after a decade of poking and digging – everyone in that village was probably able to make the tools they each needed for the daily chores of survival.

Beyond that, there's the more subtle but probably more important psychological fitness for that earlier "simpler" life. Physically, I might be able to hack it, after a difficult conditioning period. I think of myself as an outdoors person; I don't just "lift up mine eyes unto the hills"; I haul my butt up there too. I hike, I backpack and camp.

But psychologically – I have never camped out year round; I've never woken up on a rainy or a snowy morning in a rough shelter thinking: I'm going to wake up here every morning for the rest of my life. And I've never had to hunt down, and get close enough to kill with small weapons, a number of large and small mammals to take their skins for my own shelter and clothing. Or build the tools for doing that killing, skinning and clothes-making. Could I face up to that kind of "simple life," as we patronizingly think of it, or would I instead be just inclined to curl up in a fetal position and say the hell with it? I don't honestly know.

***

Looking around me today in the Upper Gunnison valley – looking at this flash of petroleum-based imported abundance I live in today, across the creek from a truly local community sustained for maybe 5,000 years – I think about growing up.

It's a good time for me to be thinking about growing up; I'm seventy. Plus. I find that incredible because, truth to tell, in my soul and mind I don't really feel much older than I felt when I arrived here as a twenty-something almost 50 years ago.

This is not to be confused with AARPy "young at heart" piety. Physically, I know I'm getting old: I'm bald; I've need glasses all the time, not just for reading; I've lost about 60 percent of my hearing in one ear; I've got a little arthritis in my right knee, left thumb and other odd joints; there's a slow rounding heaviness to my gut that no amount of physical labor or exercise seems to flatten anymore – et cetera.

So there's no question that I'm growing old, but growing *up* is what I'm thinking about – becoming mature, an adult of the species. I don't feel like the "elder" a seventy-year-old ought to be, or at least be becoming – a repository of wisdom to be passed along to the coming generations. This is a tough thing for a teacher to confess, but in my teaching I was more into cultural analysis than cultural transmission; I tried to teach the coming generations to listen carefully and critically, and to not automatically believe everything they hear from official sources the way I had tended to at their age. This isn't mature wisdom; it's just adolescent awareness refined through experience. I've finally learned to usually avoid most of the usual adolescent responses to adolescent awareness, such as shooting myself in the foot as a punishment to the species.

But, looking at the two towns across the runway from each other here, I find it ever harder to accept the conventional theology that we somehow represent a higher level of human maturation than those Archaics who survived there for 5,000 years. We perceive the long march across the runway to modern Gunnison as "the ascent of man." But looking at a society that uses these incredible quantities of the earth's finite resources just to shelter and coddle a bunch of chronically nervous and depressed humans manically busy at busywork – I'm inclined to think that this sense of being stuck in adolescence is not just my personal problem alone.

This is a thought with some scientific support. We may be what biologists call a neotenous species – meaning a species that has developed through breeding in its immature forms. Up the valley, high in the mountains above Crested Butte, there is a species of salamander that is neotenous. Salamanders are animals born to water that, in their adult phase, modify their early gill system for underwater oxygen intake to a lung system and become amphibious. But this particular subspecies of salamander, up there in a really high mountain valley where it is winter a lot more than it is not-winter, never really gets out of the water, which is usually warmer than the night air much of the summer, and protected by snow in the winter; so they remain gill-breathers, eventually breeding in the water rather than out in the amphibian edge between water and land. So eventually, this particular breed of high altitude salamanders just genetically "forgot" about growing up into the lunged adult stage.

This salamander up in the high streams of the Rockies is not the only salamander that breeds in its immature forms; there are others, who also happen to live in stressful environments – places too hot or too cold, too wet or too dry, for the salamanders to easily reach maturity. Nor are salamanders the only set of species with neotenous subspecies. David Rains Wallace discusses this topic in his fabulous book, *The Klamath Knot,* and cites behavioral evidence that the otter might be a neotenous species: it belongs to the weasel family, but never seems to grow into the solitary seriousness of the weasels, martins, badgers and other mustelids. Otters just like to play around; they act like kids all their lives.

And we humans might well be another neotenous species. Most of the archaeological and paleontological evidence supports the theory that, over most of our three- or four-million-year tenure as a distinguishable species, life was tough enough so that the species only survived through

141

our capacity for breeding in an immature stage – what today we call "teen pregnancies." If Archaic females didn't start having babies in their early or mid-teens – and continue having them regularly in hopes of a few living long enough to reach adolescent breeding age themselves – then the group diminished and either disappeared genetically into other more successful human groups, like the Neanderthals did, or just disappeared period.

We can look to other species in the primate family to imagine what mature humans might have been like, and the difference is probably nothing so dramatic as a complete change of breathing apparatus. Most of us have relatively hairless bodies compared to other species in the primate family, disproportionately large heads for our bodies, more slender bones and musculature for most of us. And we have a package of interesting (to us) and disproportionately large sexually-oriented equipage (in the air-brushed ideal) that is featured in those most adolescent fruits of civilization, which are ironically about the only things we advertise as "adult" – as in "adult bookstore," "adult entertainment."

But the more subtle but important differences are probably in the goings-on in the big brain that evolved along with these fertile teenagers. The brain's neocortex is the thing that most distinguishes us from the rest of the animal kingdom – and it is a physical thing that has been passed along, developed, evolved by breeding kids. Our brain, our mind, literally does not know, *by nature*, what it is to "grow up."

Observing in other animals – and plants, even the lilies of the field – the concept of maturity, we have tried to culturally invent maturity for ourselves, which is to say we've figured out a whole panoply of ways to play at being grownups. We look around and devise metaphors and analogies – should we be like the wolf? Are we too sheeplike? Or should we consider the lilies of the field?

In terms of social structure, our efforts to grow up seem to range between extremes set by our fellow primate species, who in their mature states range from the family-unit isolation of the mountain gorillas – the Randy Weaver syndrome – to the extreme communalism of the chimpanzees and orangutans, who invented the queue by lining up more or less politely for a turn at any female in heat.

That we play at growing up is probably good, because if we don't play at it, we may never get there – may never find, through the trial-and-error experiential analysis that is what real play is all about, the things that really utilize that incredible big brain to responsibly realize human potential within the limitations of a blessed but finite planet.

But when we play at growing up, we do it badly in at least two ways. For one, we take our "adult" play far too seriously for it to be effective play. Mostly, we insist, to the frequent point of violence, that what we overgrown but immature adolescents do isn't play at all; it's really *serious.* Which of course makes it not the kind of learning situation that good play is.

At this point in our cultural devolution, this petrifying seriousness has permeated down into all of our alleged institutions of learning where the Common Cores and over-organized summers insure that real open-ended exploration and discovery are diminishing parts of our natural childhood and adolescence. Despite a century of really interesting research into the processes of human learning, we apply almost none of that in an institutional way; instead we turn our schools and colleges into ever more indoctrinational institutions. The tendency for enlightened teachers to nurture learning despite the curriculum is currently being crimped by taking up ever more of their time and energies with preparations for exhaustive testing for "basic skills" – control methods imposed under the guise of "accountability" for them and uniformity in their "product."

Second, when we play at growing up, we can't seem to let go of the most naive and clingy habits of childhood: we need to invent an approving or at least comforting Father or Mother; we resort again and again to a childlike faith in external authority and tradition; we make a virtue of not using our big brains (as in "My country, right or wrong" or "The Bible tells me so"); we fall back on "That's the way we do things!" as though the way we do things were actually working well.

The result of all this deadly mix of childish seriousness and residual childishness is to make "growing up" as practiced by modern humans a thoroughly reductive process. When we "put aside our childish things," we are giving up the play-acts of invention and discovery, but gaining nothing in exchange (except maybe a seat on the exchange). In forgetting how to play, we surrender the rebellious curiosity, the expansive inventiveness, the amoral innocence of youth and adolescence. We bank our fires and blinder our wide-eyed vision – "Grow up," we tell each other, on those occasions when the imagination says, "Why not this. . . .." "Get real," we tell the imagination. "Look at the bottom line." What kind of an "ascent of man" is it that arrives at nothing higher than the bottom line?

And so we continue to hunker in Plato's cave, staring at shadows and forging our own manacles to control the mind – to keep that big adolescent brain from the desperate awkward acts of commencing to grow up. "Perhaps old men," said Marcel Proust, "are merely adolescents who survive for a sufficient number of years." That's me: seventy-plus.

***

Once spring afternoon I took a class out to the ghost town across the runway in a college van, and while we were there, a really vicious afternoon storm built over the mountains and came at us – wind, sleet, snow, rain, and more wind. We were driven back into the van, and back to the college where we wrapped ourselves up in hot coffee in the cafeteria and just watched it. I couldn't imagine living through that kind of nastiness (not that rare in the spring), and the less dramatic but more pervasive long cold nights of winter (not at all rare), and even the midday sun of summer, relentlesss if you are out under it unprotected.... Maybe it's better than the far frozen North of the Inuit, but it's not an easy place. How did they survive here? For 5,000 years? I can come up with two possible answers.

First, you get used to what you have. If what you have is a 1,600 square-foot house with indoor plumbing, then it's hard to imagine living all your life in a 70 square-foot pole-brush-and-mud shelter with no plumbing and no toilet paper. But if that 70-square-foot shelter is the best shelter you've ever known, then it's probably good enough. If you get used to a stove or microwave, and central heating, then a fire-pit would be hard to live with – until you got used to it.

Second, I suspect the presence of each other was important to their survival here. When the sun and the temperature both dropped so early and stayed down so long, what else did they have but each other? Talk and stories and shared heat huddled around the firepit. University of Colorado Scientist R. Igor Gamow thought that "being able to tell a story" was an important part of our cultural evolution: "Storytelling was a means of holding early groups together and, since this was an advantage, was selected for."

This is a little contrary to our modern cultural sense of why people come to the mountains. At the Telluride Idea Festival one summer, where the main topic was mountain communities, a Telluride woman – a relative newcomer, decompressing from a high-stress urban busyness – asked if "mountain community" wasn't an oxymoron. "People don't come to the mountains to be part of a community," she said. A longtime Colorado mountain-town newspaper editor, Ken Olsen Sr. of Leadville, once put it a little more aggressively: "People do not move to little mountain towns because of a love for their fellow man."

That may be true. It was true enough for me – when I moved to the mountains, a callow twentysomething trying to figure out what to do with or about two decades of pretty intensive indoctrination in the Ponzi scheme called Civilization As We Know It. Whatever that civilization is, it is not a culture built around inculcating love for one's fellow man, so I thought I was coming to the mountains like Byron or Faust, there to continue the masochistic process of alternately flagellating and comforting the proud and lonely soul I'd been taught to cultivate in high school and college.

But one thing I discovered in the mountains was what a hothouse cultivar that proud and lonely soul was. What a salamander soul, staying in the warmer water rather than getting out of the comfortable water and growing up.

***

I came to the mountains to ski, but somewhere along the line, the mountains came to me. Not in any physical sense, obviously; they just began to wake me up, infiltrate me; I began to wake up to them. One afternoon out hiking, sitting in a lodgepole forest wanting nature to speak to me and eventually going home diminished by that silly presumption. Or out fishing with the Bots and giving up trying to keep up with him and just sitting back to watch the mountains, waiting for movement and realizing I didn't have the time to wait that long. Realizing in a piece of the old forest one night that the trees were planting in me a dream of being lost there....

Winter nights on sweep with the ski patrol up on Crested Butte Mountain: dusk, maybe a wind, maybe not, maybe the disappearing day as still as a breath held for death, and the sky moving into its sherbet tones. Waiting by one of the check points for whoever was skiing and skating the road to make sure the mountain was clear, my "fellow man" a shadow going by in the dusk with a wave, then on down to the next check point, the sky a little deeper, the mountain a little larger.... Then on down to the Grubstake for a beer with those guys, another bubble of warmth and light under the night, under the quiet loom of the mountains – under these circumstances my "fellow man" didn't look so bad. There were a couple of duds, but most of them were what westerners used to call "men to cross rivers with." Go out in the mountains with, do with whatever had to be done to survive, try to grow up with.

And the mountains – which seem so easy at first, so accessible to the determined, so...just *there*, so *keeping still* as the I Ching says –

demand more and more, the longer one stays in their presence. "A society to match our scenery"? Easy enough, so long as it's just scenery. But when the novelty of great scenery wears off, and you're seeing the mountains more peripherally, as large quiet parts of the life you're living, trying to put together there, then they begin to surround you, environ you, grow over you a little, and their confusions of breezes whisper their nothings at you.

There's no god or gods there, you realize, unless you put it or them there yourself; there's no completed perfect creation there; the mountains are back beyond God, back where there's nothing but inchoate forces at play, earth and fire sticking it in the face of wind and water. In the mountains I can walk through some fragile order, order cobbled together by this mystery called life that I'm part of, something that somehow came into being at the interface of those inchoate forces. I walk up through a weave of trees and grasses and flowers trying to hold the earth together and combing the violence out of the wind and water, earth and fire – and then it just ends suddenly, that order; this upward thrusting slope of life ends like an unfinished thought, and drops away five hundred, a thousand rocky feet to another blob of trees and a beaver pond, grasses and flowers and animals far down there, like up here, trying to weave order over the fundamental realities of a raw ball of rock and heat floating in a sky more empty and cold than anything.

A universe of eternal slow meaningless struggle that generates an everchanging battlefield so charged with beauty and brokenness as to make one weep, sing, or just sit still in wonder. And it's there that the proud and lonely soul breaks too, if it's worth a damn, has any potential for truly growing up – breaks open the way the seed splits, putting up the shoot of its hypothesis in the face of the universe's indifference....

It wasn't "love of my fellow man" that drove me to a mountain town, but I have found here a higher proportion of fellow spirits than I've found before or since anywhere else – fellows (of both sexes) with a yearning to be at least something different, if not something better, than what the society we grew up in expected us to become. There were enough of us here – discovered, uncovered to each other in subtle and oblique ways – so that we could probably all agree that while, yes, it wasn't love of fellow man that brought us to mountain towns, it was interest in fellow spirits that keeps us here, as well as interest in the mountains themselves.
And here in the mountains, in posturban postmodern postAmerica, is a more likely place than anywhere else I can think of, to try to grow up to fit our big brains, if we are ever going to do that: here beyond God, beyond

progress, beyond the closed completeness and perfection of our childhood fantasies and the fantasies-exposed cynicism of our adolescence; here where life is such an obviously thin layer over the indifferent beauty of chaos – here is where we might begin to finally commence to proceed to learn to use what we have, to understand the true dimensions of what we have.

And if it takes another five thousand years, or another three million – what else do we have left to do that's worth doing? Grow up.

Sarah 1

She has the beauty of the morning of her kind:
Her feet are like roots on the ground,
Spread and gripping and bare, brown,
Quick and there after here when she wants
But stable as stone when she softly stands
To see through the eyes of the morning of her kind.

She has the body of the morning of her kind:
Sturdy she strides out to gather the day,
This over that shoulder, that over this as
Quick young things flash around her legs
Like the trunks of young aspen, limber and light
As the light in the eyes of the morning of her kind.

She has the mind of the morning of her kind:
She reads a world that never knew words
Till she and her kind gave it that grace,
Quick as the moment that might be a sun pause
Wondering what she and her singers are dreaming
As they name the world in the morning of her kind.

She has the soul of the morning of her kind:
She wakes to the sun's touch, laughing to let
It know she knows it has risen; she weeps
Quick floods and rains fall for fallen sparrows,
And all the beauty of life rises around me as I see her
See the world through the eyes of the morning of her kind.

Sawmill I: Working the Gate between Worlds

First published in *High Country News*, Sept. 16, 1985, later
anthologized in *The Landscape of Home,* a "Rocky Mountain Land Series Reader"
edited by Jeff Lee of the Rocky Mountain Land Library.

In the realm of interesting things that confuse me and confusing things that interest me, the relationships between trees and humans are high on my list.

The relationships are close. We humans are one of the longest-lived and currently most successful species in the animal kingdom; trees occupy the same crowning niche in the plant kingdom. And to what end? I once found an old 1930s "General Forestry" text at a yard sale that had a wonderful definition: "A tree is a living organism, complex in its structure, and not entirely understood as yet as to its function."

Is there anything in that definition that does not apply equally well to a human?

As with almost all plant-and-animal relationships, we humans come off as dependents – we need the trees a lot more than the trees need us. At the most basic level there's the oxygen they pump out. They aren't the only source of oxygen on earth, but they are certainly an important one. This is some mutuality to this dependency since they need the carbon dioxide we generate – and we have become substantial generators of carbon dioxide; studies currently indicate that most tree species are appreciating this and are doing what they can to take care of all that extra carbon dioxide.

But in all our other interactions with trees, they are serving us, usually in some way that demands a high level of sacrifice from them. Our least demanding uses for trees are when we use them for shade, windbreaks, and aesthetic decoration – we actually do a lot to nurture and protect them in those instances, and even to help them spread into places where they previously weren't found.

But our other principal uses for trees are for fuel and shelter, and in those uses the trees get "changed" in the most Biblical sense. Fuelwood is still the number one use of trees around the world, and a lot of land has been desertified over time just to keep humans warm and fed. Civilizations have fallen apart from that most elemental "energy crisis."

Our own Anglo-American civilization suffered that energy crisis a century or so before we began to move to America. My surname, in fact, implicates my ancestors in that energy crisis. I've parsed it etymologically: "Sibb-leah" is what "Sibley" came from (the Old-English "leah" became "ley" in Middle English). Both root words are in the dictionary today: one's "sibb" is one's clan or kin group; "leah" (or just "lea") is a meadow. So "clan of the meadow," or maybe just "people of the meadow."

But now take "meadow" back into my ancestral prehistoric Anglo-Saxon England and Europe, which was allegedly so densely forested that an energetic and adventurous squirrel could supposedly cross the island going tree to tree. In that environment, the "meadow" becomes a "clearing in the forest." And take "leah" back into the less refined grunts and sibilations of the Indo-European proto-tongue that birthed languages from India to Iceland, and you get a sound which probably underlies the words for "light" in many of those languages – thus, "the place where light comes into the forest."

When the American Sibb-leahs went into the great forests of North America – and we've been here since 1629 – that's the way we, in part, justified our devastations: "letting the light into the forest" was what the tree-mining loggers said they were doing, opening the land up for farming, recreating in our "New England" the landscapes of the old England.

So that is pretty exactly what my name means: Sibley, the Sibb-Leah, the people who let the light into the forest. One reason we left England was because there was no more forest to let the light into; it was basically all meadow, and people were sneaking out at night to tear up hedgerows, dismantle bridges; wood was still the primary energy source for heat and cooking – thus, a big chronic energy crisis that gradually drove the people to the dirty work of mining coal for fuel. Or drove them to America.

And despite an avowed love for trees, I have not really departed far from that ancestral pattern of "letting light into the forest." For the past half century I have depended partially or entirely on wood for heat. We installed a wood stove in our current "modern" gas-heated house mostly because I don't feel that comfortable depending on a bunch of petrocapitalists a state or two distant to deliver my energy. (Suppose they get a better offer elsewhere?)

Also, for maybe a quarter of those years, I have made part or all of my living from construction and carpentering, and I am not so naive as to not know where boards come from. Like all carpenters, I have shaken my head, and cussed a little, at the quality of boards that come from the lumberyard today, as though it were the boards' fault that the boards are not better. I saw a "clear" (knot-free) 20-foot white pine two-by-twelve, still as straight as when it was cut, in the old sawmill museum at Cook's Forest Preserve near where I grew up in Western Pennsylvania, and I felt the mix of lust and longing any wood butcher would feel who has dealt with late-20th-century two-by-sixes.

Boards of course don't really look like trees. Our modern shelters, in fact, have come to the point where they pretty much disguise and deny any direct relationship with anything so natural as a tree; the smooth flat surfaces, straight lines and squared corners jive aesthetically with the effort to create a constant mild climate within walls totally independent of the natural climate outside the walls. The shape of the boards as well as their function serve the purpose of establishing closed spaces that are independent of nature's way of doing things.

It's said there is "no such thing as a straight line in nature" – or a perfectly flat or perfectly smooth surface. That's not strictly true; many rock crystals have edges as straight as anything manmade, and I've seen sheet mica that does smooth and flat very well. It is probably the most dependable characteristic of nature that it always violates, sooner or later, somewhere or other, any absolute statement about what it is or isn't. But it is accurate enough to say that nature in general does not share our human fascination with straight lines, squared corners and smooth surfaces.

And the disconnect between tree and board that results from the way we transform trees into boards enables someone like me to develop, on the one hand, as something of a tree-hugger with a great love for trees

151

and forests (thirty or forty generations of cumulative Euro-American guilt), but on the other hand, as a carpenter, turning the broken bodies of trees, sliced and diced, into one-family houses big enough to have sheltered whole hunter-gatherer "sibbs." So the question arose for me: can one love both trees and good boards?

I actually got a chance to explore that question in some depth. In the course of my freelancing and oddjobbing career, I often had better breaks at oddjobbing than I was having at freelancing, and in one of those times when I needed something to put groceries on the table (not to mention a roof over the table), the husband of a friend happened to need a sawyer for a small sawmill he ran on his ranch.

Luce Pipher was the rancher's name, and he was a story or two himself – stories for another day. His ranch was the last piece of private land up on the edge of Black Mesa between the Upper Gunnison River and the Smith Fork of the Gunnison, on a creek which just a few hundred yards downstream from the ranch poured in a waterfall into the Gunnison's Black Canyon – you could, in fact, see the far rim of the canyon from the bedroom window of our cabin at Pipher's sawmill. Between the Black Canyon National Park, the Gunnison National Forest, and odd lots of land under the Bureau of Land Management, Pipher was more or less surrounded by public lands – but refused philosophically to seek grazing permits for any of that land; he ran his cattle on private land he picked up or leased here or there around the valley.

Luce's father ran the kind of barefoot and bare-knuckle family where they stopped feeding you when you got to your middle teens, so Luce left home then, but came back a few years later and bought out his father. Cattle ranching was Luce's first love, but he had all kinds of things going on the side to subsidize the ranching operation, and the sawmill was one of those things – a little operation employing two to five people depending on the season (including the logger) and capable of cutting maybe a couple hundred-thousand board feet of rough-sawn, sun-dried lumber a year.

I knew nothing about milling lumber, or the machinery involved, but Luce wasn't that impressed by my ignorance – and I reminded myself that I did have a Liberal Arts degree, which is supposed to prepare you to figure out anything the world can throw at you.

"You'll learn fast, one way or the other," he said the day I showed up to work. "Just go slow at first and try not to wreck anything." He gave me a twenty-minute walking tour of the machinery, showed me how to turn the various parts on and off, and ran a couple logs through the saw to give me the basic idea, then went back to his beloved cows and left me to some intensive on-the-job self-training.

I took it slow the first couple weeks; I was so logically and rightly scared by the machinery that it was a month or so before I started to be reasonably comfortable with those singing blades a couple feet from where I timidly pulled and pushed the levers and buttons that moved big tree bodies around and into their transformations.

The centerpiece of the mill was of course the saw itself, a circular blade four feet in diameter with a circumference of chisel teeth. It ran off a big old antique electric motor that was, in turn, powered by a big old antique diesel generator. A set of belts and electrically-controlled hydraulic elements pulled logs mounted on a carriage into the saw. Getting the log onto the carriage was all done by muscle power, with canthooks to lever the log around. Except for the teeth on the saw, the mill was entirely built from used parts, but beautifully and tightly assembled by a "master of junk" in Crawford, downvalley in the Smith Fork.

But the saw was the point of it all. The first time I looked at the saw close up that first day, it was in repose, and did not, to tell the truth, look that impressive. It didn't look flat and hard, like the sawblade in my little skill saw; instead, it looked a little warpedy, dished – alarmingly floppy, in fact. I mentioned this to Pipher that first day.

"That's right," he said. He went over to it, grabbed it between a couple of its chisel teeth, and shook it; the saw flexed, *bawong, bawong,* like a big pizza pan. "It doesn't stand up," he said, "until it's revving at speed – 720 rpm."

"Doesn't stand up"? My limited experience with steel had left me with the impression of something solid, hard and rigid, But I learned – and was to have the lesson driven home often in the months ahead – that a piece of steel four feet in diameter, spinning at 720 rpm, acts more like the pizza dough than the pizza pan. Under that much centrifugal force, its outer molecules tend to spread apart a little farther than its more central molecules. So in order for a saw to run flat and true at its operating speed, it has to be carefully hammered into a slightly cupped shape at rest.

He showed me: we fired up the diesel generator, then threw the head-rig switch; the generator lugged, then revved as the mill's vintage electric motor overcame the inertia of the saw and got it to turning. For about 10 uneasy seconds, the saw picked up speed with a sound that can best be described as beating on the air. Then, it visibly and audibly "stood up" – straightened out in its motion, and the sound of beating against the air changed to a smooth hiss.

153

It gradually occurred to me in the following weeks and months that, when the saw stood up, it become something more than just a spinning sheet of metal; it became the force at a gate between worlds – the world of nature on one side of the saw, as represented by the logs on the deck: rough, barky elements from that naturally evolved world whose shapes and textures were all derived from eons of *ad hoc* cooperation and competition for light and water, accommodation to other plants, adaptation to challenges, and probably instances of cosmic genetic inspiration.

But on the other side, beyond the saw, were the logs transformed into boards: all lines, planes and hard square edges, for assembly into the linear and planar shapes and smooth textures that hardly existed in the world before man came along.

In the two-plus years I sawed for Pipher, I never really lost my sense of amazement on making the first cut on a log: there was the log on the saw carriage, and there was the saw; I moved the log into the saw's space, and . . . except for the sudden increase of noise, nothing changed; it seemed as if the log and the saw were occupying the same space without affecting each other, holographic images just passing through each other – until I completed the cut and the slab fell away from the log, exposing a pale smooth plane and the log forever changed.

It reminded me of the pictures in my high-school geometry text: line drawings of Euclid's plane, passing like a pane of glass through cones and cylinders to create the parabolas and hyperbolas of the conic sections. In the book, the pictures seemed quite abstract, devoid of reality. But there in the mill, there was the elongated conic cylinder in the rough, shaggy, lumpy and uneven form of the log – and then after the first cut, a smooth Euclidean parabola imposed on the log. The abstraction was the saw itself, the gate between realities: the saw was geometry incarnate, the powerful realization of abstractions found hardly anywhere in nature but in the minds of humans.

I quickly learned, however, both in the sawing process and then watching the lumber sun-dry in the yard, that the transformation from rough natural tree to smooth geometric board was hardly total or perfect: a lot of the tree passed through that gate to haunt the boards. Knots from branches that were important to the tree were very counter-productive in the smooth planes and lines of the board, sometimes even falling out when they dried. And the struggles of the tree to grow straight up on a sidehill, against the pressures of snow creep, uneven shading from other trees, and other natural forces, resulted in inner tensions that all worked their way out in warps as the boards dried.

154

I learned that I myself had a great deal to do with how much of a tree's old realities came through the saw to haunt the boards in that new reality. The sawyer's first responsibility to the carpenter lay in keeping that whirling convocation of molecules that was the saw as close to Euclid's abstract vertical plane as possible. Mostly this was a matter of learning how, and how often, to sharpen the saw's teeth. These are basically little chisels, forty or so of them, a little wider than the width of the blade, that chew at the wood with a sharp *sna-a-acking* sound when they are sharp.

But when the teeth grow dull, or get chipped by a pebble in the bark (or some righteous ecoteur's spike), or even when they are not sharpened straight, all sorts of increasingly ugly things begin to happen. The saw lugs down in the wood; the machinery begins to strain. And if one side of the teeth grows worse than the other side, the saw begins to bend toward the dull side, wandering off into a warpedy plane that changes the dimensions of the board – but worse, causes the saw to rub against the wood on one side or the other, creating friction and heat.

The saw always had a thin jet of water playing on it to keep it cool, but twelve square feet of steel rubbing all the way along a sixteen-foot log at 720 rpm can generate a powerful amount of heat, which causes the hot part of the saw to expand, which throws off that delicate molecular balance, and the saw begins to beat against the air again – and if you stupidly try to run it into the log again, it can turn into the most frightening piece of powerful chaos I have ever approached, with a handful of snow or a cup of water to put against it, to extract the heat and again return it to Euclid's smooth hissing plane.

So I learned quickly that, even though sharpening was a tedious job that produced no boards, the quality of both the lumber and the experience of cutting it depended absolutely on sharpening. Hit a rock at, say, eleven-thirty and try to saw on through to lunchtime before shutting down to sharpen, and it would be one long lousy hour. If you ever buy rough-sawn lumber that varies more than a quarter-inch in its dimensions from one end to the other, you are probably buying lumber cut during an hour like that – lumber that was quite literally born in an atmosphere of "bad vibes." Don't build it into your walls.

I began to learn too that how I started into a log had a lot to do with the quality of the lumber. Being natural things, growing out of naturally uneven and hilly terrain, pushed by snow and wind and the presence of other trees, no tree grows perfectly straight; they are all a little bent by life, and that history is going to translate into a "crown" or bow in the boards that come through the gate between nature's world and ours.

155

The internal tensions of trees can be amazing. Cutting 6x6 fence posts from the buttlog of a gnarled old sidehill douglasfir once, I saw the log squeeze down so powerfully on the saw that it would have stalled it and burned out the motor, had I not hastily backed out of the cut.

The trick was to try to peel the boards off the log in a way that would result in the board warping mostly along only one of its dimensions (preferably its thickness) rather than warping along both its thickness and width dimensions, which meant that the most important moment there at the gate between the natural and cultural worlds was when I levered the log with my cant hook off the deck and onto the saw carriage; I had to make a quick judgment before clamping the log into the carriage "dogs" and sending it into the saw. By learning how to read the log – and caring enough for the tree that had been, to want the boards to be worthy of its memory – I learned I could minimize the extent to which the tree's problems in the natural world become the carpenter's problems in the cultural world.

I'd gone to the sawmill to work because Pipher had said he wanted to shut it down in the winter, which meant writing time, but I approached the work with a culturally-induced sense that it was a little beneath me – a world less intelligent than the one I, a college-educated up-and-coming writer (so I still thought of myself then), was really fitted for.

But as I began to really get into the work – the applied geometry of the work – I began to realize that it was the most intellectually demanding job I had ever had, and in a larger moral sense, perhaps the most responsible. Aside from the responsibility of keeping my own limbs out of the machinery, I had a responsibility to the carpenters who would be stuck with the boards, and I had a responsibility to the trees, to do as good a job as possible in making their broken bodies at least useful, and maybe beautiful in the way that a good house, or even a good outhouse, can be beautiful.

I left the mill after two-plus years, mostly because business got too good. I went there in part because it was promised as a part-time job, shutting down in the winter, which I wanted for writing. But because we had a great functional assemblage of junk, and because I was basically a tree-hugger at heart who cared a lot about doing the work right, we were turning out good lumber. We had one customer – a developer/builder from Gunnison, who started leaving a trailer at the yard, telling us to just call him when we had it full of 16-foot two-by-sixes, which he was using in his houses. With half-dried rough-sawn lumber, you just use bigger nails.

But the upshot of that was that Pipher decided he wanted to run the mill year round, and there went the writing season. So I left.

In addition, I had begun to see how mill accidents happen, in my own growing casualness toward the potentially deadly machinery I worked a few feet from – like the fact that it had become a mundane act to go up to the overheated air-beating saw with a handful of snow or cup of water to soothe it down. Statistics indicate that most mill accidents happen not to newcomers but to people who have been too long in the mill. Industrial workers start to put themselves through those gates, as it were – fingers, feet, hands, and all the knotty warpedy slices that come off the soul when one hangs around anywhere too long after starting to feel like just another piece of the machinery.

I loved geometry in school; I liked rediscovering it at the mill; but I am worried that too much time in a Euclidean environment – all the rough evolved textures and shapes of accommodative nature sliced and shaved down to featureless planes and predictable angles – might eventually reduce me, much as I reduced the trees, to some human analogy of the uniform standard two-by-four.

But still – I'll still say today, three decades later – I've never had work before or since that required such a balance of mental and physical work, and such a high level of dual responsibility, as I did at that job at the gate between the worlds, the natural world of the tree and the cultural world of the board. Tending the gate for all of us living or once-living organisms, complex in our structures, and not entirely understood as yet as to our functions.

Lessons Lying Under Aspens

"Consider
the lilies of the field:
They labor not, nor do they spin,
yet even Solomon in all his glory
was not arrayed such as they."

This was that early ecofreak
Jesus of Nazareth, who knew the importance
Of going to the wilderness to take on the devil.
But really, was he right?

Consider all plants, like these aspens above me:
Like all life they will work for food,
Send roots down to probe into hard rock,
Build strong stems up toward the light,
Raise water high up to tremulent leaves
That are little factories where light, air, water
And dirt are assembled into the living host,
Not just for themselves but for all of us too,
The table of life at which all living things are fed.

But no fuel-consuming pump raises that water,
No overheating drill drives those roots into rock;
Their work cleans and enlivens our air,
And in the shop of a leaf is no sweat;
If the leaf grows too hot, the shop shuts down for siesta.

To sit down and watch the lily at work – or better,
To lie down under these aspen for the larger look –
Is to know the Ecojesus truth: yes, they work,
These plants that spread the feast of life,
But not laboriously, not frantically like me at work,
Full of fears and resentments and stress;
Yes, they work, the lilies and grasses and great trees,
They work but they labor not.

Sawmill II: Junk Economics
And Sustainability

First published in *Dragons in Paradise*, First Edition,
Mountain Gazette Publishing, 2004.

Sustainability. Has there ever been a society that didn't want to be sustainable? If it is a society made up of humans that have children, then they want the society to be sustainable. I can't imagine a parent who didn't want his or her child to have a world to move into at least as good as his or her world. "A better world," we used to say, back in the good old days a few decades ago. But reality is beginning to dawn, and we are beginning to understand that, on a finite planet, "at least as good" is the essence of "sustainable." We make it better than or worse than "at least as good" on an individual basis, attitudinally and cognitively, and no amount of borrowing from the future to gild the present will ever change that.

I first began to learn about sustainability in my early thirties, in a job I felt was a little beneath me in a time-bound place I thought I was well beyond as a civilized modern of the 20th century. I was only there because I was temporarily on hard times. Right.

It was a job in a sawmill. I'd been conditioned from first grade to not want to "end up in the mill," and I had no intention of ending up in this one, and basically didn't, or haven't yet anyway. Haven't ended up anywhere yet.

But what surprised me, and eventually even intrigued me, was totally unexpected: the realization that working in this sawmill was one of the best and most expansive learning experiences of my life. It was a true learning experience in that there was no teacher, just a growing awareness of a growing awareness. And what I was learning about was another America – the untried America that has been struggling along as a "recessive gene," waiting for the cultural environment to change in its favor. A time that might be coming, if we are in fact ever going to get serious about "sustainability."

The sawmill was owned by the new husband of an old friend – one of those shewolf women who is always out hunting on the fringe of the acceptable and normal. She eventually left him for a Christian commune, but that is another story. This is his story.

Luce Pipher was his name, and he was first and foremost a rancher. Son of an ignorant but arrogant sonofabitch of the sort that haunted the back corners of the West, Luce had grown up on a porefarm up on the edge of Black Mesa between the Upper Gunnison River and the North Fork of the Gunnison, a small ranch on a creek unimaginatively named "Crystal," like a million others in the West. Just a few hundred yards downstream from the ranch, Crystal Creek dropped in waterfalls into the Black Canyon of the Gunnison River – you could, in fact, see the far rim of the canyon from the bedroom window of the cabin we lived in at the ranch when I worked at the sawmill.

Luce's father ran the kind of barefoot and bareknuckle family where they stopped feeding you when you got to your middle teens, so Luce left home then, but came back a few years later and bought his father out. Cattle ranching was Luce's first love, but he knew that a business whose markets were organized and controlled out in the cities of the plain was vulnerable, so he got all kinds of things going on the side to subsidize the ranching operation, and the sawmill was one of those things – a little two or three person operation capable of cutting no more than a couple hundred-thousand board feet of rough-sawn, sun-dried lumber a year, but as he said, "You always have a few dollars in your pocket from it."

He was the kind of man who pretty literally threw himself into whatever work he was doing, sometimes without thoroughly strategizing the operation he was throwing the body into, and when I knew him, he walked with a gimp from getting a leg pulverized in a mill belt, and he had a face that looked like it had been kicked by a horse, which it had, at a rodeo, almost killing him. He lived life flat out and hard.

When I went to work for him, he was on his second sawmill. He'd sold the first one, but years later had come onto an opportunity to pick up another. He often said that he figured he would never have a million dollars, so he at least wanted to die owing a million. Another time he said one of the few things you needed in life was a good banker – probably meaning one you could always cajole or threaten into helping you realize your life ambition. So when he went to his long-suffering banker with the proposition to buy a new old sawmill, the banker had shrugged, and he'd bought it and installed it in the old millshed, and I happened along when he was looking for somebody to run the saw.

Because I was born and bred in a civilization that equates "shiny" with good, I "misunderestimated" the mill when I first saw it. By civilized aesthetic standards – the first eyes I saw it through – it was plain ugly. A cobbled-together, unadorned assemblage of unmatched parts that Pipher told me, with a pride that at first puzzled me, had all been "junk."

"Junk," I came to learn, was a tricky word around Pipher. A former employee of the first mill told me that Pipher had fired a man once for muttering something about "junk" while working on a breakdown. But Pipher himself used the term frequently and freely, often enough with a liberal salting of deletable expletives before and after. And he used it once with me, when I'd made a comment about not just the antiquity but hypothetical parentage of an old Hough front-loader we were trying to resurrect for use in the logyard.

"The trouble with you damn hippies," he said – a "hippie" being anyone younger than he was from beyond his valley – "you just don't understand junk." So if you were going to use the term, you'd better understand what it meant.

Over the two years I worked at that sawmill, I gained at least a journeyman's appreciation of junk. The mill, to the best of my knowledge, had hardly anything purchased new except for the teeth I put in the saw when the old ones were ground down too far. It was all assembled from secondhand stuff from salvage yards and those private EAR collections

161

(Equipment Awaiting Repair) that adorn every farm or ranch that has been around long enough to be worthy of the name. Junk might be one of the most reliable products of farming.

"If you need a piece of wire," Pipher said one day (shaking off a piece that had tangled around his boot), "just take ten steps in any direction."

But junk is just junk until somebody comes along who knows how to work with it, a junk artist to beat off the rust and dust and coax it back into action. The junk artist who put together Pipher's mill was one of the great artists of the North Fork country, Ken Spencer of Crawford; he'd built the mill for himself, but he'd put it up for sale because he had another idea he wanted to build, an even smaller mill he could mount on a semi bed, to cut only aspen for a specialty market he'd discovered.

Pipher had bought the mill because he knew how good Spencer was at assembling junk. Give him a cutting torch, welder, grinder, some hand tools and a big box of bolts and nuts, and the cultural resources in the EAR yard behind any respectable barn in America, and maybe a place to buy a few specialty parts (pride made this a last resort), and he would come up with a usable version of anything you needed, from a sawmill to a satellite dish. If there'd been a good junk artist in the multitude when Jesus Christ said you can't make a silk purse out of a sow's ear, he would have asked for clarification: how big was the ear, how fancy a purse did Jesus have in mind?

Pipher himself was a pretty good junk artist, but his son Luther was better. There was a big unheated shop building near the sawmill that was Luther's domain – a massive mess of a place with some really fine metal-working machinery buried here and there in the – junk.

One day I was working on my Volkswagen in front of the shop – always a cause for snickers there in heavy Ford and Chevy country. Luther happened to be around when I finally located my problem: the fork that disengaged the clutch was worn out. "Probably take a month to get one of these," I grumped.

After the obligatory commentary on foreign cars, Luther looked at the piece, then looked at where it fit and what it should have been doing, and went into the shop. He scuffed around on the floor, picked up a few scraps of metal, went to work with the machines and welder, and in less than an hour, had assembled a new clutch fork for the Volksie that was still working when I sold the car five years later.

These were people who got a pugnacious set to jaw and shoulder if you just brought up "environmentalism," let alone called them "environmentalists." But they had an American subculture that knew and practiced a lot more recycling, on a deeper level, than those of us who accumulate virtue putting cans and bottles in the appropriate containers.

***

The sawmill, I came to see, also had other environmental implications. We only cut maybe a quarter million board-feet of lumber a year, which put us a class with the majority of mills in the nation – three-fourths of America's sawmills cut less than a million board-feet a year with fewer than 10 employees per mill. (We oscillated between two and five, including the logger, depending on the season.) But all those little mills together produce less than one-fourth of the nation's lumber; the rest is cut in big and bigger mills, with the biggest five percent of mills producing over half the nation's lumber. I visited a couple of those mills after working at Pipher's mill, just out of curiosity – huge vertically-integrated complexes spread over acres, dozens of saws for varying sizes of timber and various types of products, from huge ceiling-to-floor bandsaws down to little four-foot circular saws like ours, with planing mills and drying kilns, the works. There were more workers per shift just in the sharpening rooms of those mills than in our whole mill.

Those "big, bigger and biggest" mills were basically set up for the tree-mining era in America's natural history. As the glossy magazine ads from the big "forest products" companies point out, trees are a renewable resource, but renewability has its relative time frames. Even up in the soggy Northwest, it takes most of a century to grow a tree too big for a four-foot circular saw, and to cultivate a mature forest full of "old growth" trees that size is more of a millennial project. To develop and feed a demand for lumber that can only be fulfilled by taking out big old-growth forests is a mining venture, no matter how the companies and the Forest Service try to spin it ("sustainable yield circles" and all that).

There has always been at least one "big" sawmill in the Gunnison River Basin (never a "bigger" or "biggest") – down in Montrose or Delta or both places – with an appetite of several million board feet a year, far from the capacity of the "biggest" mills but a few quanta above our mill's capacity. There are also usually between three or half a dozen small mills like Pipher's (less than a million board-feet) scattered around the Basin, and the small mills – as I heard frequently from Pipher – "always get hind tit from the (expletive) (expletive) (expletive) Forest Service."

According to the small millers – and confirmed to some extent by the Forest Service – the Forest Service sets up two kinds of timber sales on the public lands: fairly large sales of several million board-feet of prime harvestable timber, and "clean-up sales," which involve cutting out the festering places in the forest where the pine beetle or spruce budworm have established beachheads, or in blowdowns that are vulnerable to insects or fire, and the like. The clean-up sales are usually small – just enough to take care of the problem – and they are often unattractive for mills because they require the logger to take out a lot of logs only partially decayed or broken that are marginal for lumber.

The Forest Service – which, like all public agencies today, has been downsized again and again to get rid of the fat, and more recently some muscle and bone – claims it can't afford to comply with NEPA requirements for a lot of little sales in the good timber rather than a few big ones, and there are staffing statistics to support that.

So the big mills are the only ones that can afford to bid on the big sales of good timber, and the little mills have to fight it out over the clean-up sales. An outsider might observe that several of the small mills could go together to bid on a big sale, then divvy it up, but that sensible solution doesn't take into account the extent to which a strong strain of rugged American individualism drives a person like Luce Pipher: if you can't do it on your own, it's probably not worth doing. Especially if it involves cooperating with either some (expletive) (expletive) competitor or the (expletive) (expletive) (expletive) Forest Service.

So that leaves the clean-up sales for the highly independent small mills; and that being the case, from an environmental perspective (no, Luce! I didn't say "an environmental*ist* perspective"!), the small mills are more a "part of the solution" to today's forest problems than part of the problem: they produce timber from the stressed and sick parts of the forest.

Hardcore environmentalists will argue with that. Anything removed from the forest is taking away nutrients, removing carbon from the natural carbon cycle, et cetera. And the insects and tree diseases are all part of a natural cycle that worked just fine in the forests for millennia, creating an ever-changing mosaic of old sick stands and new young stands and middle-ages stands that smoked and drank too much – et cetera, et cetera. This is the Christian Science philosophy of forest management; if there are sick trees, it is because God meant them to be sick as part of the larger picture of overall forest health, and the main management priority should be to keep humankind out of those natural processes.

But even most hardcore environmentalists live in houses, and as Aldo Leopold said, "a public which lives in wooden houses should be careful about throwing stones at lumbermen." There are ways to get wood from the forests, for houses or whatever, that are less injurious than others. A century of all-out efforts at fire suppression demonstrated that fire cannot be kept out of the life cycle of the cool and dry western forests, but better forest management – including clean-up sales – could keep manageable the fires that will come sooner or later to balance out the carbon cycle. And small forest-products operators making part of their living by taking care of the festering places in the forests makes a lot of sense to me – even though it often meant dealing with some pretty ugly stuff there at the saw, at the gate between the world of the tree and the world of the board.

***

That small sawmill on Crystal Creek made environmental sense in another way, although imperfectly, in the context of the fittingness of the "cultural ecosystem" it was part of. But it took a long time for this to sink in to my slowly evolving sense of what makes sense. And whether or not the little mill makes sense comes down to what the reader will accept as What Is Important. Values, in other words.

Consider just the boards. Our mill produced what is called "rough-sawn lumber" – one-by and two-by lumber that is actually one or two full inches thick (within a quarter-inch either way). At that point – as far as our mill took the process – it is a cultural product, for a culture that admires straight lines and smooth flat surfaces but doesn't necessarily obsess about those attributes – a quarter inch either way is close enough.

But to become truly civilized enough for the purely Euclidean spaces we lust for, the rough-sawn lumber has to go through two more "gates." It goes next to a planing mill, where the shaggy rough-sawn boards are made really smooth, at the sacrifice of up to a quarter-inch of wood shaved off of each face, so that a finished "two-by-four" actually measures 1.5 inches by 3.5 inches – but a *precise and dependable* 1.5 by 3.5 inches, none of those 4.25 or 3.75 inch wide rough-sawn two-by-fours that can give a sheet-rocker the grumps.

After the planing mill, the increasingly civilized boards are bound in bundles and put in a kiln to cook out their moisture because it is in the drying phase that the old tree tensions left in the boards reveal themselves through warping. Kilns cook the wood till their moisture content is less than a fifth of that of green wood, with the bundles bound tightly enough so the cellulose cells split rather than tightening into a warp. Once the board has been planed and dried, it is fully civilized, ready for application

165

to the cultural world of straight lines, square corners and smooth flat surfaces.

Do civilized boards still warp? Do civilized humans still warp? The question answers itself, without the impropriety of questioning the answer: freaks happen, just look the other way. We haven't yet figured out how to totally control nature, but the best minds in the best universities are still working on it. I've visited the Forest Service's big Forest Products Laboratory in Madison, Wisconsin, where they are essentially trying to figure out how to economically dissemble a tree down to the individual cellulose cells and reassemble those cells into building products that have no warp, no knots, none of the "imperfections" of nature.

Within that civilizing context, civilized economics suggests a vertical integration of the steps necessary to civilize a board – if the logging, sawing, planing and drying functions can all be vertically integrated, then economic efficiency, and therefore productivity and profitability, the arch-values of civilization, are nurtured. That is the economic reasoning that drives the big mills, where the sawing, planing and drying functions are vertically integrated, often with laminating shops for putting together big laminated beams out of regular lumber and other specialty divisions applying the fruits of the Forest Service's industrial research.

But while economy of scale is theoretically served by huge centralized mills, the raw resource itself is less conveniently organized – especially now that most of the big old-growth forests are mostly mined out. So vertical integration in the logging and hauling steps is less economically efficient; most of the big mills have their own woods crews, but also depend on very competitive independent logging contractors bidding each other down for a lot of their supply.

But the changed nature of the resource base – otherwise known as America's forests – from high-density old-growth timber to a lot of pretty decentralized smaller trees, is changing the way the big players in the lumber industry operate. They are getting away from the huge mills of the 19th and 20th centuries, and going to smaller mills closer to the woods – smaller in size, but high-volume, high-tech mills that are largely automated, computerized, and capable of scanning and cutting a steady stream of even-aged, even-sized, tree-farm trees far faster than even the least conscientious and caring human sawyer could ever do.

The logging operation is also getting more mechanized. Rather than the heroic old image of loggers going out to take on monster trees in an environment of difficulty and danger, the cutting for the big industry today is as likely to be done by big mechanical feller-bunchers trundling through the woods, grabbing a tree in steel arms and sawing it off at its base, then going to another and "bunching" it with the others in its arms and sawing it off, then hauling the bunch back to the staging area where the trees are rammed through another machine that strips their branches and bark, then loaded off to the computerized mill. Volume is all, in dealing with the new decentralized, diminished and unminable forest resource.

But meanwhile, back at the ranch – a different set of values drove the economic environment around the mill where I worked. First of all, there was no effort at all on Pipher's part to integrate his mill vertically for the further civilizing of our rough-sawn boards. We sawed the lumber rough and green, and people either bought it that way and stacked it tight for drying themselves, or just nailed it up green with big nails before it started to warp and battened the cracks against the inevitable shrinkage, or bought it off the lot where it had been sun-and-wind dried. We were upfront about what they were buying – lumber whose predictability was not guaranteed – but there was an element of *caveat emptor* to it. "Sun-dried" is a virtue with tomatoes, I guess, but it's a little hard to sell a two-by-twelve that has sun-dried into a kind of Moebius strip turning back on itself. On the other hand, when I had actually read a big log right, and sawed off a set of two-by-twelves that had sun-dried into boards with only a modest crown and a depth-bend that any respectable carpenter could compensate for with bigger nails, I could sell those off the lot with pride.

But if there was no attempt at economic vertical integration in the "forest products" business as I experienced it, there was a lot of "horizontal integration" between forest products and other products.

As I noted earlier, Pipher considered the sawmill to be part of the support mechanism for his cattle ranch. It generated a comparatively dependable cash flow for the kind of "mountain ranching" operation that, by all civilized standards, hardly qualified as a business if the expectation of reasonable return on investment is a defining characteristic of a business.

Mountain ranching actually combines the most difficult qualities of both the pastoral and farming aspects of what we call agriculture. It's pastoral to the extent that it involves herding cattle around mountain highlands to graze land too marginally productive for growing anything humans can eat directly. But because it's up in the mountains where winter snow precludes winter grazing, the ranchers have to be farmers too, growing hay on their valley land all summer to feed their cattle all winter.

So the mountain ranchers' costs are considerably higher than the costs for ranchers down on the plains and deserts where, as Pipher put it once, "your only expenses are horseshoes and salt." But the mountain ranchers get basically the same prices for their cows as the guys down on the plains and deserts because ranchers don't get to set their prices based on their costs; they take whatever is being offered through a ruthless commodities market that many of them are too proud to stoop to understanding and trying to hedge against. The prices they pay for their farming and ranching equipment are also set outside of their valleys, so they basically have no local control or impetus coming or going in the ranching business.

But hanging out around Pipher for a while, I came to see that ranching is not so much a business as it is an occupation, in all the larger senses of the word. It is a way of keeping the family, the extended family, a fair portion of the whole local community, occupied – but more than that, it is part of a way of sustaining occupation of the land. And the real measure of an occupation of that sort is how many different ways you can come up with for sustaining your occupation, not only in space but through time.

So a sawmill becomes a logical step in such an occupation. For one thing, all ranchers need a certain number of sheds and shelters and cabins spread around, and rough-sawn lumber is certainly adequate for such structures; it would be almost an insult both ways to buy fully civilized, planed and kiln-dried boards for such buildings.

For another thing, a lot of sawmill equipment has other useful applications, not just in the ranching operation but elsewhere around the community. The front-loader we used in the yard to move logs and piles of boards around, for example: when we shut down the mill at the end of the day, as likely as not Pipher or one of his sons would be there to change the loading forks for the big bucket, and would go dig a basement for somebody who was going to put up a house, or fix up a ranch road somewhere. Or a pair of them might take the loader and the mill dump truck (for hauling slab too thin and barky for firewood down to the "midwinter lightning-strike pile") up to the probably slightly illegal gravel pit by Crystal Creek to dig a load of gravel for somebody's driveway.

Pipher was even learning how to use the energy of the sun. Another of the "goddam hippies" inhabiting one of the cabins on the ranch paid his rent by retrofitting the cabin for passive solar heat. Once Pipher saw that that worked pretty well, he had the guy design and build him a passive solar house – his fourth or fifth house, like all the others built with rough-sawn from the mill. If lumber was stacking up in the lot, Pipher would just haul it to some piece of property he'd picked up somewhere along the line – someplace not quite good enough for grazing – and build another house, either to sell or to live in for a while until he built another one. A lot of the non-lumber costs (wiring, plumbing, windows, et cetera) got worked out in complex trades with people around the valley – the barter economy in places like that can be phenomenal. And when nothing but money would do, he'd go back to his banker.

But at any rate – this hard-bitten self-proclaimed hippie-hating anti-environmentalist built himself a solar house, but would have hurt anyone who called him an "environmentalist" because of his interest in "renewable energy." He liked the idea because the sun gave away its energy free, and he hated having to buy energy from the big entities beyond his control that charged for it. It was just part of his occupation: if it's there, and it's usable, then figure out how to use it.

But it was all a fairly intelligent occupation for the most part – possibly excepting the little gravel pit. He borrowed some grass and some wood and some energy from the environment, but he didn't use a whole lot of anything, and he did operate – as do most of the ranchers I know in their second, third or fifth generations on their land – with a sense of wanting to sustain that borrowing through time. Five generations on the land becomes a kind of immortality.

It was always precarious, both in terms of human economics and natural ecosystems – nobody getting really rich, some real (and often ignored) poverty, and spots of environmental damage that ebbed and flowed. There's a chronic drought in the Southern Rockies as I write this, and I would guess some inadvertent (and genuinely regretted) damage is being done to the range and forests in places just because there is always going to be an "adjustment lag" in the changes necessary in the human economy when the "natural economy" changes. Someone will try to slip through a dry summer without reducing the size of the herd at a loss, and it's sometimes okay – unless there's a second dry year following. Or an August gullywasher hits the wet meadows when they are vulnerable and washes a gully that will lower the water table and another wet meadow will become a dry sage flat. (And it might not even have rained half a mile away; there is almost a "judgment of God" aspect to some things that happen in the high country.)

Nonetheless, despite a certain dependence on fossil fuel products, that valley economy the sawmill was part of was as close as I've ever been to an ecologically sustainable human economy. It has most of the qualities of what the futurists at Rocky Mountain Institute over by Aspen call "resilient systems," systems capable of adjusting to and surviving changes in either the natural environment (drought, floods, global warming) or the cultural environment (terrorism, bad prices, huge deficits). Those qualities include small units dispersed in space, short linkages between modules, simplicity and reparability, diversity, self-reliance, decentralized control and quick feedback. Not to mention cycling a lot of junk back through the system. If Thomas Jefferson had visited that valley – he'd have nodded. "Yes. This is close to what I meant."

It's all actually not bad for a bunch of cowboys who really liked the bumpersticker, "Are you an environmentalist or do you work for a living?" I'd want to pick my moment and my evening with considerable care before saying it out loud in the Boardwalk or Needle Rock Inn in Crawford, but most of what I think I really know about the economics and politics of sustainability in complex natural and cultural systems, I learned there at and around that sawmill near the edge of the Black Canyon of the Gunnison. It had a way to go before the occupation of the land became a true inhabitation, and then there was the fossil-fuel problem. But it was sure a lot farther along that road than the huge but fundamentally simplistic eating machine of a civilization I'd grown up in.

The Horse: Form and Function

"Just a thing for converting hay to horseshit,"
Bill said to me, looking not at me but at the horse,
Which we both were watching, leaning on the fence
At the back part of Bill's thirty-five
Being paid off month by month from his job
Digging coal for power plants he never saw.

"Never really seem to have time to ride her,"
Bill grumped, reaching into his pocket for his can,
For more of the stuff that takes ten minutes
Off the long hours and adds ten to the short ones.
But while he was thus occupied, the horse just
Took off. Went running up the field, an easy lope
That would have been no harder for the horse
With a man on his back, even one with a belly like Bill's.

We both watched. Mane catching the wind: thinking
What reason for a mane if there's no air to catch;
Tail streaming out behind.... It was just worth watching.
It was just goddam beautiful. And at the far fence,
The horse stopped. Stood there looking
Beyond the fence. At what, who knew. But then,
Even at that distance we could see it: Lifting its tail
And dropping a load. "Like I was sayin'," Bill said.

Lying Down with Fire

Published in the *Whitefish Review*, Volume 8, Issue 1, Summer 2014.

*S*urreal is a word best defined by example: sweltering in an open sleeping bag, in a clearing in Idaho that is actually an abandoned homestead orchard, with several hundred other people, all surrounded by the winking, glowing and popping, muttering presence of a forest wildfire which, like those of us in the clearing, has "lain down" for the night — that is *surreal*. No one was really sleeping; not even the fire — especially not the fire. Just resting up for when the sun returns and our surreal contention recommences.

Surreal: sub-real, the reality underlying reality. When you are half-awake, half-dreaming, surrounded by an elemental presence like a dozing wildfire, new depths to what passes for reality open under and over you. You feel what a thin and fragile layer life really is, pressed between a planet beneath you of rocky crusts floating on a core of fire, and a restless swirling deep gulf of atmosphere above you, also stirred aswirl by a more distant fire.

Surreality takes over, till morning, when the sun comes up like a smoked Japanese flag and you feel the heat start to stack up again in the atmosphere and the air again gets restless and the wildfire beyond your clearing starts to stir again in its intrusion into the planet's thin skin of life. But reality returns with the sun; there's breakfast and Army coffee, and there are your tools stacked and ready, all sharpened overnight, and there are hundreds of you, moving out in tens and twenties, to try to wage orderly war against what's wild in wildfire, that affront to what's civilized in civilization. That thin layer of life between surrealities again thickens to mere reality: a forest around, burning in an unregulated way, needing to be brought under control.

You can even forget, as the orders for the day are laid out in an orderly way and you all march off with your tools in hand, how yesterday ended in a not very orderly retreat from the chaos of a forest possessed by fire. Fire everywhere, fire chimneying up both sides of hills to consume and starve itself at a ridge, fire throwing out burning cones and twigs to spread itself ahead of itself, fire cooking pine sap out of lodgepole and igniting the vapor in huge gouts of flame flaring up slopes ten feet above the trees. You can forget the pell-mell retreat back to that clearing you're leaving now, to go see if the fire today is going to be more scaled down to what several hundred firefighters can actually try to control. You can forget what you couldn't forget in the surreal night: that yesterday the fire came entirely too close to roaring right over your crew.

I'm thinking about that experience because this summer marks the 20th anniversary of the death of 14 firefighters who died trying to put out — or actually, at their time of death, trying to escape — a 1994 wildfire that consumed a steep slope of scrub oak, pinon pine and juniper on public land on Storm King Mountain, just west of Glenwood Springs in our Colorado Rockies.

It never should have happened. A subsequent investigation concluded that "the South Canyon tragedy (on Storm King) resulted from a series of judgments, decisions, events and actions with serious cumulative impacts." The firefighters were members of a "hotshot crew" from Prineville, Oregon who had just arrived in Colorado and gone straight to work on the fire. In addition to being in unfamiliar geography, they had apparently not been properly briefed on the day's weather forecast, which included the arrival of a front with increased winds. Running a fireline strangely low on a steep slope, according to the memorial website, they found themselves outflanked by a secondary blaze that started below them and ran up the slope faster than they could run for the ridge, over which they would have been safe, at least for the moment. Why were they building that line below that ridge, the logical place to be taming a wildfire?

A similar set of questions arose just last summer when 19 firefighters from another hotshot crew died south of Prescott, Arizona, in a fire in similar terrain — the scrubby chaparral, scrub oak, and pinon-juniper forest that is common to so much of the arid and semi-arid West below seven thousand feet elevation. It's a dry scruffy forest made for fire: Native Americans burned it regularly on purpose, to keep the brushy stuff young and tender for the deer they depended on.

There are two questions that don't seem to get asked in time: first, why are humans being sent in to fight wildfires in such places? And second, is it even possible to fight wildfire in such places, under certain conditions of fuel, temperature and wind? In other words, is there enough likelihood of containing a fire under those conditions to warrant the risk of sending in the troops?

The answer to the first question is usually the same: firefighters are being sent into nasty situations in scruffy non-commercial timber to protect property; the fire is threatening homes. The subsequent investigation in the Arizona fire last summer indicated that the majority of the buildings threatened by the fire had inadequate fire clearings around them. Of the 100-plus buildings that burned, only a few owners had made a serious effort to protect their property themselves (and most of the protected homes survived). The investigation concluded that the hotshot team had been "forced into a losing battle" to protect structures that were "indefensible." The Prineville hotshots were in a similar situation: fighting a fire that the Bureau of Land Management hadn't even bothered to fight until property owners in a nearby development had expressed concern. (Ultimately no buildings were lost in that fire — just 14 lives.)

An answer to the second question — should people be sent in to fight some fires at all? — is more complicated, and involves human nature as well as the nature of the forests. And the nature and function of fire in those forests.

All known life on the planet is based on carbon compounds and water. Given that our bodies are roughly two-thirds water, it is more than just a poetic fancy to say that life is water's way of using carbon compounds to create containers in which it can escape the downpull of gravity. Water encapsulated in carbon can swim against gravity in 300-foot trees; it can crawl out of itself onto the land, eventually to stand up like a human to look around and think about it all.

But there is a cycle to such things. We probably all learned about the water cycle in school, long enough ago to forget its specifics but recall its generality: what comes down eventually goes back up to come down

175

again. But carbon has a cycle too: every carbon-based life-form pushes some genetic heritage forward for a time, then dies and leaves continuity to the living; the dead are recycled through decomposition into mineral compounds and carbon oxides (mostly dioxide) which are then absorbed into other oncoming life forms — the resurrection through rot, gospel in the Church of the Conservation of Matter and Energy.

The carbon cycle runs into problems, however, in the so-called Temperate Zone. The cycle depends on old life dying and rotting in dynamic balance with new life coming on and growing, and that doesn't happen — especially in the cool high and dry forests of the interior West. Old life dies on schedule but does not rot fast enough; the small life that takes on the rot phase works best in warm muggy climates. So death piles up in most of our western forests — turns gray and hard rather than brown and spongy. And the oxidation process that carries carbon back into the atmosphere to feed new life (is carbon dioxide the soul of carbon-based life?) is woefully slow — until so much carbon-based death is lying around as duff and downed stuff that only a process of rapid oxidation can redeem the cycle. A lightning bolt, a careless match, an antisocial pyro — it doesn't matter: the forest longs for, lusts for it. In a dirty, messy way, fire brings balance back to the carbon cycle for that part of the life project.

But tell that to a hotshot fire team in full retreat with the full force of rapid oxidation licking at its heels. I speak from some personal experience. I spent a few summers and falls as a young man fighting wildfire. It amounted to economic development in Crested Butte, the mountain mining town in transition to a resort town where I found myself in my 20s. For several years in the 1970s we had a "hotshot crew," most of us more or less trained by the Forest Service. It provided erratic but always welcome income to an ever-changing roster of a 22-person crew of firefighters — members dropping off or rejoining as they got or lost better jobs locally.

Human psychology needs to be considered in this. A thirty-year-old was an elder in this group — not that there was any respect accorded us older guys. It says a lot to say that we liked the "hotshot" designation. *We* were hot, and we mostly saw ourselves as being as wild as the places where we went to fight fires. It maybe says all that needs to be said about the psychology of the Crested Butte Hotshots that it became a tradition to bring back (whenever possible) a burnt log from the fire to pitch through the plate glass window of the Grubstake Bar — paying for which took a fair chunk out of fire checks that wouldn't be received for a few weeks. If you need another indicator of crew morale, let's just say that emergency supplies for the crew always included a substantial stash of "uncontrolled substances." A fire was an adventure away from home.

Some of our cocky attitude about fires stemmed from the fact that mostly we fought little lightning-strike fires in the forested mountains and mesas around our own valley — the kind of fire a crew can actually put out in an afternoon and evening, and be back in town before the bars closed. But we got a good reputation for being in good enough shape and woods-savvy enough to give good work on those fires, and we began to get the call for larger fires in the surrounding region.

Then in August 1973, with the Cascades and Northern Rockies in a serious dry spell with fires everywhere, we got put on a leased commercial plane and flown and bussed into the depths of Nez Perce National Forest in Idaho, somewhere in the Salmon River watersheds (when there was water to shed), for what developed into a "project fire" — a big regional convocation of fires all over the place, joining up here, splitting around a mountain there, lurking and sneaking to explode up hillsides everywhere, and generally creating an environment of chaos. The Hotshots were, in short, invited in to participate in fighting a real wildfire unleashed.

We arrived mid-morning — after a night spent trying to sleep on planes and school buses — at an abandoned homestead clearing of maybe forty or fifty acres with a decaying orchard. The atmosphere was more heat than light, in a world so gray-brown with smoke that we could only see the tree-ragged mountains ranking around us in vague silhouette. "Where's the fire?" we asked. Smartasses, hotshots. The Forest Service man in charge of that sector of the fire waved an arm vaguely, encompassing the immediate universe. We didn't know how accurate that was until that night.

We were equipped with shovels, pulaskis and a couple chain saws, and sent out to build a fire line on a ridge that the fire command — someone somewhere else looking at the big picture — anticipated would burn that afternoon when the fire "woke up" from having "lain down" overnight.

It was probably a good enough plan at the fire-command level, but from our perspective we didn't even know whether our local commander had us on the right ridge or not. It made us nervous when the ridge dipped downward, and we found ourselves building line down a slope rather than along a ridge. But the fire, some fire, was sure enough coming up the hillside toward us, faster than we were building line on what began to look less like a ridge and more like just a forested mountainside.

I am neither excessively stupid nor excessively "macho" most of the time. But caught up in the literal heat of the moment with that fire, I found myself doing stupid things that could only be described as "trying to prove something" to this wild raging force that suddenly seemed to be right there with us, among us. I was a sawyer that day, supposedly cutting down trees in a swath to either side of the "mineral dirt" path the rest of the crew was chinking out with shovels and pulaskis; but I found myself using the saw like a short-handled scythe, cutting down and stomping brush and forbs flaring ahead of the infiltrating fire.

A safety officer saved us from this madness of continuing to obey an order to build a fireline already breached — running *up* the hillside from somewhere below, he shouted for us to abandon the line, get back up the hill. A spot fire from a flaming flying cone or something had started below us, and was coming uphill on *our* side of the line with serious intent. That was when the planes started coming over us — very close over us.

The aerial attack is a pink slurry of water mixed with a bonding substance, usually fertilizer. The slurry can be delivered as a mist, a spray, or a splat, depending on the altitude from which it is released over a fire. That afternoon they were coming in so low that it was mostly a splat. We had to stop and lay facedown every time we heard the sudden roar of the big plane coming over apparently no more than a hundred feet above the taller trees and diving down our ridge. The splats that hit our backs became a pink badge we wore for the rest of that fire. Looking back once, at a plane steeply climbing out of the valley, it occurred to me that I had never before seen the top of an airplane in flight. We got splatted, but so did the fire behind us, enough to slow it a bit, and we managed to run, stagger and stumble back up to the old homestead clearing while the fire burned both sides of our anonymous ridge rather than just one side. Lines were abandoned elsewhere too that afternoon. The fire held the forest. I don't know what having those planes that day cost us taxpayers — I'd guess in the high tens of thousands — but if the Prineville or Granite Mountain Hotshots had received the same, they might have lived.

We had been first to arrive at the old orchard clearing that morning, but by the time we got back late in the afternoon, there were several hundred people milling about. A National Guard unit had arrived, with a full complement of the stuff that accompanies the cannon fodder of a modern army to the field — mess tents with big pots of Army coffee and garbage cans for boiling tons of the frozen packaged meals they used to give out on airlines, assembly lines for slapping together sandwiches for hundreds of sack lunches, shower tents, mountains of sleeping bags, rain shelters being set up (dream on), a small machine shop for sharpening blades and sawteeth that operated at a grinding whine more or less through the night not far from where we were assigned to sleep.

But it was not a night for sleeping anyway. We were just lying down with the fire, surrounded by the fire's wink and mutter. The fire had humbled us that day, chasing us up the hill – but also humbling us with the astounding beauty of great gouts of pure flame, Edenic angels flying up a mountainside above tall trees, igniting clouds of resin-vapor cooked out of the pines. There may be fates worse than death and one might be life after flight from the freedom the fire promises to old trees. Is carbon dioxide the soul of carbon-based life? No – better to just embrace the humility: when high temperatures, wind, and the fuels from a century of fire suppression conspire to give fire its day, don't get in its way.

On our fourth day in Idaho that year, the fire simply left, or died, or went somnolent, whatever wildfire does when it loses its wildness. A drop in temperature, a rise in humidity, wind not being fed by fires that weren't rising to the bait of the day — whatever: the fire was gone. We puttered around for a couple more days, cleaning up around the edges of the burn, toppling smoking snags back into the burn, breaking up smoking branches and logs and applying a little water here and there ("Drink lots of coffee, and don't waste a drop!"). But the fire was gone. Did we miss it? Yes, in a morbid way. Did we think we had beat it? We knew better.

I came to think that our hotshot crew was a counter-productive workfare system for independent individuals who hate the idea of being on welfare. The little lightning-strike fires that we could put out were mostly doing good work for the forest, cleaning up the forest floor, balancing out the too-slow resurrection through rot with some rapid oxidation. When enough little cleansing fires got put out by hotshots like us, the result was inevitably a big fire from which we could only retreat. If we were fast enough and had air support.

Of course, some of the little fires can go on, with the right weather conditions, to become big fires if left to burn. In the two decades since the South Canyon fire, the West has experienced some of the largest fires ever recorded, and some of the most destructive of property — which is mostly an indication of how far humans have pushed into the "wildland-urban interface". But the size and intensity of the fires in the last two decades is also a function of the warming and drying of the region as a manifestation of global climate change. Many of those fires are simply too big and too intense to attack.

More and more "prescription fires" are being lit to clear out the fuel buildup, although prescribed burning is truly playing with fire. Los Alamos was almost destroyed in 2000 by a prescription burn that got out of control and burned over 40,000 acres and more than 200 homes — a big reason we no longer call them "controlled burns". But as the ability improves to predict weather events ever more accurately and even more locally, this does become a more viable option; all we need is a "conservation corps" of a million young people to tackle the backlog of fuel buildup. This would be steadier work than "hotshots crews" — but it wouldn't be so cool. It would be more like just a job.

And that is probably part of the reason why, even though land management agencies and hotshots alike are starting to ask the right questions about forests and fire, they still tend to rise to the old call when they smell the smoke. And it is part of the reason why, despite the fact that the agencies are getting more proactively selective about where they will send young people to defend property, young people are still going to get their adrenalized butts in tight places trying to defend the indefensible, and sometimes there will be no escape.

Surreality — the reality below reality, rationality, reason. Like we always do with things we hate or fear, we've invented rationales for the often futile and always dangerous act of throwing ourselves against wildfire. We fight it because it destroys resources, destroys life. Remember Bambi and Smokey. And the sanctity of private property. But basically we fight it because it is wild, uncontrolled, a gaping gate revealing the underlying chaos of the planet's infrastructure. We fight it because it's unacceptable to our sense of the way things should be.

But to lie down with a fire at night, to rest, to doze and wake and dream and wake again and doze with the surrounding fire and its glowing crackling vision for the forest, somewhere between the fight and flight – you may glimpse, as through a glass darkly, the stodginess of our sense of how things should be, in the face of the changeable nature of still evolving nature, the need for the uncluttered resurrection in the fire's wake. Is carbon dioxide the soul of carbon-based life?

Hartman Rocks

I lift my eyes to these hills
To see beyond gods and such folly;
I come up among these rocks
To take peace in their absence of plan.

Here in this thrust and boil of stone,
Long cooled but still settling out,
And the penetrant thrust and twist of root
Sorting mineral from dust beneath sun
And the dry vagrant prowl of insistent air
And this tree's hope against hope for rain:
Here in this mishmash of eternal fiddling
I am finally free from God, destiny, free.

Philosophers ask what life means, or meant;
These rocks make me think: accident.
In the beginning was no word, just swirl
And press of rampant roiling energy
Rearranging itself in random shots
Ever more solid and slow till its latest form
Is this long drawn death in beauty and brokenness
Here in these rocks that rise in ruin all around.

No: the word, if it comes at all, is dragged here
By such as me: a buzzing busyness at surface
That interrupts this bright waiting silence
Not at all, or not enough to matter.

The Valley of the Shadow

Published in *Mountain Gazette*, March 2006, substantially revised 2014.

It was just an afternoon ski up the Slate River valley, but like a lot of things these days, it made me think about dying.

A narrow valley, and the mountains to either side go up so steeply to the sky that the low winter sun doesn't linger long in the afternoon. I'd thought I might ski up to the old Pittsburg townsite, not because there would be anything going on up there but just because it's a kind of a marker, a long-abandoned outpost of mostly human culture in otherwise omniscient nature; it's a good place to go to and turn around if you're just out for exercise, or for the beauty of the day. It's also where the road doubles back on itself and starts to seriously climb out of the valley toward Paradise Divide; you don't just start up that part of the road in the late afternoon in December unless you're seriously prepared for something more than a little leisurely mucking about on skis.

But I was still a couple miles down from the old townsite when I realized the night was coming down the valley faster than I was going up it. There it was, just ahead: a very distinct transition. I was gliding down a slight slope in the bright, if deeply slanted winter sun, and not far ahead was a deep blue twilight. Far and high up the valley the sun still lit the tops of the distant peaks, but filtered as it was by the deep twilight below, it was not a warm light. Beautiful, all of it, achingly beautiful, but cold, cold.

So I glided to a stop that afternoon, in the deep orange penumbra of the coming night—and was immediately chilled: got out the windbreaker, got my gloves out of my pocket. The sun was still on the steep north slope just above me, but I could watch its not-so-slow retreat up the slope. And I thought, that day: a good place to turn around—try to stay ahead of the advancing shadow going back down the valley.

***

I don't consider myself to be an especially morbid person, but I've been thinking about dying pretty often, these days. This is still a largely abstract preoccupation with me, but I have friends for whom it is less abstract, friends who are going to die within the next year, and who know it and know why. Some of them younger than I.

In my mid-70s now, I'm a little like the old truck we use for hauling wood in the fall – always something wrong with it, which I fix but discover something else on the verge of going wrong with it, but it always starts and gets out there and back, maybe with a little tinkering en route.

My longtime doctor and I aged more or less together over the past 40 years, and we both retired. The new guy that bought his practice seems qualified and smart but lacks the empathy the old one had. He told me, on a recent checkup, that I'm in the 18 percent probability range for heart trouble; if I wanted to change my lifelong bad habits in terms of diet, alcohol intake, exercise, et cetera, I could maybe reduce that to 15 or 16 percent. But the real problem, he said, is "you're a male in your 70s." So much for that: not so much a problem as just a fact of life, my life.

I know that one of these years, I'm going to go to the doctor for the annual checkup and he is going to find something he doesn't like. Or I'm going to wake up realizing I've been putting off asking the doctor about a nagging something or other that, instead of going away after a few days or weeks, seems to be hanging on or getting a little worse.... And then I am going to have to make the kind of decision about myself that I've had to make all my life about my automobiles: should I fix it up one more time (assuming it is fixable, and even though there are noises and rattles indicating other incipient breakdowns on the horizon), or is it time to just trade it in? Except that, with me (other than the possible parting-out of used organs), there's no trade-in value.

184

Junking it, is what it amounts to, and what I wonder, fear about myself, is whether at that point I'll have the gumption (and today, the necessary guile and prior planning) to stand up to the heroic health industry and the perfervid Christians and conduct myself through a reasonably dignified process of dying.

I hope of course that I'll be one of the lucky ones, like a couple of friends who simply seem to have gone to sleep, one in a movie theater, the other in his easy chair at home, not so much as an outcry or a groan from either; they just quickly and quietly left. But that is not the usual situation. Every Friday afternoon, I go with a group of friends to the old folks home – the "Living Care Center," it's called – and sing old songs to people who going through a much longer and more difficult process of leaving, an earthbound purgatory. Many of them are no longer here in any really meaningful sense – autonomous organs continuing to thump along in human shells essentially empty.

That's what I think of these days, when I think about death: my own: whether I will be brave enough to carry out a decent death as a final obligation, maybe to the planet but certainly to myself: to die in a timely and dignified way, to go with grace.

***

This is of course one of those conversations that is generally considered to be culturally inappropriate. Bring it up, and it's like a fart someone couldn't quite hold back; everyone is faintly embarrassed, and someone else starts talking about the weather, or how it's time to get dinner on the table.

But the topic is here, more and more. My partner and I have been talking about it—quite a lot, in fact, because she has finally finished going through what many of our friends today are going through: the death of very old parents. Or to say it as it really is—the long, slow, and often painful death of parents who know they have outlived their productive years, who know that every additional year of their poor excuse for living diminishes what they have to leave for their kids or for the things they really believe in, who have ceased to really enjoy life and are horrified at the looming prospect of the Happy Golden Years Managed Care Facility, but who are too polite to object to the strenuous efforts of a health juggernaut that will do everything it can to keep them alive forever or at least till their annuity and other assets are milked dry. And there's the aggressive contradiction of religion too; the supposed belief in an afterlife,

185

but no tolerance for those who might wish to transcend both their pain and the burden they place on their loved ones by trying to go with grace to that afterlife.

One of my friends recently had the trauma of losing both of his parents within a matter of weeks—both through the relentless accumulation of natural causes, but with the second death undoubtedly facilitated by grief at the impossibility of imagining life without the partner who left first. But traumatic as that was for my friend, I think he was luckier in a way than my partner because the same process lasted, off and on, a decade for her.

Her father died in his eighties, a brilliant, energetic and creative man who lived long enough to see the juggernaut of civilization trundling away from—and in some ways, over—the ideas to which he had dedicated his life. His wife (my partner's mother), who had dedicated her life to him and his work, lived on beyond him a decade without really wanting to at all, or so she said. She said she wanted to be dead; she started to wear the "Do Not Resuscitate" bracelet—but at some point, for whatever reason, took it off, and so was resuscitated once from a minor (but sufficient) stroke. After that, she survived a couple other incidents through nothing more nor less apparently than her body's habit of being alive. She all but stopped eating—took in nothing, my partner claims, but coffee and chocolate. She became so physically emaciated that it was literally dangerous for her to go out on a windy day. But until cancer came to her pancreas finally, in her early 90s, her heart kept thumping along in a low-pressure way, pushing enough blood through a relatively functional system to keep her brain and body alive.

I escaped this thing that so many of my peers are experiencing; both of my parents left when I was still in the decades between being their responsibility and being able to take on their care as part of my responsibility. My father died in his mid-60s of an undiagnosed prostate cancer that spread to his bones—a couple years of pain, including the pain of chemo and every other all-out treatment to fight the inevitable. My mother died much younger, at 48, of the complications associated with *lupus*, when I was still in my early 20s—a long, lingering, sad death from one of those mysterious auto-immune diseases in which the body essentially turns against itself.

Both of them were robbed of a sense of completeness to their lives. I remember my father, when he called to tell me about the diagnosis, saying he had hoped for a few years after retirement to "sort things out." And my mother—I just think about an easel up in the attic with a half-finished painting on it. A kind of a Norman Rockwell picture of a young girl with dance slippers slung over her shoulder looking at a ballet poster. And a drawerful of stories and poems. But mostly, had she been unladylike enough to mention it, her sense of incompleteness would have been not getting to see—for better or worse—my sisters and me grown and out in the world.

But they—and I—were at the very least spared this strange situation facing people today, moving into their eighties and beyond, and their grown children, confronted with a ridiculous paradox: a society that seems to appreciate nothing but youth and its follies on the one hand, but on the other hand seems to have a fanatical will to keep the aged alive for as long as possible, in diverse situations of cultural irrelevance and even disrespect, culminating in the "nursing homes" where they are treated in the same kindly but patronizing ways we treat slow children.

And this in a world that so obviously needs, more than anything else, fewer people.

***

So I'm thinking about this; my partner and I are thinking about it. We have, in fact, worked with a lawyer to draw up "medical powers of attorney" for each other so powerful that they would, in effect, let us each be the other's "executor" in the most basic sense of the term—help with the syringe, the overdose, the pillow, whatever works. That's just the ideal, of course, and of course it'll never fly in the current political/medical environment, enforced by inconsistent politicos who focus their mercy on human vegetables but can't extend it to healthy young people who need good educations and good jobs to go to.

But the afternoon ski up the Slate River did suggest an alternative. It made me think, for example, of one of the books by a great nature writer who was doing nature-writing before nature-writing was cool, Farley Mowat, and *The Snow Walker*. Mowat had a penchant for the far frozen north, and *The Snow Walker* is a set of essays that, as I remember, stemmed from a season (up where it's all one season) trading stories with far northers in a trading post where he worked.

The title essay—"The Snow Walker"—was a terrible sad story, of a tribal band of far northern native Americans who were starving to death in an unusually severe winter when the animals that nurtured them didn't show up where and when expected—possibly because the far north was still in the process of adjusting ecologically to the efficiency we had

187

brought to the region in the form of the repeating rifle. The band finally headed south to try to find a trading post where they could beg or borrow some sustenance. It was a literal death march, and periodically, through that terrible journey, one or another of the elders would just leave in the night—go to "meet the Snow Walker." And when one of them would do that, almost invariably according to their legend, the next day a lone fat buck or some other animal would amiably show itself, close enough for even a starving hallucinating hunter to draw an accurate bead, and the people would eat again for a couple days.

The Snow Walker. A euphemism for death, and raised as I was on Dickensian ghosts and other death images, I imagined the gaunt Grim Reaper, the tall black cloak empty of features, the armless sleeves that spread to enfold one.

But suppose the Snow Walker is actually—Santa Claus? Same neighborhood: a fat jolly spirit that opens a door out of the night and welcomes one into another kind of warmth? I've read, from the stories of those who have been brought back from the edge of death by freezing, that the last thing you feel is warmth – probably your body's last hypothermic gasp. But why couldn't death be as generous as St. Nicholas – if not an actual gift to the still-living as in the story, at least a gift to the dying?

***

Timeliness, timing, of course, is the problem. When one is young, it is easy to believe "you won't see *me* getting old and useless." And there are certainly "untimely" deaths, moreso for people who hang out around mountains—falls, accidents, the mysterious heart failures that seem to strike vital and healthy men between 45 and 55, the ugly systemic malfunctions that took both my parents untimely.

But for the rest of us—how will we know when it is "closing time"? Actually, I think my partner's mother left an inferential clue. Her family had been typical enough of the postwar American families—there was no discernible reason for unhappiness, therefore no acknowledged unhappiness. But she had lived in the kind of strange estrangement from her two daughters that one often sees in once-ambitious women who become homemakers and support systems for partners working out their ambitions. My partner's mother had been studying to be an actress, a serious classical actress, but had married in college and had become a wife and mother instead. So it is our hypothesis that she took off her "Do not resuscitate" bracelet because she still had unfinished business, making a better peace with her daughters. My partner wanted that too, and made several trips back to Madison during her mother's last year, and was with her – reading to her from Chekov – when she finally let go. "There," Sonya tells her Uncle Vanya at the play's end, "beyond the grave, we shall say that we have suffered, that we have wept, and have known bitterness, and God will have pity on us; and you and I, Uncle, shall behold a life that is bright, beautiful, and fine. We shall rejoice and look back on our present troubles with tenderness, with a smile—and we shall rest."

So—taking care of business, the business of making the best of the messes of life: maybe only then can we put on the bracelet, really decide to let go of life, when we've taken care of the business of living. "It is time I wrote my will," said Yeats, somewhere in his sixties, but sometimes I think I'm still trying to *discover* my will; there's still unfinished business.

***

So, again, how will I know when it's time? If I wait till I think I've finished my work – I've got so many "writing projects" started that, were I permitted to stay till I finished them all, I'd be about 125 years old. But I also know that many are called to great ideas, but few are chosen; many of my great ideas, maybe most of them, probably aren't going to be done right (or at all) by me. Or I'm probably not going to do right by them. Probably. Unless, of course, in the process of working on them, they became infused with my peculiar brilliance, or, or, or.... Thus doth consciousness make cowards of us all.

Do I, in other words, really think I can come to a place where I believe that the earth is done with me—a place where I believe I am done with the earth? I can only say I think about it a lot these years.

The ski up the Slate River helped me think about it. I felt how cold the coming night was, but also saw how beautiful. For the time being, the parts of me that feel the cold and the parts of me that see the beauty are still bound up in this concatenation of contradictions generally known as me. An occasionally interesting but often tedious writer, an iconoclast whose unique visions are damped down to negligible by an unaccountable sense of personal inferiority, an aging orphan son who never felt like a father even when he became one, a sometime teacher who hates discipline and "rigor," an almost, a not-quite—I've begun to really appreciate the observable truth of the compost bin: that matter and energy are constant; that the assemblage of matter and energy into forms like me is often interesting but always imperfect; that what is ultimately important is the fact that every iota of matter and energy gets a lot of different and often interesting opportunities. My church is the church of the conservation and transformation of matter and energy.

But do I have the courage of that conviction? When I look up the Slate River valley, as I did that day, beyond the nearer night to the sun on those peaks beyond—maybe. Maybe some day I'll muster the gumption to leave a few cryptic notes ("Don't call the rescue people; I'm off to see Santa"), and ski up to the old abandoned Pittsburg townsite some brilliant afternoon, and when I get there, just make the turn that goes on up toward Paradise Divide, and go and go till it's just time to sit down under a tree and watch the moon reflect its glory, life's glory, and there give my last unconditional gift hypothermally to the universe. Life grant me that grace.

After Life

After we wake up from living
We no longer need to make fire
For the heat we no longer need
In the bright crystal morning ahead.

Unseen but felt we mourn our loss
With those we've lost, till we wake up
Again to all possible, and leave wondering then,
On the backs of deer or hummingbirds.

And we go till, freed, we forget ourselves
In places so lovely, so fine, we want to be
Everywhere there for a while, a night or a moon,
Or to maybe be somewhere a tree for a life.

And we're a tree, then, some of us, for a fractal
Leaving of time, and, if doubly blessed, something
Of those we loved will come to lie under us,
Or in our branches build nests, or just sing.

The First River of
the Anthropocene

A short version published in the *Mountain Gazette,* May 2012,
substantially rewritten for this edition in 2014.

Climate change that is almost certainly anthropogenic (caused by us): shouldn't our first response to that be at least a chuckle? I mean, for as long as we have been consciously studying the world around us, we've been saying, "Everyone complains about the weather but no one does anything about it." Now, we are finally all doing something about the weather!

Well, I think it's funny – worth at least a chuckle, if only because we usually think better when we approach something in a good humor rather than a grump. A chuckle at our own unintentional overreaches might be a more constructive response than the current polarizing demi-religious political war that is shaping up, between the told-you-sos trying to scare us into action over it and the committed know-nothings and vested interests denying that it is even happening. Exactly what we're doing about the weather, we don't know; and it was not part of our intentions when we started burning fossil fuels a couple hundred years ago and pumping all that banked carbon back into the carbon cycle. But now that there is a very high probability that we are in fact changing that first and largest of all the

193

evolving planetary systems through our actions, we really do need to step way back for the bigger picture. And when we can do that with a laugh together, even a rueful laugh, we're usually in a better frame for looking at the big picture thoughtfully, than when we're pulling back into battle line.

As is often the case with our major environmental changes, there are almost certainly some unanticipated consequences of warming up the atmosphere that we will rue. But we should also contemplate the possibility that there might be some unanticipated positives in some places. For example, most scientists seem to agree that pumping that formerly banked fossil carbon back into the carbon cycle is countering and possibly reversing the long slow slide back into another episode of Big Ice over most of our northern land masses. This should give comfort to all of us who feel deep within that, like the New England farmers say, "the glaciers aren't gone; they just went back for more rocks."

The point I want to suggest is that climate change, whether anthropogenic or just another of those inexplicable "acts of God," is not necessarily all "good" or all "bad"; it is – just change: something else to learn to adapt to, the way we've been adapting to and otherwise surviving natural and cultural events for many millennia. When one looks at what we know about the long and checkered natural history of the planet, there is no obvious planetary reason why our land masses should be scraped bare of all life by massive ice sheets; and if putting some of that banked carbon back into the atmosphere precludes that gross stupidity, we may be doing the planet – or at least ourselves on the planet – a longterm favor. Of course, since we've done it clumsily and unintentionally, we will have to pay for that in the short term by also learning to live with consequences like oceans several feet higher – unless we can actually accept what's happening and manage to stop raising the planet's temperature, maybe reverse it a little, to keep the polar ice from completely melting.

Truth to tell, we really don't know what all of the consequences will be of the changes we've imposed on the planet – not just the climate changes, but the anthropogenic changes to all the ecosystems we have elbowed our way into. We have wanted to believe – more and more desperately as the impact of our works has become more and more evident – that we are so small and the planet is so large that all the works of man are insignificant, incapable of changing much. "A little chipping, baking, patching, and washing," said Emerson of our works (on the eve of the Industrial Revolution); "in an impression so grand as that of the world on the human mind, they do not vary the result."

But our earth scientists have weighed the evidence, and the varied results of our works – the deserts we've accidentally enlarged, the ecologically diverse prairies we've replaced with monocultures, the oceans where we are now literally scraping the bottom for food and other resources, the forests we've turned into fields, the amount of land we've paved over, et cetera – and now of course our loading of the atmosphere with climate-changing greenhouse gases – the scientists have weighed all of this, and concluded that we are *in fact* changing the planet on a geological scale. After serious study and considerable debate, they have christened this geological epoch "the Anthropocene."

The Anthropocene: deny it if you must, but you'll probably better sustain your ignorant bliss if you drop out of this essay at this point. The rest is for those of us who accept that judgment of science, who are willing to acknowledge that we are in fact changing the planet, and who believe it is like that old hippie Stewart Brand says: "We have to figure out how to do well at it."

***

Much of what is written about our anthropogenic changes on the planet employs the methods of the old Puritan preachers trying to reform their congregations by scaring them with images of being barbecued for their sins over the flames of hell by an angry god. But rather than indulging that envirowriter tendency to start by scaring readers with descriptions of the full catastrophe of how our planet-changing activities might play out, I am going to instead ask the reader to use this penultimate climate change – capping all of our other anthropogenic changes on earth's ecosystems – as an opportunity to just shut up for a bit on the "woe woe is us" routine, and to take a long look at the larger picture of humankind's cumulative adventure on Planet Earth. We may be at a time when we need to remember the engineers' old saying: "When you're up to your ass in alligators, it's hard to remember you set out to drain the swamp."

So what was it we were trying to do when we discovered that we had inadvertently changed even the weather, along with most of the other ecological systems on the planet?

I would argue, I guess, that I don't think we ever really articulated what we were going to try to do before we just set about doing it. But based on the cumulative evidence of what we have actually done, we can say this now: some eight, ten, twenty thousand years ago, we set out to change the nature of the planet, to convert an ever larger portion of its

195

resources to our own species' growing needs, stemming from populations growing rapidly in a warming world mellowed by the departure of the Big Ice.

Our far distant ancestors may not have thought of it like that, but they were confronted with a choice:

either submit to the controls and limits that "natural" ecosystems place on successful species (numbers limited by food supplies, density-bred diseases, deadly competition among expanding groups, et cetera), thereby letting "nature" set limits on our success; *or* apply our natural gifts (the big brain with its capacities for analysis and creativity, our communication skills, our manual dexterity, our omnivorous appetites, our toolmaking capacity) to creating new socio-economic systems that enabled us to support ever larger and denser populations.

So rather than continuing a trend toward snarling bands of hunter-gatherers fighting each other like the wolf packs were doing (and are doing again today) over increasingly crowded territories, we chose the latter; our distant ancestors sussed out the efficiencies and defensive advantages of farming over foraging, herding over hunting, and we humans began to change the planet to better meet the needs of our own growing populations. Those new strategies worked so well that within a few thousand years we outgrew those agri-cultures, and are now deeply invested in a 6,000-year experiment in even denser living – an experiment that has left the planet littered with the ruins of many urban experiments, but we keep trying.

We have, in short, given ourselves license to change nature itself to free ourselves from nature's perceived limits. When we perceive the world around us attempting to limit us in some way – new diseases, food shortages, water shortages, et cetera – we impose technological, political, and other cultural changes on ourselves *and* on the world around us to counter those limits. We now appear to be closer than we have ever been over those 6,000 years to succeeding with the urbanization experiment – and perhaps more culturally fragile and over-extended. And since the measure of success is always an expanding population, we always seem to be needing to evolve even denser, more ordered and managed cultural systems for adapting the planet to our needs.

Is this a fair description of what we are doing in the Anthropocene? By our works shall we know ourselves. Is it "wrong"? "Evil"? We can definitely say our changes on the planet were often wrought ignorantly, clumsily – we have often succeeded so well in our efforts to rearrange the planet that we have imposed serious problems on ourselves: mass cliff-drive slaughters of megafauna that eventually left us eating squirrels and roots; famines caused by soil exhaustion, monocultural diseases and water problems; energy crises from depleted wood supplies; desertification from bad land use; wartime devastations from the ozymandian arrogance of the alpha types we allow to ascend to power in our urban concentrations, et cetera.

But in cataloguing these sins against the planet as well as against ourselves, it would be good to keep them in the context of the long history of a planet that has had frequent major episodes of volcanos, earthquakes and other tectonic lurches that have reshaped the planet; extreme weather events and longer-term climate shifts (including the Big Ice) that have wiped out whole ecosystems; a meteor collision that wiped out half the animal kingdom; not to mention the steady tedious labor of wind and water to reduce all the planet's landmasses to sea level, or the geological fact that those landmasses themselves are just drifting islands of stone on the molten core of the planet.... We've done unintentional but undeniable damage to our planet, but it is all pretty mild compared to what the random forces operant on the planet have done with no help from us or anyone. A look at the Grand Canyon ought to comfort the soul of any farmer feeling guilty about having unintentionally facilitated the gullying of a field.

It seems important to acknowledge this underlying planetary chaos, because our appreciation, or even acceptance, of our own works seems to be undermined by an archetypal story – totally unsubstantiated by planetary reality – that somehow the earth was beautiful, perfect, and orderly, until we humans came along and mucked it all up. The Garden of Eden, from which we were evicted for the sin of original and creative thought. We need to think this through a little coherently. We can envision a "Garden Earth" because we are capable of conscious critical and creative thought; we can look at the world around us and envision ways in which it could work better – for us, at least – and we possess an unprecedented dexterity for devising tools to carry out those visions. We can in fact dream of a "rational planet," an earth without the disruptions and chaos that we ourselves, along with those random planetary forces, bring to parts of the planet – an earthquake here, a nuclear meltdown there.

But when and where did the mental crosswiring happen that led us to think this probably impossible dream of a Garden Earth is a *memory* of an Edenic Paradise Lost? And I will note that this is not just a belief of fundamentalist Jews, Christians and Muslims. The "Gospel of Ecology" (a Rod Nash term) that drives the more evangelical wings of the environmental movement proclaims a "Paradise Lost" story that simply

197

replaces "God" in the story with "Nature." This is not going to be helpful in the Anthropocene.

***

So where does this leave us today? We are, yes, apparently up to our asses in a multitude of manmade messes – but focusing on that is distracting us from the fairly astounding achievements that have brought us to the point where the planet that felt too crowded to a few million humans ten or twenty short millennia ago is now supporting (sort of, more or less) billions of us – and many of us in circumstances those ancient ancestors could not even have dreamed of.

I personally don't pretend to like all of our achievements, and I wish we were making a better effort as a species to control our numbers. But the species has chosen the course we are on, and to think we can just back out of it now – run the film backwards like the Internet coyote story – would not restore a garden earth that has never existed. A half-built house, just rising out of its basement foundations, usually looks like a mess too – mud and dirt everywhere, stacks of stuff lying around, no real sense of the overall vision – but that doesn't mean it is a wreck, a disaster. You do need to have some blueprints on hand, however; and if the basement was badly built, you need to correct the mistakes there before proceeding on with the rest of the building.

So it is time to evaluate the Anthropocene project – not ignoring the alligators, but with more attention to the garden vision that has moved us historically to want to "rationalize" the planet.

I can think of no better or worse example of us at work in the Anthropocene than the river whose headwaters I've inhabited for most of the past half century. The Colorado River, which I have been studying in an on-and-off way since the late 1970s, and for which I've spent most of the past decade actively involved in planning the near future of its headwaters. There is probably no other river that has been leaned on harder for human purposes – a river so wild and chaotic a mere century ago that its central reaches were the last blank spot on our map, and now, a century later, a river almost completely controlled and manipulated for human purposes (including being operated in certain blessed spaces as a "wild river"). It could be called "The First River of the Anthropocene."

It is also a river that has been the focus of a river of angry tears and lamentations from the Corps of Envirowriters, whose unstated end argument would appear to be that the best thing for us to do would be turn it back into the wild and chaotic river it was a century-plus ago.

In the interest of full disclosure, I have to say that I have shed my own literary tears for the Colorado River. Back in 1977 I wrote an essay for *Harper's Magazine* about the Lower Colorado River, arguing finally that "this cannot go on this way," an essay that became a PBS film in 1981. Also in 1981, environmental journalist Philip Fradkin brought out *A River No More*, lamenting what we have done to the Colorado. Not long after that Marc Reisner wrote the environmentalist epic *Cadillac Desert* lamenting what we've done to the entire American West with emphasis on the Colorado River. A few years after that, Colorado journalist Jim Carrier wrote *The Colorado: A River at Risk*; and just a few years ago we got *Dead Pool: Lake Powell, Global Warming, and the Future of Water in the West.* Even more recently, we've got Jonathan Waterman's *Running Dry*, and – well, I could go on and on. And those publications are just the more in-depth (or at least longer) lamentations; the number of passing media articles and presentations about the sad fate of the Colorado River might not outnumber the stars in the sky, but they probably outnumber the articles about the Anthropocene.

Meanwhile, some facts: over the 35 years since my own lamentatious essay in 1977, those regular predictions of near-death notwithstanding, the Colorado River now provides some of the drinking water for around 10 million *more* people than it did in 1977 – some 35 million of us today (and most of us using less water *per capita*). If you're eating fresh produce in mid-winter, you have to thank the lower Colorado River in part. The southwestern cities that depend in varying degrees on the river – the cities that most of us depend on directly or indirectly for the complex networks of finance and transportation and communication that operate our societies – have mostly at least doubled in size in that time.

Yet, also meanwhile, the Colorado retains much of its spectacular beauty. It has almost as many stretches of good whitewater floating and fishing as it did in 1977; some of its fisheries are better today than they were then; some new "wild and scenic" stretches are being protected along the river; it also has more flatwater recreational opportunities for those who like that kind of thing.

I am certainly not deluded that everything is fine in the Colorado River Basin and all of its technological extensions outside the natural basin – far from it. There are major problems that we need to address on the river, from the headwaters all the way down through that vast manmade delta where the river disappears into the cities and farms of the southwestern deserts. The creeping consequences of diverting too much water from the headwaters for out-of-basin metropolises, the deterioration of mountain streams from cattle and other human activities, the salt-loading from some irrigation runback on top of the natural salinity of the river, evaporative losses that further degrade water quality, siltation behind reservoirs and a *lack* of silt in the Grand Canyon, loss of both riparian and aquatic habitat for wildlife – there is no shortage of significant problems facing us up and down the river. But, with the exception of the more recently "discovered" global climate change looming over everything, these were already recognized problems 35 years ago, and some of them – irrigation-induced salinity, loss of habitat, degradation of streambeds – are being addressed with some success.

The point is, we don't seem to be looking at the big picture so much as we're looking at the alligators. Our enhanced post-1970 level of "environmental awareness" has been important in motivating those improvements and corrections to our often naïve and clumsy works on the Colorado River, as well as the rest of the planet. But we do seem to be doing our good works to the same old "river-no-more" dirge – doing what we do to undo our damage, trying to put things back the way they were, restoring the edenic garden that never was rather than getting on with completing the Anthropocene reconstruction of the river we've begun and cannot afford to back out of half-done.

An example of what I would call "positive Anthropocene action" has happened right here in the Upper Gunnison valleys, on the Taylor River, a tributary of the Gunnison River. The Taylor watershed is one of the great snowcatchers in the Southern Rockies, the west slopes of the highest range on the Continental Divide. Its tributaries gather into a broad open park, then drop down into twentysome miles of beautiful canyons, a world-class stream for fishing and an exciting stream for whitewater floating. To look at it today, you would not know that it is now a "man-made river."

The Bureau of Reclamation built a dam at the top of that stretch of canyons in the 1930s, to provide late-summer storage in Taylor Park for the Uncompahgre Valley Water Users Association a hundred miles downstream, at the other end of the Gunnison Tunnel the Bureau had built at the turn of the 20th century to move water from the Gunnison River canyons over to the Uncompahgre Valley. The Taylor Dam was hustled into construction by West Slope Congressman Edward Taylor to prevent a transmountain diversion into the Arkansas Basin, but it effectively killed the Taylor as a river, turning it into an irrigation canal only carrying significant water when water was called for from downstream to keep the tunnel full. But when the Bureau in the 1960s built the Curecanti dams (now the "Wayne N. Aspinall Unit") in the Gunnison's canyons above Black Canyon National Park, all parties involved realized that it would make more sense for the Uncompahgre Valley Water Users to store their Taylor River water in the much larger Blue Mesa Reservoir, fifty miles closer to where the water would be ultimately used.

This was arranged through an agreement in 1975, and it meant that the Taylor Dam was no longer needed for its original purpose. One can hear the chorus that would erupt today: "Tear it down! Free the river!"

Instead, a "local user group," made up of Taylor River irrigators, the local anglers club, a couple rafting companies, the reservoir concessionaires, and some wealthy second-home owners – your standard democratic group of special interests – proposed to the Bureau of Reclamation that the storage at the top of the canyon be managed with releases that matched the natural hydrograph to a great extent but with more late summer flows for rafters, fishermen and irrigators, and with wet year yields held in storage when possible for dry years, evening out the extremes.

The Bureau went along with this, and every spring now, the "Local User Group" members listed above sit down together to plan how the Taylor River will be run through the summer and fall, to give all the diverse users as much of what they need as possible, while also "running it like a river" with attention to its environmental health. The result is a beautiful "manmade" river – as natural looking as any fisherman or floater could want for the aesthetic aspect of their recreational pursuit, yet it is entirely operated by the Bureau of Reclamation - an Anthropocene stream.

A century or so down the road, the reservoir will have silted in, preceded by a diminishing capacity for the kind of management now being practiced, and it is probably not too soon to be thinking what to do when that eventuality is upon us. But that would require us to be "thinking Anthropocene," rather than writing it off as just another "damnation" of a river.

Another insight on what the Anthropocene will probably be is taking shape up in the headwaters of the Colorado River's mainstem, where significant quantities of the tributary waters have been diverted through the Continental Divide to the cities and farms east of the Southern Rockies. The megalopolis spreading north and south from Denver has grown largely on water from the Colorado River mainstem and its tributaries – the Fraser, Williams Fork, Blue and Eagle Rivers. Half a million acre-feet of water a year – 160 billion gallons – goes through or over the Divide from those streams, and barring tunnel collapse, so long as there is a Denver, that water will never again water the West Slope.

Had Colorado's Front Range megalopolis been limited by its "natural" water supply, it would have probably been three or four water-conscious cities of maybe a million people total, instead of a metro region pushing four million with the attitude that water is not a limiting factor in urban growth. Where would the other three million people have gone? Well, if we were really trying as a species to take care of business *within* the limits of nature, most of them would probably not even exist due to some cultural or natural imposition of birth control. But we do not choose to so constrain ourselves, and we continue to operate most of the arid West on the welcome-wagon philosophy: let the people come; we will find the water for them somewhere.

In a cumulative way, however, this creates real problems in the watersheds of origin. Roughly 60 percent of the Fraser River, for example, high in the Southern Rockies, is diverted through the Moffat Tunnel for the Front Range metropolis. This creates problems for the people in the Fraser valley, which has a local economy that has depended on the river for agricultural, recreational and environmental uses, not to mention the aesthetic qualities associated with a river running through a mountain valley. The diversions so reduce the quantity of water in the river that the remaining water gets too warm for the cold-water fish the anglers want, and often too shallow for floating boats. Those depletions, compounded by historic agricultural uses, often dewater stretches of the river entirely.

This is all very legal under Colorado water law, but most of the Front Range cities, at this point in time, are acknowledging a moral responsibility for mitigating those impacts – on the one hand, acknowledging that no one should build their future by depriving others of a comparable future (or present); and on the other hand, acknowledging that the "mountain playgrounds" are part of the reason the cities attract people to fill their jobs and purchase their real estate.

This obligation was most recently acknowledged in 2012 with a Colorado River Cooperative Agreement between Denver Water and 37 headwaters municipalities, utilities, counties, and other user groups on the West Slope. Under this agreement, Denver Water will be taking a modest additional amount of water (~18,000 acre-feet) from the West Slope in above-average runoff years only; in exchange, they will be investing millions of dollars in West Slope water problems.

Much of this money will go to towns and utilities to improve their treatment plant efficiency – their ability to do more with less water. But a lot of it will also go to what are being called "enhancements," but can only be described as reconstructing the river: narrowing its channel to deepen it, adding meanders and riparian plant life to shade and cool it. In essence, stretches of the headwaters streams will be "downsized" to fit the amount of water remaining after the cities have taken their cut. It is an expensive process, estimated at around a million dollars a mile.

Other things will be happening up here in the headwaters region, once we get serious about the Anthropocene. Meteorologists estimate that roughly 40 million acre-feet of precipitation falls on the West Slope of the Southern Rockies every year, but up to three-fourths of that never appears in the streams that feed the Colorado River; instead it gets carried back into the atmosphere as water vapor through one of two processes. Some of it is *sublimated* from the solid state (snow) directly to water vapor without first going through the liquid phase. Sublimation happens to windblown snow; it also happens to snow that piles onto tree branches rather than falling onto the ground snowpack. Most of the rest of the 25 or 30 million acre-feet of precipitation that "disappears" is used by the trees of the mountain forests themselves, which need a lot of the water for their own nurture and growth, but also evaporate a lot of it through their own evapotranspiration "micro-climate" mechanisms.

An "early Anthropocene" action in response to that knowledge might be – well, has been – to simply remove all the trees from the mountains, which does in fact significantly increase the runoff – in the form of a fast, destructive and uncontainable muddy flood that eventually brings down most of the mountain slopes along with the water. We've demonstrated that often enough to know better.

But ... do we need *all* of those trees to hold the mountain in place? The Forest Service has experimented with careful thinning of forest stands and the creation of small openings to allow more of the snow to fall on the ground rather than getting stranded on, and sublimated from, branches. It is possible to increase the water yield this way, and such treatment can also improve the health of the stands – in aerial views after the recent bark beetle pandemic, those experimentally treated stands were still mostly green. But like everything else in the Anthropocene, to treat millions of acres of forest to increase the water supply would be labor intensive and very expensive.

The Nature Conservancy is currently pioneering another Anthropocene treatment in the Upper Gunnison Basin: reversing gully

203

erosion in once wet mountain meadows. The goal is to restore high water tables in eroded meadows, increasing high-altitude ground storage to "naturally" regulate the release of water to the streams below, and also improving the habitat of the meadows for both domestic stock and wildlife (including threatened species like the Gunnison Sage Grouse). Again, there is no shortage of places gullied by some combination of hard human use and extreme natural storm events. And again, the work is expensive – it's amazing how hard it can be to find rocks in the Rocky Mountains, in the right places for plugging gullies. And then there's the intensive and expensive heavy-lifting labor aspect of it.

It is my personal bias that a lot of concentrated, intelligent and expensive work in the headwaters regions of the Colorado River – small high-altitude reservoirs like Taylor, increased high-altitude groundwater storage and restoration/reconstruction of degraded streams – would solve a lot of problems for the entire Colorado River Basin. But there are other situations farther down the river that demand attention.

The Grand Canyon situation, for example. On the one hand, it should probably be regarded as miraculous that a two-hundred mile "wild river adventure" exists in the midsection of what is supposedly "a river no more." The miracle is engineered, as it were, behind the scenes by the National Park Service – a to-the-hour scheduling process to keep a conveyor belt of public and private trips moving down the river, but spaced so that each party sees no more than a handful of other people in their own wild river adventure. And it is still a wild enough adventure to be dangerous; people continue to die untimely in the Grand Canyon. This is wilderness adventure in the Anthropocene, and it must be acceptable because most people are ecstatic when they come out the other end, and many come back to do it again and again.

But the Grand Canyon wilderness adventure is seriously threatened by the presence of Glen Canyon Dam just upstream – a classic "early Anthropocene" misadventure of the right hand not knowing what the left is doing. The dam by no means supports the potentially beneficial situation downstream that exists with the smaller dam on the Taylor River.

Glen Canyon Dam is undermining – a literal and intentional use of the word – the Grand Canyon in two ways. First, it has stopped the flow of silt through the canyon. The Colorado in its pre-Anthropocene days was a steep and "immature" river, still digging out its channels – a task complicated by the intrusive rise of the Colorado Plateau. The natural history of the Colorado River prior to the Anthropocene was planetary chaos exemplified. In its efforts to move the Plateau and the Southern

Rockies down to sea level, the river moved so much silt, sand and gravel that it threw a dike across the Gulf of California, cutting off the northern third of the Sea of Cortez, which eventually dried up under the desert sun, creating the sub-sea-level Imperial Valley. The bottom of that "valley" is now the very salty Salton Sea, created originally by another bit of expensive early-Anthropocene bad planning by early settlers, and since sustained by final irrigation runoff.

But in the process of moving all that silt out of and through the Grand Canyon, the river, in its fluctuating annual flood-to-trickle extremes, deposited sandbars throughout the canyon, which are essential today as camping sites for the thousands of wilderness adventurers that pass through the canyon every year. But now that the dam has stopped that abundant flow of silt (which is instead filling in the reservoir behind the dam), the river is moving those sandbars bit by bit farther down the river, with only small amounts of new silt coming in from small Canyon tributaries.

This problem is exacerbated by the fact that Glen Canyon is a power dam, providing "peaking power" for most of the American Southwest. This means fluctuating flows for the canyons below the dam, and the pulsing fluctuations further hasten the erosion of the sandbars.

Is this a solvable problem? Maybe – for a price, probably a big price. Occasional "flood" releases from Glen Canyon Dam have been tried to stir up sand and silt that has slipped to the river bottom for redeposit on the sand bars. That has helped a little, but basically nothing will help except infusions of new silt. So – barges to float silt from the upper end of Powell Reservoir down to some kind of a glory hole from which it would be washed past the dam and into the river as a slurry? Rock crushers up the Paria River tributary to create new gravel, sand and silt to wash down to the mainstem with a small water diversion from Powell Reservoir? Like all of the headwaters options, any solution would require massive infusions of money. It would also require some studied finesse on the quantity introduced, since any silt added below Glen Canyon is going to eventually be filling up Mead Reservoir behind Hoover Dam.

Farther down the river is the delta situation. One of the most damning laments the lamenters have to throw at the "river no more" is the charge that it "no longer flows to the ocean." An Anthropocene question to ask is: So what? Why would a freshwater river *want* to flow into the ocean? With only three percent of the world's water fresh enough for plant and animal uses, why would *we* want it to flow into the ocean?

What is lamented is the loss of a rich and lively delta region in which the Colorado River used to spread out and disappear before it became the First River of the Anthropocene. Most of us, including most of those lamenting its loss, never saw that final efflorescence of the wild Colorado River; but Aldo Leopold saw it, and said it was good, so there is a growing sentiment that it ought to be restored.

Recently, to celebrate a new agreement on drought-sharing between the United States and Mexico, a "pulse flow" of water from the seriously diminished storage behind Hoover Dam was sent down to the old delta region, to see what restorative activity it might inspire; but in terms of a more lasting solution, this was like taking out a bank loan to throw a party celebrating a bankruptcy. Less celebrated but probably more important is La Cienega de Santa Clara – the Santa Clara Marsh engineered in a small piece of the old delta using brackish water from irrigation runoff too salty to reuse in fields. Migrating birds do not mind that it is a manmade marsh, and there is more "leftover" water in that region that could be ditched into other parts of the delta region – all at a cost of course, as usual.

What gets overlooked, however, in this unfolding story of the First River of the Anthropocene is the vast new "delta" region into which the Colorado River now disappears – into the desert rather than the ocean. A delta that begins on the east with water to Phoenix and Tucson, sweeps west and south through huge productive agricultural areas in both the United States and Mexico, and finishes up on the west with water for Los Angeles and San Diego. Millions of people are living and working in places to which the early explorers gave names like "The Journey of the Dead"; we are eating green produce in the winter because of this vast manmade delta.

***

Now a question: why is our regret at the loss of the old delta not more balanced in our minds and hearts by amazement and maybe a little pride in this new delta we have wrought from the desert? This points to what might be the central problem of the Anthropocene: our growing disaffection for the whole project. A cultural focus on the "alligators" has left us more depressed than impressed by what we have wrought on the planet. We seem to not like ourselves or our works very much – even as we take the benefits of the Anthropocene for granted: the abundant food, water on tap, lights and heat at the flick of a switch, et cetera, et cetera.

Our unanalytical lack of appreciation for our own works is matched only by our uncritical appreciation for anything we regard as "natural," not a work of man. I recently read an essay, for example, that called the Grand Canyon "America's cathedral." Our *cathedral*, our common place of worship? I will certainly concede the mesmerizing beauty of the Grand Canyon, having seen it from both the rim and the bottom. But – good grief: it's *erosion*; we should worship such a massive example of the planet methodically tearing itself down? Not to worry of course: I know and you know that, megamillennia hence when the Colorado River has carried the rest of the Colorado Plateau – and the Southern Rockies – down to the ocean (along with the Grand Canyon and all our dams), there will be some other tectonic belch or lurch that will cause a third new set of mountains to crumple upward, and the whole mindless, beautiful business will start over. But should we *worship* at that profane process of beautiful destruction?

Why not make Hoover Dam America's cathedral instead? The dam and the vast irrigation works downstream that it enabled, and the aquaducts out to the great cities of the Southwest? I myself find beauty in those incredible structures – not the same kind of beauty that I find in the magnificent erosions of the Southwest, but a beauty caught in the clean hard lines of the dam and its smooth bland and massive temerity in challenging the wild river to stand in and push rather than cut and run.

But no – I don't like that idea either. If we must have a cathedral, I want it to encompass both the Grand Canyon and Hoover Dam. Not to mention the little headwaters spring (dug out and boxed by some nameless human, from which I drank for four very good years at the Rocky Mountain Biological Lab here in the Upper Gunnison), and the Taylor River, and – well, the entirety of the First River of the Anthropocene.

What I really want is for us to stop mooning about a "river no more," and get down to finishing the First River of the Anthropocene. A step on the way to our Garden Earth. We've made mistakes in the first century of that work – starting with that piece of foundational infrastructure called the Colorado River Compact. But the errors of omission and commission can be fixed, minimized or revised.

I am aware that there is little hope, here in the mean time, this meanest of times, of getting our federal government – that wholly-owned subsidiary of the dragons of vested interest that squat on most of the world's wealth – to participate in any intelligent work on this, or on anything.

But we have learned enough through our interactions with the Colorado River at this point so that a lot of what needs to happen can happen at the state and local levels, with the infrastructure already in place to now adapt ourselves to our own works and what they need to work better.

The great and growing cities ringing the river's "natural" basin, for example, know that they need to continue ratcheting down their per-capita consumptions, through measures that will make developers howl, but which will sort would-be newcomers according to their willingness to embrace "living intelligently in the desert" rather than "living mindlessly in an artificial oasis." Thousands of farmers using the river's water know that they cannot forever control four-fifths of that water to grow whatever they want to (even if it is a water-intensive crop in the Mojave Desert); they can either start figuring out how they can keep farming with less water, or the 95 percent urban majority will send in experts to do it for them.

And up here in the headwaters, we have lots of gullied places to fix, lots of small storage projects to work on, to keep as much of the water as possible as high as possible for as long as possible, because water in the headwaters is pure possibility, pure potential, and we don't need multi-billion-dollar projects to do that work.

One of the reasons for de-gullying dried-out meadows is to make them wet again, and thereby to create habitat for wildlife – including the Gunnison Sage Grouse, a threatened, maybe endangered, species. Many inhabitants of the Upper Gunnison have been working hard, across old social divides – ranchers and environmentalists, local business people and college professors, college students and everyone else. Some of them are involved out of fear of what might happen if the federal government "lists" the species and sends in its experts to impose their ideas on how to save the little bird.

But a lot of the effort is because a lot of Americans – not the ones creating "the mean times" at the national and state levels – have decided that we don't want to be alone in the Garden Earth we all envision "as through a glass darkly" (or mistakenly believe we remember); we want to get there with as much of the rest of the kingdoms of life as possible, and will put in time and tax dollars to help carry forward species whose survival we have endangered – usually as unconsciously and inadvertently as we've changed the climate.

As a member of a couple of quasi-official water organizations in the Gunnison River Basin, I'm spending some of my retirement time working on getting volunteer groups out to work on the "wet-meadow" project in the Upper Gunnison (funded at this point by The Nature Conservancy). I put in a couple days late this summer up in the high country building small rock dams to stymie small gullies, working one day with a group of students from Western Colorado State University in Gunnison, another day with a group of high school students and two of their teachers. Both days, we also had a group of adult volunteers – mostly retirees like me – who came over from the Denver area. It's as good in its way as going out for a hike or bike – and better in other ways: a full body-and-mind workout with knowledge of something accomplished to justify the tired muscles.

One thing I wondered about, out there: would it help inspire these volunteers (and the hundreds we optimistically hope for in the future), or discourage or even anger them, if I were to suggest that we – along with the Bureau of Reclamation managing the dams, the utility managers down in the desert cities working on long-term conservation plans, the responsible farmers downstream from our valley all the way to that great manmade delta trying to improve irrigation efficiency and use – that we are all working on the First River of the Anthropocene?

No, they might say: not us, we're just working to put things back the way they were (in the Garden), despite the obvious geo-bio-logical history showing that things have never been "the way they were" for very long on our restless planet. Maybe that doesn't matter; maybe all that really matters is the presence in the mind and heart of a holographic shard of the garden place the planet might be – between geological episodes and other random disasters.

But we do need to keep in mind the natural history of our species, which makes the striving and vision at the heart of the First River of the Anthropocene (often obscured by "alligators") just the latest chapter in an epic we launched on those ten or twenty thousand years ago, when we decided to stop fighting for hunter-forager territory and started farming the planet – decided to challenge the forces of nature that would limit our numbers to what fit the status quo of the day, and began to adapt nature and the planet to our needs and vision. A story that either continues as an ongoing epic, or crashes and burns in a species tragedy more spectacular than that of the dinosaurs.

***

The First River of the Anthropocene is of course only a very small piece of Planet Earth in the Anthropocene Epoch. It's just a little farther along in the transition to – whatever we are able to make of it. And a little messier because so much (maybe too much) has been done so quickly. Probably some of it will have to be redone, or just undone, in order for us to move the project forward.

But I can't help but think we would be better able to face the whole global task of forging on with what is everywhere begun if we could learn to look at what we've done as creatively as we look critically at what we've undone.

I was moved some years ago by stumbling onto an essay by Julian Huxley, one of that famous family of thinkers and doers. Through us humans, Huxley said, "the universe is becoming conscious of itself, able to understand something of its past history and its possible future."

Can we really walk away from that? That gift and that responsibility? Slouch off in abject concession to the rich white dragons squatting on the world's wealth, the retroenviros with their jeremiads and lamentations, the fundamentalist know-nothings, the militant authoritarian fear-mongers? How do we reopen our once-open exploration of the universe of possibility? How do we infuse the currently somewhat helter-skelter Anthropocene with the vision of the Garden – the Garden that never was, yet, but might be?

It is as if man had been appointed managing director of the biggest business of all, the business of evolution —appointed without being asked if he wanted it, and without proper warning and preparation. What is more, he can't refuse the job. Whether he wants to or not, whether he is conscious of what he is doing or not, he is in point of fact determining the future direction of evolution on this earth. That is his inescapable destiny, and the sooner he realizes it and starts believing in it, the better for all concerned.

- Julian Huxley, "Transhumanism"

Cro-Magnon in the Interglacial

The world is turning to water and warmth;
The ice cliffs which came from as far as the memory went
Now soften, retreat, drip and trickle, collapse with sullen roars;
The sun has seized the day, grown strong and cruel to the ice,
And the sun's green things leap into the breach in surges,
Fighting their own fights, grass against brush, trees marching in,
And even at night the world sleeps to the rustle and whisper
Of life's great rebellion as it joins the sun against the ice.

And here at the beginning of a new age of not-winter
Cain dreams. And Abel is nervous as Cain dreams.

      Cain stares into the little fire of sticks and bones
      And dreams it large, dreams it myriad,
      Fires so large and so many they consume the night,
      Turn night to day and the season to not-winter forever.

      Cain stares at the forest marching in against the ice
      And dreams it changed, dreams it rearranged
      In stickbuilt lattices mounting to the sky to help
      Turn night to day and the season to not-winter forever.

      Cain stares at the shiny glob melting from rock in fire
      And dreams it changed, dreams it shaped into
      Fire-forged tools and devices against the ice to
      Turn night to day and the season to not-winter forever.

Cain dreams, and Abel is nervous as Cain dreams
Not to mention a little pissed
Since Cain is slacking even more than usual.
But when he asks, "What's wrong, brother,"
Cain looks at him like he'd never seen him before.

211

Then says, "I'm thinking," as if that excused it all.

Abel knows better than to press, and goes about doing
What has to be done whether fairly shared or not.
But at night at the fire, with the night pressing in,
Watching Cain wander off in his lostness of thought,
Asks again: "Thinking what?" Cain snaps back to there,
Angry at the interruption – then, night all around, softens.

"I'm dreaming," he says, "of paradise on earth."
Abel stares for a moment, then looks down at the fire.

"I'm imagining a world that works for us."
Not knowing what to say, Abel stares into the fire.

"I see ways to so warm the world that the ice will never return."
Abel understands that, looks up and smiles.

But Cain, staring into the fire, doesn't see the smile.
As he doesn't see the receding ice contract to a kernel
Of coldness that comes to lodge in his heart
As he lives out his dream of paradise
Cold in the warmth between ice and ice.

Night Skiing and
The Disorientations
Of Lunautic Perception

First published in *Mountain Gazette 92*, March 2003,
Significantly revised July 2004 for *Dragons in Paradise*, and again in 2014.

Lunautic. Loo-NAH-tick, not LOON-a-tic.

I forget the moon behind me for a moment, and look out ahead to the darker part of the sky where I can see past some distant star to a dimmer star, and on past that into the bottomless night, and I wonder if I would see the same thing if I'd grown up in some prior time, when people weren't indoctrinated to believe that the night is bottomless, and that we perch precarious on the side of a spinning ball of stone looking out into that night, rather than standing down on a stable ground looking up at it.

And thinking about that, I look back over my shoulder, lunautic, at the full moon, and again almost fall down, but get my ski pole in the right place to catch myself, and concentrate again for a minute on skiing, looking at the trail and those ahead of me, hearing the breathing and shish-slish of whoever is skiing behind me. My shadow paces me, leading a little off to the left if I let it.

A full-moon ski, in January in the Upper Gunnison valley above Crested Butte, and it's not even cold. Compared to what it should be, could be, anyway. The usual moderately nasty post-sundown river of cold air was flowing down the valley when we started – but that's eased off now, and it wasn't even zero scale, let alone some more customary January temperature in the Upper Gunnison. Couldn't be global warming, of course; Congress would be doing something about it.

Lunautic – as in argonaut or astronaut. Lunautic: moving with the moon, moving by the moon. We're up the Slate River valley beyond Crested Butte: one of those longdrawn mountain valleys carved by snow and ice piled beyond our imagining in these droughty times, with the finish work done by a few millenia of wind and water and the gently penetrating roots of trees. The mountains rise around us ghostly in the monolight of the full moon. Under the moon, in the snowy time, the world is white and blue-gray, until you get into the woods where it's just plain dark, and scary as hell if you think you're on a downhill track but aren't really sure if you're moving, or if you are, how fast. Up the Slate, moving with the moon.

But now, we're out in the open, and the wash of the moon is cold on the slopes rising steep around us. These slopes I'm looking at: I'm part of a small local faction that advocates developing them for downhill skiing. Am I loony, lunatic, or just lunautic? I want the development here because it would keep the inevitable expansion avalanching down into one already moderately overrun valley, rather than spilling it over into another adjacent valley, which is what the ski resort has proposed in the past. I look up at the slopes, which are looking at the moon, don't appear to care one way or the other.

I try to imagine lifts running up them, here, there. It's easy enough to imagine, and it doesn't look all that different. Does it ruin it? Yes and no: I have to admit that, back when I was still up for that kind of skiing, I'd love to have lift-skied some of these long steep leeward slopes (after dropping a couple depth charges on them to see if they wanted to avalanche). Now, I'm more inclined to say, enough is enough, but that's not yet an acceptable concept in America; you don't stop this stuff; it's like diarrhea, you just try to get it in the right place. Better here, funneling down into Crested Butte where it's wanted, needed, than opening up the holy semi-whole East River valley, under Gothic Mountain.

There's already a subdivision planned for the hillside just behind us here, now in moon shadow. The loyal opposition has managed to get the house size down from a possible 20,000 square feet to 12,000 max, and has raised some interesting questions about the water supply – but that's about as far as that's going to go, and if the houses are going to be there, and the road plowed out to them, then we'll just have to start these full-moon skis a little higher, wherever the new end-of-road trailhead will be.

The Slate River trailhead in winter is already a few miles past where it was when I first skied here; and the first subdivision extending the trailhead was, is, a kind of well-planned commune of hardcore environmentalists who all walk or ski in from a common parking lot. There are in fact enough decent environmentally concerned people in this world to more than fill this valley all the way up, and someday, when the upvalley avalanche of developments for good people from this side meets the upvalley avalanche of developments for good people from the other side, all of them people who really love the mountains and contribute to the environmental organizations in their valley – I'll be dead by then, thank goddam.

I decide to think of something else. I look up at the people ahead of me, all of us head-down and concentrating on skiing, and I think how silly it is, to be out here on a full-moon night, but doing something that forces a fairly high degree of concentration down where one's feet are. Fixated on the ski track and watching one ski slide into view, then the other: I think how silly that is, and decide to look over my shoulder at the moon, which is looking over my shoulder at me and, I imagine, sneering at me for looking at my skis instead of at it, or the world, or vice versa – and I almost fall down again. Flail my poles, skip sideways on one ski to catch my balance, violent moves an older guy ought to be too smart to be making himself make... Is my shadow laughing at me?

The moon. I am glad sometimes that I don't live closer to it. I mean "closer" in the sense of actually having to pay attention to it, as the only occasional source of light in an otherwise dark night, coming and going on a schedule of its own. I live in the modern world where, for the time being, lights come on and go off independently of the sun and the moon, their presence or absence. We have developed our finite resources to a point where, for a few years, we could probably survive, physically at least, without the sun or the moon for light. But there was a lot of time – most of our time as a species – when the moon was missed when it wasn't there; the first real record we have of scientific thought, mathematical thought, is a bone with 28 notches carved in it.

The moon. Glad as I am that I don't have to live closer to it, I still note its presence in my own cycles. I rejoice in the new crescent moon, that fingernail at sunset: I always think when I see it – ascendant now for the next week plus. When I think about it, I think that I wax with the moon, and wane with it, which is a good reason to not think about it too much: for every day waxing, a day waning? How can one get ahead like that? The crescent moon makes me feel good if I don't look at it too long; it makes me think that great things might happen in the next ten days or so to full moon. And full moon for me is like Christmas for kids – this is it; it's all downhill from here, until the next lunautic crescent.

The moon we call "gibbous" – the moon on its way back to disappearing, a moon still roundish all around but no longer round – I don't just dislike the gibbous moon; I kind of fear it. I remember driving to Denver once, and coming to that wonderful place on US 285 where the city unfolds and spreads all the way to Kansas, the only really beautiful way to see Denver. But that night a dark orange gibbous moon was hanging huge over the city, looking like special effects from one of those sci-fi movies about alien attackers. The most malevolent moon I've ever seen. Gibbous, gibber, madness – the gibbous moon is the moon you see when you wake up at night at the wrong time of month having to go to the bathroom, and you don't get back to sleep till dawn, with nothing but lunatic gibbering going on in your head....

If I look at the lovely early crescent moon too long in the evening, the dimensional magnitude of the universe starts to creep up on me. Or just the magnitude of the relatively minute solar system. In the first day or two of crescence – in Colorado, anyway – you can see the whole moon, not just the crescent, because the soft light reflected from the earth makes the part not lit by the sun just visible – the dark side of the moon lighted by earth. "Earthshine" is the technical term.

So a kind of celestial triangulation begins to form somewhere between the eye and that part of the brain or the solar (?) plexus where our megabalance seats itself: the softly lit ball defines a line between where I am and where the moon is, but that brilliant almost detached edge of yellow-white light is an arrangement between the moon and the sun that so recently seemed to sink so intimately down just over that hill there on the horizon – yet, projecting the angular relationship between the moon and the sun from that crescent sliver, I can see, if not believe, that the sun is not just down there behind the hill, but is also way, way out there: we're a triangle in which the short leg between me and my reflection on the moon is very, very short, and the leg down to the distant sun is long, long, long. No wonder it's cold in the winter.

Then, shortly, on those crescent nights, the moon is gone too, and if you're still sitting thinking of angles and distances, you do become aware of looking down and out into space, not up into it, and from a spot on the side, not the top, of this ball of rock turning at between five and six hundred miles an hour at this latitude.... It makes one want to hold onto something, a big rock, a god, something. Life is precarious, on the side of a ball of fire-fueled rock both spinning and revolving around a much larger ball of burning gases that is virtually indistinguishable in a galaxy adrift in an expanding universe whose dimensions are so unimaginable as to be as good as god.

***

Hanging on to my balance on my skis, the moon looking over my shoulder, maybe laughing but more probably totally indifferent, I wonder if I would feel this precarious if I'd grown up in an earlier world where people believed that the sky was just a kind of a bowl over a flattish earth: a bowl across which some Apollonian deity daily dragged the sun, then back under the earth through the night to do the whole show again next day. Did they ever see the night sky as something into which we might fall – if not forever, for a finite but expanding amount of time? Or would that have been too much for a young species? Or did the species start out with a terrifying sense of falling into the abysmal depths of the night sky? Who, in the process of falling asleep, hasn't suddenly jerked awake, a feeling of falling, asleep? And is that why we invent stories about cerulean bowls, a lid of light over the night beyond, and Apollonian sun-chariots, stories to pull over ourselves like warm blankets against the night?

Apollo the sun god – Mister Up-and-at'em, up and doing, early bird gets the worm, footprints in the sands of time aren't made sitting on your ass, et cetera. I give him his due all day, under his sun: Apollo, class president, captain of the football team, groom of the head cheerleader, general of the Rotary and first piston in the economic engine plowing the earth, Apollo's the one we all cozzen up to because we're all afraid not to. Lincoln pegged the sons of Apollo perfectly: "the family of the lion, or the tribe of the eagle...(which) thirsts and burns for distinction, and...will have it, whether at the expense of emancipating slaves, or enslaving freemen."

But Apollo loses his grip on my heart and mind and balls as he hauls the sun over the horizon, and the sky begins to go translucent and open up (especially if the crescent moon is hanging there and alcohol's blue burn flares to supplant the sunyellow coffee charge of the day).... Then comes Zeus's other son, fair Apollo's dark half-brother – Dionysus who hangs with the moon and the moonshine and all the interesting women – the women Apollo publicly shuns, the only beings he really fears, these women who would rather dance with Dionysus than be honored and worshipped on Apollo's pedestal....

The moon is still there, over my shoulder, my shadow still pulling me off the left a little.

Back when I wanted to be an engineer, at Carnegie Institute of Technology in Andrew Carnegie's Iron City, I got my mind infected by Dionysus at a performance of "The Bacchae" – that terrible terrorist play of vengeance, Dionysus' revenge against Apollo's servant Pentheus who knew nothing if he didn't know how to Just Say No to that side of the soul that comes up with the moon. Like a kid tearing wings off flies, Dionysus destroys Pentheus' rational clean well-lighted world with slow relentless grace, and after that performance, understanding nothing, I first looked over my own shoulder at the Dionysian moon and began to stumble onto that theretofore religiously and conscientiously ignored side of the soul. Like so many sophomores, I stopped just saying no, vaguely concerned that it might be saying no to a lot of life.

And I look out at the moon again now, this wholly lunautic night: look over my shoulder and down and out at the moon from the rolling side of this earth and I stumble again. Shadow's fault. The full moon lacks the delicate subtle spatial significance of the crescent moon, its triangulated intimations of infinitude; but that's okay, especially when you're out under it skiing and worried enough about falling down: you don't need to be thinking about falling off too.

I realize I'm starting to work up a sweat; the people up front are setting a pretty good pace. Under the guises of getting a drink, adjusting layers, blowing my nose, et cetera, I gradually work my way back to the end of the group, where I can set my own pace, including the occasional full stop to let the cold blue fire of the night burn itself on the retina of my brain.

Stopped there, free to front, confront the moon in its own kind of vibrant stillness, I reflect on my own adventures and misadventures with the godly brothers Apollo and Dionysus. Forget the father god – Zeus, Yahweh, whatever you want to call him – he's what he is, and ever will be, but we have to make our peace with his sons, who both say, each saying in his way: declare an allegiance with my brother *only*, and I'll come destroy you.

I know people destroyed by each of these brother gods – people destroyed by the constrictions of common sense, people destroyed by the excesses of nonsense; people who drank themselves to destruction and people who rationalized themselves into a dry sad old age; people who loved too many too much too often and people who died devoid of understanding the question. Apollo of the sun, Dionysus of the moon – learn to love the twilight, and the morning when the gray starts to go pink, the times of translucent and transparent transition between dark and light.

Stopped there this wholly Dionysian night, I watch the others ski on down the valley, back toward the cars. I wasn't stopping there in any terminal way; I knew I would be there when we all reconnoitered at the designated place in town, and said wow, great, wonderful, cocooned again in the babel of people, booze, food, music, and I was. But I hung back so a piece of me could stay there where I stopped, lunautically sundered to lope off up the hill to sniff the sky, and wait there till I came again to stay.

***

I can never figure out whether I am strong enough or smart enough to learn what the lunatic world has to teach, or whether I'd rather just make up stories under the well-lighted lid where I can hunker. I feel like we are close, but just not quite there. We get lost in nostalgia, security yearning, god dreams, stories like warm blankets of blessed ignorance. And the moon meantime goes gibbous, disappears, then again begins its quiet crescent pass toward fullness.

Stopped there, the moon ignites the memory of another night moon burned on the brain – very late one night in a bar in town, when – no real hope left, as usual, of getting laid – I remembered that it was a full-moon night outside, and stepped outside for a breath of air and saw Gothic Mountain, Fuji-like from Crested Butte. And with Dionysus' blessing, I ran home and stuffed my sleeping bag, a tarp and a jacket, a canteen and a partial box of Cheerios into a pack, and ran back to the bar in time to catch a ride up to Gothic town, cradled by Gothic Mountain, I walked on up the valley in the moonlight, full summer moon then, and started up the mountain – just went up, no trail or anything, just up the side of the mountain, to climb it to the moon....

I stopped that night on an open bench only a few hundred feet up. My feet not fueled by the same fire as my brain. And I woke up in the morning to a sky still open between night and the coming lid of daylight. I huddled cold and vaguely sad in my soggy bag, muzzily munching my Cheerios, a little hungover, abandoned again by the dark god of drink and dance I'd tried again to follow to the moon, and would again and again. No father god, just the bipolar brothers that haunt our days and nights, the gods of up and down, light and dark, who drive us strange between light and night, left brain and right in terminal tension, like paired stars circling each other but fending off some consummate fusion for fear of – loss. Loss of whatever.

But the sun god came that morning with an almost Dionysian diffidence. No great swelling dawn like thunder up out of whatever wherever. The sun that day – like always in the mountains, actually – didn't come up, but came down, meandering leisurely but careful down over the high westward rocks above, down into the trees and eventually down to where I sat waiting. As if to say – "Oh! Hello. Well. Bless you, my son" – and then wandering, wondering on down, to nudge awake the outliers and villages and towns and cities all the way to where his leisurely retreating brother of the once and future night was moving on ahead.

And I, like the mythic high-altitude black butterfly, absorbed the random wanton indiscriminate energy trailing behind these brethren, and rolled up my bag and started up again, on up the mountain so much more finite under the sun than under the moon, but no less real.

New Moon Song

That barest line of newest moon
That fingernail light in the western sky:
It never fails to make me glad
Although I have no clear translucent why.

I think I flow and ebb with moons;
My brain expands and shrinks inside
As moonlight time from dusk to dawn
Backs down across the night to finally hide.

The sliver moon last night glanced down on
A world more blessed with beauty than sense
In the way the day had by then been undone,
But the sky so translucent bottomless deep
Made me think or hope there's more than this
For life, there's better than beauty to come.

Benediction

Let peace come down
With the quiet insistence of night
Imposing its cool on the sunshot earth
And sponging the rawness with dew

Let love come down
Like a star's just now seen light
Laying its beam on the darkening earth
For all who will see and be new

Afterword

By Ed Marston, publisher emeritus of
The High Country News

It was a cold winter's afternoon, and we were returning to Paonia from somewhere to the east or south – Colorado Springs or Santa Fe, and of necessity passing through Gunnison, Colorado, icebox of the nation.

We stopped for coffee, before pushing over Blue Mesa Reservoir and Black Mesa, and picked up one of the local papers. A line of type leapt out: "Was the 20th century the only way out of the 19th century?"

My heart jumped, as a prospector's would. Finding a line like this, and the talent it implied, in a local weekly was less likely than finding a gold nugget in a stream.

Then my sense of discovery disappeared. This was no new nugget. It was a quote from George Sibley, promoting his latest theatrical

223

production: *Gunnisoon,* in which early Gunnison area settlers awaken, terrified, after a century's sleep to find themselves in a ski town.

I couldn't discover George as a new talent because I had known him for a long time, as friend and editor. One of my biggest defeats as an editor came at his hands. Traitorously, he had published in the *Mountain Gazette* an article about his early days in Crested Butte, titled "Mendicant Mountain." I saw it in the Mountain Gazette and asked him for permission to reprint in *High Country News.*

I thought it brilliant – the third best article he had written – but I also thought it too long. I could easily cut 1,000 words out of its 6,000-word length. It seemed to wander. It seemed at times to double back on itself, like a meandering stream. It seemed to take 10 words where I would use five.

So I cut it to 4,000 words and was left with a dead, lifeless thing. So I cut only 500 words, and it became merely comatose.

You can judge the full article for yourself in this book. I won't say it doesn't have a little fat. But I couldn't find it then and I don't see it now. Think of the article as a hike. George built in places to stop and admire the view, to turn around and see where we had come from, to wander a bit to see a hillside or a grove from a different perspective. Yes, he is taking us someplace. But if we don't understand the trip, reaching the destination will be meaningless.

I am writing this in advance of seeing all the essays that will be included in this anthology. So I don't know if George will include anything from his first book, *Part of a Winter,* about four winters he and his first wife Barbara spent as winter caretakers for the Rocky Mountain Biological Laboratory, up the East River Valley in the old mining town site of Gothic. This was back in the days when the central Rockies had winters, and it was George's job to shovel roofs so they wouldn't collapse under the weight of snow.

The title came from a relative who had spent 36 years of his life running a snowplow on the mountain passes around Silverton, Colorado, to keep them clear of the ever-ready-to-run avalanches. (One of the avalanches is named after that relative, who "discovered" it by getting caught in it.) He described his decades in Silverton as "part of a winter." George is revealed by his choice of that line as title. He is not minimizing what he and his family did by living through a few winters in Gothic. He is simply putting it in context.

I best remember George's description in "Part of a Winter" of his wood gathering. He would go out on skis to drag back dead trees for the cabin's stove. As winter progressed, he saw he was creating [the map of a tree among trees, like] a railroad system with a main trunk-line which ran back to the cabin, but with many spurs that enabled him to reach dead standing trees close to the main trunk. The image of George on skis creating his railroad system in that isolated mountain valley is as vivid to me today as it was the day 20 or so years ago that I read it.

What are we to make of his snowy railroad? Traditional nature writers don't isolate themselves in deep snow for months in order to build even a metaphorical railroad. But there is nothing traditional about George. He modestly burst on the journalism scene in 1977 with an article in Harper's Magazine about the development of the Colorado River and Hoover Dam, the massive structure that created southern California.

You might expect a diatribe, or at least irony. Instead, as I remember the article three decades later – shame on me for not rereading it since – it balanced hindsight critique with admiration for the vision and achievement of those who did the work.

Is George, then, that most boring of people: an apologist or explicator of the wonders of the industrialized world? Far from it. Such a person would not question whether the 20th century had to lie between the 19th and 21st centuries, with the clear wish that there had been a different kind of 20th century bringing us to a different kind of 21st century .

Neither, though, is he a romantic looking for societal salvation in Wilderness and dandelion tea.

In his book, *First Summer in the Sierras*, John Muir hikes through the ravaged foothills on his way to the high country. Miners using high-pressure hoses – water cannons really – had eroded canyons into the foothills to extract the gold. Muir is full of admiration for what these men have achieved with some canvas hose, brass nozzles and wooden sluice boxes. He admires human energy, and he doesn't care that much about the foothills. His love is of the higher elevations.

George is like Muir, but to my mind better. He admires the energy and ingenuity that has led to our industrialized society, but he deplores its excesses. He wants to do things right, which means he wants to live right and work right.

That desire is on display in what I think is another of his three best pieces: "Working the Gate between Worlds." ["Sawmill I" in this collection.] As published in *High Country News* in 1985, it was a pure piece about an indigent writer in his early thirties come to rural Crawford, Colorado, finding employment running a small sawmill for a rancher named Luce Pipher. Luce was as rough as the unplanned boards that

225

George learned to extract from the trees Luce's logger dragged in from the woods, as George had once dragged in trees from the snow-bound East River Valley.

If you measure the dimensions of a two by four that you buy in the lumber yard, you will find that it is actually smaller than two by four by about a half inch each way. It went into the planing mill as a true, rough-skinned two-by-four, but came out smoother and smaller. George produced true two by fours. Moreover, he became so skilled at reading the tree and cutting it to minimize its warping and bending, that builders in western Colorado learned they could use his rough, cheaper boards as construction lumber and still put up true structures. (I've checked this out with local builders, who still miss George's product.) Business boomed for Luce, and George found himself working into the winter, his writing time. So he quit.

Modestly, George does not use himself as an illustration of how societies create wealth. But George in the sawmill is the perfect example. An accountant would say that Luce's capital hadn't changed when he hired George. The leaning shed and the patched together sawmill [(see "Sawmill II")] still had the same monetary value. But when Luce added hippie George to his operation, its ability to produce wealth soared.

Did George share in the increased wealth? I don't know, and George doesn't say. It has apparently never been George's desire to get rich. I'm not sure it's even been his desire to get comfortable. I think he likes struggling with his old and decrepit Subaru, the way a monk likes shrugging his skin within a hairshirt.

George is driven by the desire to understand the world, to explain that world to people who may be interested, and to improve the world in light of that understanding. In that sense, he's an idealist who does not understand what drives others of us to look out so strongly for ourselves. He is confused because he understands so clearly that there is no salvation for the individual, but only for the group.

This collection of essays, then, is about our collective salvation. It is set in small Rocky Mountain towns because it is here that George can most clearly see how our society works. Writer Robert Heilbroner wrote a book of biographical sketches titled "The Worldly Philosophers." It was about the philosophers who explained our world to us: Adam Smith, Thomas Malthus, John Maynard Keynes, and others. For those of us who have chosen to live in small towns in the Rocky Mountains, George Sibley is our worldly philosopher, our economist. Reading this book won't help you to outsmart the stock market. It won't make you happier. It may even make you unhappier.

But it will definitely help you understand your life. What more can we ask?

GEORGE SIBLEY – ABOUT THE AUTHOR

George Sibley was born and raised in Western Pennsylvania, but indisputable math indicates that he was conceived in Colorado, by two Colorado natives; he considers himself a default Colorado native. After graduating from the University of Pittsburgh in 1964, he returned to Colorado, where he has lived ever since, primarily in the Upper Gunnison River valley on Colorado's West Slope. Skiing brought him to the Upper Gunnison, but he stayed for the valley. In his earlier years he worked in Crested Butte as a ski patrolman, then newspaper editor, then a freelance writer for a variety of publications, most of which did not pay very much, so he also worked at a variety of odd jobs, part-time or seasonal, including construction, bartending, forest-fire fighting, and back-country winter caretaker.

In the late 1970s, he and his partner Barbara Kotz and their son and daughter, Sam and Sarah, moved for several years to the adjacent North Fork valley, where he worked as sawyer at a small sawmill with winters off for writing. That was followed by a few years in pursuit of the higher education at Colorado State University in Fort Collins, Colorado.

In 1988 he got the chance to return to the Upper Gunnison valley, to teach journalism and writing courses, and regional and environmental studies at Western State College of Colorado in Gunnison (now Western State Colorado University). He also coordinated special projects for the college, including the college's annual fall Headwaters Conference, summer Water Workshop, and spring Environmental Symposium.

He retired from the college in 2007, and became involved in western water issues; he currently serves on the board of the Upper Gunnison River Water Conservancy, and is education coordinator of the Gunnison Basin Roundtable.

As a writer, his most recent major work was *Water Wranglers,* a commissioned history of the Colorado River District and the development of Colorado's share of the Colorado River, published in 2012. Books prior to that were the first edition of *Dragons in Paradise* (2004, Mountain Gazette Publishing) and *Part of a Winter* (1977, Crown Publishing), both essay collections about life in the Colorado Rockies. He has also written numerous essays and articles that appeared in nationally distributed publications (*Harper's Magazine, Technology Illustrated, High Country News, New Age Journal* and *Old West*), and in regional publications like *Colorado Central* and *Mountain Gazette*. A list of his essays and other writings is available at www.gard-sibley.org/george.html.

He lives in Gunnison with his second partner, Maryo Gard Ewell, a longtime Colorado arts administrator and friend. He continues to "essay" when not immersed, as it were, in water issues.

CPSIA information can be obtained
at www.ICGtesting.com
Printed in the USA
LVOW13s2317190117
521609LV00006B/148/P